Labour Market Reform in China documents and analyses institutional changes in the Chinese labour market over the last 20 years, and offers evidence that further labour market reform is necessary if China is to sustain its high growth rates.

The book first assesses the problems associated with the pre-reform labour arrangements. The book investigates the impact of rural economic reform on rural labour market and urban labour market reform, and its inadequacy. In particular, it provides an in-depth analysis of how current ownership patterns of urban enterprises hinder further labour market reform. Finally, the book examines the new phenomenon of rural–urban migration and its impact on rural and urban economic growth, and models its effect on urban employment, unemployment and earnings.

XIN MENG is a fellow of the Department of Economics at the Research School of Pacific and Asian Studies, The Australian National University.

T0312072

TRADE AND DEVELOPMENT

A series of books on international economic relations and economic issues in development

Academic editor
Ron Duncan, *National Centre for Development Studies,*
  The Australian National University

Advisory editors
Ross Garnaut, *The Australian National University*
Reuven Glick, *Federal Reserve Bank of San Francisco*
Enzo R. Grilli, *The World Bank*
Mario B. Lamberte, *Philippine Institute for Development Studies*

Executive editor
Maree Tait, *National Centre for Development Studies,*
  The Australian National University

Other titles in the series
Helen Hughes (ed.), *Achieving Industrialization in East Asia*
Yun-Wing Sung, *The China–Hong Kong Connection: The Key to China's Open Door Policy*
Kym Anderson (ed.), *New Silk Roads: East Asia and World Textile Markets*
Rod Tyers and Kym Anderson, *Disarray in World Food Markets: A Quantitative Assessment*
Enzo R. Grilli, *The European Community and Developing Countries*
Peter Warr (ed.), *The Thai Economy in Transition*
Ross Garnaut, Enzo Grilli, and James Riedel (eds.), *Sustaining Export-Oriented Developments: Ideas from East Asia*
Donald O. Mitchell, Merlinda D. Ingco, and Ronald C. Duncan, *The World Food Outlook*
David C. Cole and Betty F. Slade, *Building a Modern Financial System: The Indonesian Experience*
Ross Garnaut, Gui Shutian and Ma Guonan (eds.), *The Third Revolution in the Chinese Countryside*
David Robertson (ed.), *East Asian Trade After the Uruguay Round*
Chris Manning, *Indonesian Labour in Transition*
Yiping Huang, *Agricultural Reform in China*
Richard Bird and Francois Vaillancourt, *Fiscal Decentralisation in Developing Countries*
Gordon de Brouwer Financial Integration in East Asia

Labour Market Reform in China

XIN MENG

Department of Economics, Research School of Pacific and Asian Studies,
The Australian National University

CAMBRIDGE
UNIVERSITY PRESS

CAMBRIDGE UNIVERSITY PRESS
Cambridge, New York, Melbourne, Madrid, Cape Town, Singapore, São Paulo, Delhi

Cambridge University Press
The Edinburgh Building, Cambridge CB2 8RU, UK

Published in the United States of America by Cambridge University Press, New York

www.cambridge.org
Information on this title: www.cambridge.org/9780521121118

First published 2000
This digitally printed version 2009

A catalogue record for this publication is available from the British Library

Library of Congress Cataloguing in Publication data

Meng, Xin.
Labour market reform in China / Xin Meng.
    p.   cm.
Includes bibliographical references.
ISBN 0–521–77126–9 (hardcover)
1. Labour market – China.   2. Rural-urban migration – China.   I. Title.
HD5830.A6M46   2000
331.12'042'0951–dc21   99–29696   CIP

ISBN 978-0-521-77126-9 hardback
ISBN 978-0-521-12111-8 paperback

Contents

Figures

Tables

Acknowledgements

I am indebted to many people who have assisted me with this book. I am especially grateful to Professor Bob Gregory, who gave up so much of his time discussing economic issues related to the book and pointing me in the right direction. I am also very grateful to Professor Paul Miller, Professor Heinz Arndt and Dr Cezery Kapuscinsky, who always read drafts quickly and carefully and gave constructive comments and suggestions.

I am obliged to Dr Frances Perkins, who commissioned a report on Labour Market Reform in China, which subsequently developed into this book. I would like to thank my co-authors Dr Mike Kidd, Dr Harry Wu and Dr Frances Perkins for allowing me to re-write and expand the ideas from the work we did together.

Finally, I would like to thank Corrie Reiman for his encouragement and help on English editing of the early draft chapters. My thanks also go to Ms Dayaneetha DeSilva for her helpful and thorough editing of the final version of the book.

To my daughter Ningning

1

Introduction

Purpose of the book

China is in transition from a planned economy towards a market-oriented one. The economic reforms begun in the late 1970s have brought about remarkable economic growth, initially through transformations in the agricultural sector and subsequently through rapid export growth. The proportion of exports in the country's GDP has quadrupled in less than two decades, to 20 per cent in 1997. Whether China can sustain its rapid growth rate will depend heavily on the government's willingness to pursue further internal structural reforms.

Unlike its East European counterparts, economic reform in China has proceeded in a piecemeal manner, with the aim of establishing a 'socialist market economy under state planning'. This goal has been poetically described by China's most influential economist, Chen Yun (1995):

> The bird must not be held tightly in the hand or it will die. It should fly, but only within the cage: without a cage, it will just fly away. If the bird is a market economy, then the cage is state planning. Naturally, the size of the cage has to be appropriate.

While the reforms have not been sweeping, partly to avoid socio–political upheaval, keeping 'the bird in its cage' is inherently problematic. Recent economic growth has not been accompanied by significant labour market reforms within state enterprises, which have remained heavily over-staffed and inefficient. This book contends that achieving sustainable economic growth will require a more thorough overhaul of the current labour market arrangements.

This book covers new ground in documenting and analysing institutional changes in the Chinese economy over the last 20 years from a labour market perspective, and offers empirical evidence that further labour market reform is necessary if high growth rates are to continue.

1

Plan of the book

Prior to the reforms, rural and urban labour arrangements were inefficient and resulted in low productivity in both rural and urban sectors of the economy. Chapter 2 of the book analyses the drawbacks of these pre-existing labour market arrangements, and the remainder of the book is then divided into three parts.

Part 1 examines the impact of rural economic reform on labour markets in rural agricultural and non-agricultural sectors. It describes how economic reform brought about institutional change in the rural agricultural labour market and analyses the changes in labour supply behaviour and income distribution patterns (chapter 3). Emphasis is also given to institutional change in the rural non-agricultural labour market – in particular, employment and wage determination patterns in this sector (chapter 4). Finally, an interesting phenomenon that has emerged in the rural labour market – the widening wage gap between the rural agricultural and non-agricultural sectors – is analysed (chapter 5).

The implementation of urban labour market reforms and the impact of enterprise reform on the urban labour market are studied in part 2. The major reform measures implemented in the urban labour market since the beginning of the economic reform are introduced and their impact on wage determination in the state sector scrutinised (chapter 6). Following this, the impact of the current enterprise ownership structure on the determination of compensation and employment at the enterprise level is investigated (chapter 7). Particular attention is subsequently given to the important issue of necessary and possible paths for reforming China's urban social security system (chapter 8).

Part 3 analyses the unfolding patterns of rural–urban migration since the reforms began. The impact of massive rural–urban migration on China's economic growth is studied through empirical testing of a three-sector model (chapter 9). The issue of how to efficiently allocate migrant labour to regions with varying rates of economic growth is discussed: the main constraint in this regard is found to be a lack of reliable and impartial information about job markets in various parts of China (chapter 10). Finally, emphasis is given to the existing segregation of the rural migrant and urban resident labour markets and the impact of eliminating such segregation on the urban labour market – in particular, on unemployment, hidden unemployment and labour costs (chapter 11).

The book concludes in chapter 12 by providing an overview of its main findings and its contributions toward enriching our understanding of Chinese labour market reform.

2

Pre-reform labour arrangements

Before economic reform was initiated in 1978, China did not have labour markets in the conventional sense. Labour mobility was non-existent and all wages were centrally fixed by the government. When the Chinese Communist Party (CCP) came to power in 1949, China pursued a Stalinist economy, whereby assets and property belonged to the people. Consequently, workers were their own employers and they could not 'sell' their labour to themselves. Labour was thus not considered a commodity and wages were not perceived as being the price of labour. Furthermore, given the premise that workers were the ultimate owners of property, they could obtain work whenever they needed to. In addition, no one could dismiss anyone else: full employment and lifetime tenure were fundamental features of this system.

The implementation of these Stalinist policies on a country-wide basis was no simple matter, not least because of China's huge population. Difficulties arose not only because of the requirement that each person be given a job for life, but also because of imbalances between the treatment of the rural vs. the urban labour force. Housing, medical expenses and food were heavily subsidised in the urban sector. As a result, urban workers were more costly to maintain in comparison to rural ones.

This dichotomy reflected the Chinese government's strategy of mutually exclusive rural and urban labour markets. As a corollary, rural people were excluded from working in the cities, and received no social security benefits. The reason for this 'neglect' appears to be that, given the nature of traditional farming techniques (labour-intensive, with small-size plots), the marginal rate of technical substitution between land and labour was relatively high. Hence, it was easy for the agricultural sector to absorb the abundant labour supply and avoid open unemployment. This encouraged the government to leave rural residents out of any consideration of the design and development of social security arrangements.[1] Perkins and

---

[1] Interestingly, there is not much in the way of documented justification for this policy.

Yusuf (1984) suggest another reason. They argue that China had very low grain output in the early 1950s and was not in any position to implement a policy of large, forced grain deliveries from the rural areas. Preventing rural–urban migration thus had the dual advantages of keeping more people in the countryside to increase grain production while limiting the number of city dwellers who needed grain products. Both of these considerations may have played a part in China's highly restrictive labour mobility policies in the pre-reform era. Whatever the reasons for the policy, the complete immobility of labour was a major constraint to economic growth in pre-reform China.

Inter-regional labour migration within both rural and urban sectors was also restricted, as was labour mobility among firms within each urban region. There were some exceptions – for example, rural university graduates or army officials could gain urban residency. Various formal promotions and a few cases of family reunion also qualified for limited inter-urban migration.

These restrictions on labour mobility were implemented through the *household registration system* (or '*hukou*'), which forced individuals to register with local authorities to gain residency, thereby determining where they lived and worked. Basically, people spent their lives in the place where they were born. These restrictions generated serious problems for the Chinese economy including considerable hidden unemployment in the countryside and low productivity and inefficiency in the cities. They also meant that labour arrangements and income determination systems in the urban and rural sectors differed markedly.

Pre-reform labour arrangements in the cities

Employment

Central planning meant total government control over every aspect of labour arrangements: job-seekers would be assigned employment. Assignment was normally through educational institutions (high schools, technical schools, or universities) or through local communal offices (*Jiedao Banshichu*) where people would register their residency. The State Ministry of Labour and Personnel assigned an employment quota to each provincial or city government. This would trickle down through the system until the quotas were finally allocated to each school or local communal offices.[2] Jobs were then allocated to individuals who belonged

---

[2] There was some flexibility in the size of the employment quota at each level.

to each particular school or communal office and who needed a job. Individuals were not allowed, and were also unable, to find jobs by themselves.

Major employers such as the state or collectively-owned enterprises or government departments were not allowed to recruit freely. Every workplace was given an annual employment quota, which was a result of negotiations among firms, their associated government departments and the local Bureau of Labour and Personnel. However, the final decision was made by the local government departments and the Bureau of Labour and Personnel. Once assigned to a job, employees were not allowed to quit, change jobs, or move to another firm other than by way of a promotion. Moreover, firms were not allowed to dismiss workers unless they had committed criminal acts.

By having such an authoritarian structure of job allocation, and by restricting rural–urban migration, the ideological goal of full employment was achieved during periods when the economy was running smoothly. However, when the Chinese economy was thrown into upheaval by political forces (as happened during the Great Leap Forward and the Cultural Revolution), special arrangements had to be made to maintain the facade of full employment.

In the case of the Great Leap Forward (in the late 1950s and early 1960s), grain output declined by 24.4 per cent, industrial productivity fell by 5.4 per cent and the national income fell by 4.1 per cent between 1957 and 1960. To maintain full employment and to increase agricultural production in the face of this disaster, about 20 million urban employees were forcibly transferred to the agricultural sector (Chen and Yu 1993).

There was a similar response during the Cultural Revolution, when production stagnated and schools and universities closed down. Hundreds of thousands of young urban people had nowhere to go. Once again, the government's solution was to move them to the countryside, where they were not needed: about 17 million high school and university students were treated in this manner between 1967 and 1970 (Chen and Yu 1993); here, they became part of the hidden rural unemployed. When the Cultural Revolution came to an end, all those who had been forced into the countryside created a huge unemployment problem when they returned to the cities, and the massive influx forced the government to belatedly admit that China did have an unemployment problem (Feng 1982; White 1988).

Figure 2.1 presents total urban employment as a percentage of total employment for each year since 1952. The two distinctive periods of

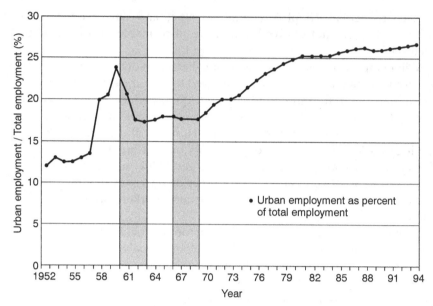

Figure 2.1 Share of urban employment, 1952–1994
Source: SSB (various years a), table 1–8.

economic upheaval, between 1960 and 1963 and between 1966 and 1969, are evident (the shaded areas in figure 2.1). The share of urban employment to total employment declined from 23.6 per cent in 1960 to 17.3 in 1963 and again from 18.0 in 1966 to 17.5 in 1969.

Urban wages

Wages in the urban areas were also centrally determined and controlled by the Bureau of Labour and Personnel, with two major implications. First, establishments had no right to determine their employees' wages (Shan 1991). Wages were based on personal criteria such as educational levels and work experience (Shan 1991).[3] The wage-setting system provided a precise wage for each individual. Second, urban establishments were given an annual total wage bill quota by the Ministry of Labour and Personnel. The wage bill quota was a direct function of the enterprises' employment allocation – that is, the fixed employment quota times the precise level of wage for each individual employed in the enterprise.

---

[3] In the case of government officials, 'work experience' implies the period since the individual joined the Communist Party and became 'Revolutionary'.

However, firms were not financially independent. All monies earned were given to the government. In return, all costs were covered by the government. Wages were thus effectively funded by the Ministry of Finance, via the provincial Bureau of Finance, the local Bureau of Finance and then on to each firm. If, for instance, a firm was allocated a higher employee quota, an appropriate increase in the wage bill would be automatically forthcoming.

The grade wage system that was introduced in the early 1950s, and continued with hardly any changes until the late 1970s, was based on the Soviet model, having eight distinct levels for factory workers and technicians (working-class wage ranking) and 24 levels for administrative and managerial workers (cadres' wage ranking) (Wang and Li 1995). Seniority and qualification were the two main determinants of the grade system, which also accounted for relevant industry and regional differentials. 'Seniority' had two different meanings here. For those who started working after 1949, seniority meant the length of time that they had been in any state or collectively-owned workplace. For those who had joined the CCP before 1949, seniority implied the period since the individual became a member.

Both education and seniority played an important role in the wage determination of those who started working after 1949. A university graduate obtained a cadres' level-23 wage for the first year after graduation and 1 year later would automatically be promoted to level 22. Blue-collar workers and normal school graduates with 9–12 years of schooling received the apprentice's wage level on entering a firm. Similarly, a technical school graduate with 9 years of normal schooling plus 3 years at a technical school would receive level 3–4 of the working-class wage level.[4]

Regional wage differences were based on the cost of living, using the early 1950s' measures of consumer prices in each region. Beijing, for example, was ranked in region 6, whereas Shanghai was a more expensive region and was placed in region 8. The higher the price, the higher the rank and the higher the wage levels. On the other hand, industrial wage differences were related to specific differences in working conditions.

An illustration of this grade system is given for administrative and managerial workers for four regions in table 2.1 . The table uses grade 24 as a benchmark to show how the wage distribution differed within each region. At the bottom of the table, the regional income differentials are also presented by using grade 24 in region 4 as the benchmark.

---

[4] The rankings for the 8 working-class levels were placed in ascending order – that is, the lowest was level 1 and the highest was level 8. The rankings for the cadres were placed in descending order, with level 1 being the highest and level 24 the lowest.

Table 2.1.   *Examples of relative wage grade level for administrative and managerial staff, by regions (all indices are relative to the lowest level)*

Grades	Regions			
	4	6	8	10
1	15.48	13.48	13.41	13.47
2	13.96	12.15	12.09	12.15
3	12.44	10.83	10.77	10.83
4	11.06	9.63	9.57	9.62
5	9.94	8.66	8.62	8.66
6	9.24	8.05	8.00	8.04
7	8.07	7.03	6.99	7.03
8	7.21	6.28	6.25	6.28
9	6.55	5.71	5.68	5.71
10	5.66	4.93	4.90	4.94
11	5.21	4.55	4.52	4.55
12	4.61	4.01	3.99	4.00
13	4.14	3.62	3.59	3.61
14	3.69	3.21	3.19	3.21
15	3.31	2.88	2.87	2.88
16	2.94	2.57	2.55	2.57
17	2.63	2.30	2.29	2.29
18	2.34	2.03	2.02	2.03
19	2.08	1.81	1.81	1.82
20	1.87	1.63	1.63	1.63
21	1.68	1.44	1.44	1.44
22	1.32	1.30	1.29	1.29
23	1.15	1.15	1.14	1.15
24	1.00	1.00	1.00	1.00
24	1.00	1.21	1.28	1.34

Source: Author's calculations based on relevant documents.

Wage increases were awarded only according to government regulations. For example, after 3 years at apprenticeship level, individuals received an increase in wages to level 1 of the working class, and 3–5 years later their wage level would automatically increase by a level; in the cadre class, all university graduates had their wages increased to level 22 after 1 year of service. Apart from these wage increases accruing to seniority, there were also occasional uniform across-the-board wage increases, by means of a central government policy directive. In principle, wages were effectively fixed for very long periods (Korzec 1992). During the Cultural Revolution, for example, there was no general wage increase for almost 12 years. As can be seen in figure 2.2, the urban average real wage level was almost held constant for the whole period 1952–78. The shaded bar in figure 2.2 represents the end of this period and the beginning of the period of economic reform.

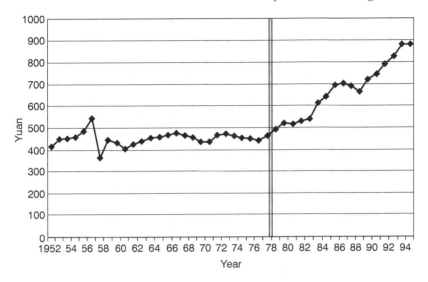

Figure 2.2 Urban average annual real wage level, 1952–1995 (yuan; CPI 1951 = 100)
Source: Author's calculations, based on SSB (various years a), tables 1–10, 1–31.

In addition, the rigid wage determination system had been accompanied by a piece-rate wage system in some places and by a bonus system in others before the Cultural Revolution. The Cultural Revolution, however, abolished all of these incentive systems.

Social welfare

To keep wages low, most welfare benefits – such as housing, medical care, pensions, and sometimes even schooling and hospital treatment – were provided by the state-owned enterprises as an internal social security system. Each enterprise functioned as a microcosm of society, whereby all welfare was provided within the enterprise and accounted for as part of labour costs. Workers – and, in some cases, most of their family members – were employed for a lifetime with one workplace. As labour was completely immobile and enterprises were not financially independent, this system ran smoothly in its own peculiar way. Since open unemployment was non-existent, no unemployment benefit scheme was needed. However, every worker was entitled to a pension upon retirement. Depending on seniority, the pension was set at a percentage of the individual's last salary before retirement. Like the wage bill, funding for pensions was allocated by the government according to the number of retired employees and their previous wage and seniority levels.

Free medical care was provided to all employees and their direct family members. Hospitals were government-owned, which permitted inexpensive medical services and medicine. Firms used special government funds to pay hospitals annual amounts to cover the medical expenses incurred by their employees and family members.

Housing, on the other hand, was less equally distributed among employees than any other form of welfare. Although everyone with a job was entitled to highly subsidised housing, demand always exceeded supply. The reason for the excess demand was twofold. On the one hand, as housing was highly subsidised, rent-seeking behaviour always led to a high level of demand. On the other hand, the heavy industrialisation strategy adopted by the Chinese government in the pre-reform era focused government attention on investment at the expense of consumption. Housing was one of the areas which were largely ignored. It was reported that *per capita* housing area in urban China reduced from 4.5 m^2 in the early 1950s to 3.6 m^2 in 1978 (State Statistical Bureau [SSB] various years a).

Problems with the pre-reform urban labour arrangements

The labour arrangements of pre-reform China can be contrasted with a labour market system that places a greater emphasis on creating productive efficiency by the efficient allocation of labour. Such a system should result in the right person being allocated to the right job, generate the right technical proportion of labour to capital and provide labour with an incentive to increase productivity. If workers are not motivated, they will not work to their full capacity, and sometimes may even deliberately under-perform. This is the so-called 'shirking problem'.

The pre-reform urban labour arrangement in fact promoted shirking and inefficiency. The labour assignment system did not allow employees and employers to choose each other, resulting in mismatches between workers and jobs. Moreover, once mismatches occurred, the system did not allow for any corrections as individuals could not change their jobs while employers could not fire their workers. The rigid labour assignment system also allowed the government to allocate labour regardless of a firm's requirements. With increasing population pressure and an escalating labour force participation rate, full employment could be achieved only if the government forcefully assigned labour to firms. This resulted in widespread over-staffing.

China's pre-reform labour arrangements were also unsuccessful in inducing the labour force to be productive. A successful incentive system should reward productive effort and discourage shirking on the job. However, in pre-reform China, workers had to make an effort without commensurate economic reward, and the end result was that no one was prepared to put in any effort. Nor had the system any way to punish shirking. Economic theory suggests that an individual's working effort is positively correlated with productivity and negatively correlated with utility. An incentive system can thus be successful only when the rate of return to effort offsets the disutility of effort (see, for example, Stiglitz 1974, 1975; Solow 1980, 1985). The opposite of productive effort is shirking, which is positively related to an individual's utility, but negatively related to productivity. The system's disregard for individual differences in productive performance became more pronounced during the Cultural Revolution when the piece-rate wage and bonus systems were abolished.

Although it may be argued that the pre-reform wage-setting system appears to be similar to that in a market economy, in that wage levels were related to an individual's level of education, training and work experience, there is an essential ingredient missing. In a perfectly competitive world with full information, individuals receive a wage which is equal to the value of their marginal product. Human capital theory suggests that individuals will invest in their own education and training in order to increase their marginal productivity and, thus, their lifetime income. Hence, we observe a direct relationship between human capital variables and wages. However, schooling and work experience are indicators only of *potential* productivity: to ensure that individuals utilise their full human capital stock it is essential that there is a mechanism which encourages individuals to work efficiently. In a market economy, the threat of job loss is one such mechanism.

In the case where labour mobility is rigidly constrained, as in pre-reform China, the link between human capital and labour productivity is broken. When firms are not able to hire or fire employees, it is not easy to punish inadequate workers. Hence, a high level of human capital stock does not necessarily guarantee high productivity. Similarly, when workers cannot choose jobs which may best suit their abilities and/or interests, a poor worker–firm match may result. This may, in turn, reinforce shirking as the worker may not be interested in the job. Therefore, without labour mobility, human capital can be a measure only of *potential* labour productivity. From this perspective, the underlying flaw of the pre-reform labour system in urban China was the lack of labour mobility generated by workers being unable to choose their jobs, and by employers being unable to dismiss unsatisfactory workers.

Pre-reform labour arrangements in the countryside

The urban industrialisation strategy adopted by communist China was intended to develop heavy industry at the expense of agriculture. Prices for agricultural products were deliberately kept low to subsidise the cost of living and production in the cities. At the same time rural–urban migration was severely restricted and the rural population was excluded from favourable employment arrangements implemented in urban areas. However, as arable land was kept constant and population growth was very rapid, the amount of arable land per farmer declined considerably, thus reducing the average productivity of labour.

By 1980 the amount of sown area per labourer was approximately half of that in 1952 (table 2.2). This rapid decline implies a rapid decrease in the average productivity of rural labour. According to Rawski's estimates (Rawski 1979), the average labour productivity (per man-day) within the agricultural sector declined from 1.46 yuan in 1957 to 1.24 yuan in 1975. In other words, during this period, the amount of hidden unemployment in the rural sector increased significantly.

The rural agricultural sector

Redistributive land reform at the beginning of liberalisation in 1949 established a small family-farming system. At that stage, decisions regarding labour allocation and income distribution were made within the family. However, this system did not last long. Between 1955 and 1957, China launched a large-scale agricultural cooperative movement and soon after, during the Great Leap Forward (1957–9), the people's commune movement swept across rural China. This resulted in the economy and administration of a given rural area (about 4,000 households and a population of 20,000 on average) being put under a single entity, the commune, within which there were no independent property-owners. An attempt was made to apply communist principles of production and income distribution[5]: 'from each according to their ability, to each according to their needs' (Luo 1990; Griffin and Griffin 1984).

The Great Leap Forward was an economic and social disaster which resulted in the loss of 30 million lives (Johnson 1988). In order to recover

[5] During a brief period (1958–9) all members of the commune ate together, with the food being provided free of charge from a communal kitchen (Johnson 1988).

Table 2.2. *Changes in rural labour force and sown areas in China, 1952–1995*

Year	Rural labour (10m persons)	Sown areas (10m Mu)[a]	Arable land per rural rural labourer (Mu)[a]
1952	18.243	211.844	11.60
1957	20.566	235.866	11.50
1962	21.373	210.343	9.84
1965	23.534	214.936	9.13
1970	28.120	215.231	7.65
1975	29.946	224.318	7.49
1980	31.836	219.569	6.90
1985	37.065	215.439	5.80
1988	40.067	217.303	5.40
1989	40.939	219.831	5.37
1990	42.010	222.543	5.30
1991	43.093	224.379	5.21
1992	43.802	223.510	5.10
1993	44.256	221.611	5.01
1994	44.654	222.361	4.98
1995	45.042	224.818	4.99

Note: 1 Mu is approximately equivalent to 0.67 hectares.
Source: SSB (various years b).

from this catastrophe, another restructuring of the rural institutional system was implemented. Between November 1961 and February 1962, rural ownership was changed to a three-tiered system to reflect the corresponding administrative hierarchies: communes, brigades and production teams. The basic accounting unit was also changed, first from a commune to a brigade, which generally had a population of 1,000–2,000, and then from a brigade to a production team, which consisted of approximately 30 households or about 150 people (Byrd and Lin 1990b). The production teams were relatively free to allocate land, labour and other publicly-owned properties. However, communes and brigades were part-owners of the production teams' properties. In addition, they provided economic and administrative supervision to the teams. Often communes or brigades used production team land, labour or outputs without offering any compensation.

The reduction of the size of production units from the commune or brigade to the production team during this period should have increased the efficiency of agricultural production. The income distribution system, however, continued to provide inadequate incentives for individual workers. This, together with the low output prices and rapid population growth in rural areas, led to low agricultural productivity and a low rate of rural development. A vicious circle thus developed: with constant or even slightly decreasing arable land areas, rapid population growth and poor production and income distribution systems, agricultural productivity dropped lower and lower, generating a very low income for the rural population, so that investment in agriculture was scarce. This, in turn, reduced rural labour productivity and further depressed rural sector income.

The rural non-agricultural sector

The predecessor of China's rural non-agricultural sector was the rural sideline production and handicraft industry, undertaken by millions of individual Chinese farmers as part-time jobs.[6] Between 1955 and 1957, those working in the handicraft industry were organised into specialised 'sideline production teams' under agricultural producer co-operatives (Byrd and Lin 1990b).

China's commune and brigade enterprises (predecessors of the township and village enterprises or TVEs) began in the late 1950s during the Great Leap Forward. In order to fulfil the ambitious 'industrialisation' target set by the Communist Party in a bid to catch up with industrial countries, each commune and brigade established its own steel plant.[7] Most of the men had to work in those plants; only women and children were left in the fields. By the end of 1959, there were 700,000 small industrial enterprises in rural China, employing more than 5 million farmers. The total output value at that time (evaluated by the government, not by the market) was over Y10 billion, being 10 per cent of total national industrial output value in that year (Zhang 1988).

These impressive statistics were, at best, a veil. The steel produced by these small plants was of such low quality that it was never used in any further production. In the meantime, agricultural production was set back by the siphoning off of manpower, funds and materials. A nation-wide economic crisis ensued. In 1960, finally acknowledging the gravity of the situation, the central government called for a readjustment of the national economy. As a result, most of the commune and brigade enterprises were closed; only a small number of enterprises remained, particularly those producing agricultural tools, repairing agricultural machinery, or processing food.

It was not until 1970 that a new peak of rural commune and brigade

---

[6] In 1954, 10 million farmers, more than 5 per cent of the total rural labour force, were engaged in such work (Byrd and Lin 1990b).

[7] The main target was that the total national output of steel in China should meet that of the United Kingdom in three years, and that of the United States in five years.

enterprise development appeared. Again, it was called for by the central government in an effort to speed up agricultural mechanisation. Most of the enterprises established during the 1970–7 period were associated with agricultural production, such as agricultural machinery, farm tool production and the manufacture of chemical fertiliser.

Labour allocation and income distribution

As mentioned earlier, communes and brigades had the greatest impact on the factor allocation of production teams. Farmers were organised in production teams and team leaders allocated individuals to work particular fields. However, some kinds of production, such as irrigation construction and other non-agricultural production, was organised by the communes or brigades. To do so, the communes or brigades had to order the production teams to provide labour input. The basic structure of this labour allocation situation is depicted in figure 2.3.

During this period, income distribution in the production teams followed a work points system: the work points of each individual labourer were evaluated against each day of work among the members of the team. A healthy man, aged 20–45, usually earned 10 full points per day. A healthy woman in the same age range usually earned 8–8.5 points per day. However, the monetary value of these work points was not known until the end of the year. At the end of each year, the net distributable income of a production team was divided by the total work points earned by all members who worked in the production team.

Income was calculated in terms of grain and cash. The distribution of grain was based on 'to each according to their needs' and the distribution of cash was based on 'to each according to their contribution' (Putterman 1990). Everybody in a production team was entitled to an amount of grain according to their age and gender. Children, the old and women were supposed to need less than strong young men. The age and gender composition of each household also determined its grain ration for the following year. The cost of the grain products obtained by each household could be calculated according to the price and quantity. This cost was then covered by the total value of work points earned by the total members of the household. In some cases, the total value of work points earned by the household members was less than the cost of grain they obtained, while in other cases it was more than the cost. When a household earned less than the grain product they needed to consume, they owed the production team. On the other hand, if a household earned more than it needed, it obtained extra cash. In any case, the distribution of grain was guaranteed.

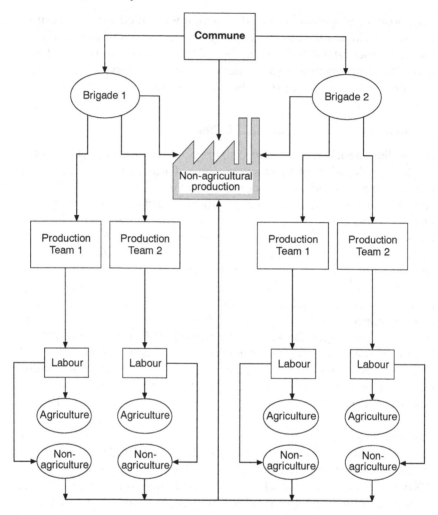

Figure 2.3 Schematic representation of labour allocation, pre-reform rural China

However, it was often observed that when more and more households earned less than they consumed, a production team would have nothing to pay to those who earned more than they consumed. Thus the money the households earned could not be paid.

The income distribution system for commune and brigade enterprises was even more complex than that of the agricultural production teams. Workers in these enterprises, drawn from various production teams, were paid within the same work points payment system as those who worked in the fields. Enterprises had to transfer a certain amount of their revenue to each of the production teams in proportion to the number of workers supplied. Once again, workers were not paid until the end of each year and were paid directly by their production team according to the work points they earned from the team. They were not paid directly by the enterprise.

The main difference between the work point system and a normal wage system is that value in the work points system cannot be determined in advance. The work point system affected individual incentives in the following ways:

- The value of each work point was determined not only by an individual's effort, but also by the efforts of all his/her co-workers. The nature of farming is such that it is difficult to monitor individual performance. Consequently, members of a production team had an incentive to shirk in the hope that the work of other people would pay their contribution and in the belief that no matter how hard they worked, the results of their extra contribution would ultimately be shared by all the members in the team. This is the so-called 'free-rider' problem.
- Grain was distributed on a *per capita* basis and was paid for by work points earned by households. Households not earning enough work points to pay for food were, in principle, required to pay back the production team from the next year's earnings. However, in practice, this was rarely enforced. Therefore, those who earned more than enough to pay for the grain ration had to bear the burden of those who had not earned enough (Lee 1984).

The pre-reform labour arrangement and income distribution systems in the rural areas, like those in the cities, thus discouraged an increase in labour productivity and income. Figure 2.4 shows that over more than two decades of the pre-reform period (1954–78), the annual growth of rural *per capita* real income was about 2.5 per cent p.a. This rate increased to 7.3 per cent over the post-reform period (1978–95). Such slow growth in the pre-reform rural income was one of the most important factors that drove the economic reform process.

Time for change

The main problems with China's pre-reform labour system were the extreme immobility of labour and disincentives embedded within the income distribution system of both rural and urban economies. This

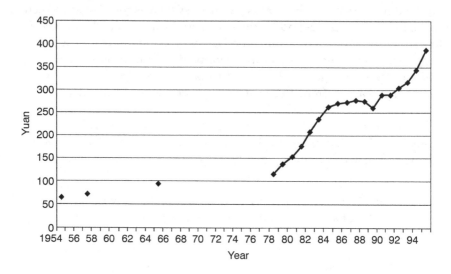

Figure 2.4 Change in rural *per capita* real annual income, 1954–1995
Note: Using 1954 price as deflator.
Sources: *China Rural Statistical Yearbook* (1989); SSB (various years b).

labour arrangement system generated hidden unemployment in the rural sector and progressively reduced rural labour productivity, pushing rural people into a vicious cycle of increasing poverty. At the same time, it reduced labour productivity in the urban sector and generated a serious problem of urban hidden unemployment. These arrangements were only part of the whole centrally planned economic system, which was the main obstacle for China's economic growth. However, as the labour arrangements were such a politically sensitive issue to the Chinese Communist Party (CCP) (White 1988), reforms in this area have been, and continue to be, a very painful and prolonged process.

Part 1

Economic reform and the rural labour market

The segregation of the rural and urban economies in China was one of the most distinctive features of the Chinese economy in the pre-reform era. This feature did not change at the beginning of economic reform. Up until the late 1980s, rural–urban migration was still rigidly controlled. While nation-wide data on rural–urban migration in the 1980s are not available, limited rural–urban migration can be demonstrated using data from a nation-wide survey of 222 villages called the Hundred Villages Labour Survey Data (HVLD).[1]

The HVLD data show that permanent migration of farmers to urban areas accounted for only 1.75 per cent of the total labour force in the 222 villages surveyed in 1986. This was the situation after a decade of reform. However, by the beginning of the 1990s, encouraged by the high demand for rural labour in the urban areas, rural–urban migration had become uncontrollable, presenting new challenges for labour market reform.

Owing to the volatile nature of China's labour markets in the reform period, this book first studies rural and urban labour markets separately.

---

[1] The 'Nation-wide 222 Villages Labour Investigation', carried out by the Institute of Rural Development of the Chinese Academy of Social Science, covered 222 villages in Shanghai, Jiangsu, Zhejang, Fujien, Hebei, Shangxi, Inner Mongolia, Heilongjiang, Guangxi, Ningxia and Qinghai provinces in China. This data set (HVLD) is drawn from this investigation. See Yu (1989).

3

The rural agricultural labour market

Economic reform began in the Chinese countryside as a result of a grass-roots' reaction from those enduring extremely poor living conditions. Between 1976 and 1977, a production team in Anhui province secretly initiated what was, in effect, a partial privatisation movement. The farmers in the team were so impoverished that they did not particularly care if they were caught and punished by the Party. They divided their team's land into equal-sized small pieces on a *per capita* basis, and each family member was given their share. The production team made contracts with each family. By the end of the year each family was required to pay an amount of grain as taxes to the central and local governments, and the amount of grain required for the so-called 'collective accumulation' for the production team, the brigade and the commune. In a radical departure from what had gone on before, the rest of the output was to be family income. Since both production and income distribution systems shrank to the smallest unit where each member's effort was directly rewarded, not surprisingly the total output of the production team more than doubled by the end of the year, and the farmers in the team had enough to eat. Many teams followed the year after, and were all successful at increasing output and family income. At last, the central government realised that this was the only way for Chinese farmers to escape from lifelong poverty and hunger. In 1978 the Chinese government introduced the 'household responsibility system' (HRS), based on these spontaneous experiments, to the whole country.

Labour arrangements under the HRS

Under the HRS, land is owned by the collectives and contracted out to households. The contract requires households to fulfil a state production quota for certain agricultural products, and to deliver a levy to the collectives. Households are free to decide on their resource allocation, production structure and income distribution among family members, provided that the quotas and levies are met. The introduction of the HRS meant that labour allocation and income distribution became household decisions. Families decided who worked on which plot of land or which off-farm activity according to individual members' abilities. Their efforts were directly rewarded in the form of household income.

If one assumes that a household is an integrated decision-making agent who seeks for household rather than individual utility-maximisation, the 'free-rider' problem can easily be solved under the HRS. Many studies have shown that the dramatic increase of labour productivity in rural China after economic reform is a direct result of these institutional changes (see, for example, Lin 1988; McMillan, Whalley and Zhu 1989). Few studies, however, have investigated the changes in rural household income determination and labour supply behaviour as a direct result of the introduction of the HRS.

If farmers behaved in an economically rational way under the new HRS, then household labour allocation and income determination behaviour in the agricultural sector should be similar to behaviour in a market economy. In other words, income should be related to labour productivity and labour supply should respond to the wage rate. The following sections test these hypotheses.

Does the HRS reward productivity?

As noted in chapter 2, the work points system evaluated individuals' work according to their age, health condition and gender. Furthermore, the grain ration system was based on different allowances for children, the aged and adults. Thus, under the old system, one would expect that rural household income (grain and cash) would be determined mainly by the number of household labourers, household age and gender composition. The more labourers, the more work points earned and the higher the income. Age should exhibit an inverse-U-shaped relationship with household income as a result of both the grain distribution and work points system. The higher the percentage of female labourers in a household, the lower the household income level because women were paid lower work points and obtained a smaller grain ration than men. There was no relationship between household income and labour productivity.

Under the HRS, however, one would expect household income and labour productivity to be related. This implies that in addition to labour inputs and age, the average educational level of household labourers would contribute positively to household income. According to human capital theory, an individual's education and work experience enhance his/her labour productivity. Thus, under an effective incentive system, these human capital endowments will be rewarded. More importantly, under the HRS, a household as a production and income distribution unit will try to allocate its labour inputs (both male and female) to maximise utility. It is not in the household's interest to discriminate against its female members; instead, everyone would be allocated to the tasks where they had the highest productivity. Thus, unlike the work points system, one would not expect the gender composition of a household to affect household income.

This section tests the above hypothesis by estimating a household net income equation. In rural China, most production still takes place within the household, while some household members worked at Township-, village-, and/or Privately-owned enterprises (TVPs) or other places. Household net income[1] thus normally comes from two sources: net income from household agricultural and non-agricultural production, and the income earned by work elsewhere.

We will assume that households maximise their utility subject to budget and time constraints. There are also other kinds of constraints on the household's ability to allocate their labour to maximise household utility. One possible constraint is that there might be a limited number of jobs available in the TVP sector and rural–urban migration might not be completely free of restrictions. Another constraint is that farmers were obliged to pay tax in the form of grain. This prevents them from giving up farming completely even if their marginal productivity was higher in other sectors.

Suppose a household net income function can be specified as:

$$HNI_i = f_i(NI_i^H(Q_i), E_i) \tag{3.1}$$

where HNI_i is the ith household's net income

        NI_i^H is the ith household's net income from household agricultural and non-agricultural production

        Q_i is the ith household's production function

        E_i is the income earned by the ith household's labourers who work elsewhere.

Following the new growth theory (see Romer 1986, 1990; Lucas 1988; Caballe 1993), apart from normal physical inputs, human capital should contribute significantly to household production. Human capital endowments are measured by years of education and experience (Becker 1962; Mincer 1974). The production function is, therefore, specified as:

$$Q_i = g_i(L_i^H, K_i, LL_i, EDU_i^{HA}, EXP_i^{HA}, EXP_i^{2HA}) \tag{3.2}$$

---

[1] 'Net income' is defined as household total income *minus* household production cost.

where L_i^H is labour inputs used in household production
        K_i is capital stock
        LL_i is arable land contracted by the household
        EDU_i^{HA} is average years of schooling of those who work in
                     household production
        EXP_i^{HA} is average years of labour market experience of those
                     who work in household production
        EXP_i^{2HA} is the quadratic term of EXP_i^{HA}.

Outside earnings of labourers in household i is also a function of the average human capital endowments of household members who work outside of the household. Thus:

$$E_i = \alpha_0 + \alpha_1 EDU_i^{OA} + \alpha_2 EXP_i^{OA} + \alpha_3 EXP_i^{2OA} \tag{3.3}$$

where EDU_i^{OA} is average years of schooling of those who work out-
                     side
        EXP_i^{OA} is average years of labour market experience of those
                     who work outside
        EXP_i^{2OA} is the quadratic term of EXP_i^{OA}.

The data used for the empirical test are from a sample survey of about 1,000 rural households across five of China's provinces, namely Guangdong, Jilin, Jiangxi, Sichuan and Shandong. The survey was conducted in 1994 and 1995.[2] There are some data limitations which affect how the hypothesis can be tested and the way the model is set up. The most important one is that the income is reported at household rather than at individual level. Second, although the total number of work-days of home production and outside work are available, it is impossible to tell which individuals worked in which activities and for how many days. Thus, in the empirical test only one household income equation combining income from both sources can be estimated. In addition, the variables used for human capital endowments have to be household averages rather than separate variables for those who worked in household production and those who worked outside. In addition, it is assumed in the test that all households use the same production technology. This is a strong, but necessary, assumption as the data do not allow us to estimate separate production functions for each household. We specify the household agricultural and non-agricultural production function in the form of a Cobb–Douglas specification.

Taking the Cobb–Douglas specification of the production function and assuming that the quantities of labour, capital and land have logarithmic relationships with output, and further assuming that the human capital

---

[2] See the appendix (p. 33) for the background to the survey and more details about the survey data and definitions of the variables used in the study (tables 3A.1 and 3A.2).

variables have semi-logarithmic relationships with household income, the household net income equation can then be written as:

$$\ln HNI_i = \gamma_0 + \gamma_1 \ln L_i^T + \gamma_2 \ln K_i + \gamma_3 \ln LL_i + \gamma_4 EDU_i^{TA}$$
$$+ \gamma_5 EXP_i^{TA} + \gamma_6 EXP_i^{2TA} + v_i \tag{3.4}$$

where the superscript T represents the total number of household labourers who work in and outside the home, TA represents the average of the total number of household labourers and v_i is an error term. The average years of labour market experience per household labourer is defined as the average age of the labourers *minus* seven *minus* the average years of schooling (Mincer 1974). The inclusion of labour inputs and the set of human capital variables capture the impact of these variables on both household production and on the variations of a household's outside earnings. Four other variables are also included. These are the household female labour ratio, *flr* (number of household female labourers divided by the total number of household labourers); the agricultural work-days' ratio, *agrwday* (number of household agricultural work-days divided by the total household work-days); a dummy variable for 1995, *year*; and a set of dummy variables for regions, *region*. The first of these variables is included to test whether the gender composition of the household matters with regard to household income determination. The second variable is important as agricultural and non-agricultural activities may generate different income for the household. Regional dummy variables are included to capture the regional differences in income level. Finally, as the data for the two years (1994 and 1995) are pooled, a time dummy variable is included to capture the possible changes in real income over time.

The income variables collected in the survey are the annual income of households. Labour, therefore, is measured as total household annual work-days, while capital is measured in terms of different types of material inputs. The final form of the household income equation may be specified as follows:

$$\ln HNI_i = \gamma_0 + \gamma_1 \ln wday_i^T + \gamma_2 \ln K_i + \gamma_3 \ln LL_i + \gamma_4 EDU_i^{TA} + \gamma_5 EXP_i^{TA}$$
$$+ \gamma_6 EXP_i^{2TA} + \gamma_7 flr_i + \gamma_8 agrwday_i + \gamma_9 region + \gamma_{10} year + v_i \tag{3.5}$$

Equation (3.5) can take two forms – the dependent variable can be specified as household net income or household net income per labourer. The latter is obtained by adjusting the relevant independent variables in (3.5) accordingly,[3] which gives us (3.6):

---

[3] For example, in the total net income equation, 'labour input' was defined as total household annual work-days, while in the net income per labourer equation, it is defined as household annual work-days per labourer. However, as household total years of schooling and experience do not make sense, these two variables in both equations are defined as average years of schooling and experience per labourer.

$$\ln HNI_i^A = \gamma_0 + \gamma_1 \ln wday_i^{TA} + \gamma_2 \ln K_i^A + \gamma_3 \ln LL_i^A + \gamma_4 EDU_i^{TA} + \gamma_5 EXP_i^{TA}$$
$$+ \gamma_6 EXP_i^{2TA} + \gamma_7 flr_i + \gamma_8 agrwday_i + \gamma_9 region + \gamma_{10} year + \nu_i \qquad (3.6)$$

where the superscript A represents the average of the total number of household labourers.

By controlling for all the input variables, including human capital variables (average years of education per labourer and potential labour market experience per labourer), (3.5) and (3.6) should provide a reasonable explanation of household net income determination. In particular, a test of whether the HRS constitutes an attractive incentive system can be carried out by examining whether labour inputs, household human capital endowments and household gender composition are significant determinants of household net income.

The summary statistics for the variables used in the study are reported in appendix table 3A.1. Equations (3.5) and (3.6) are estimated using the OLS procedure. The results are reported in table 3.1.[4] The t-statistics reported in the table are corrected for heteroscedasticity using the 'White' correction procedure (White 1980).

The two equations perform equally well in terms of the adjusted R^2s and the impact of the determinants of household income and household income per labourer is very similar. However, as the model specification is more consistent for the net income per labourer equation owing to the fact that the schooling and experience variable cannot be used as an aggregate, the following discussion will mainly focus on the net income per labourer equation.

Both labour work-days and land inputs contribute significantly to the household net income. A 1 per cent increase in labour work-days and land increases income by 0.23 and 0.47 per cent, respectively.

Capital inputs, on the other hand, have varying impacts. The use of seeds, plastic film and manure does not seem to affect household income, or household income per labourer – that is, the coefficients are statistically insignificant. Furthermore, the use of animal and tractor inputs has opposite effects. An increase in tractor ploughing increases household net income per labour but an increase in animal ploughing has the opposite effect. These different outcomes may reflect the level of technology adopted by different households.[5] However, when a separate household income per labourer regression is estimated for those households who used

---

[4] There seems to be a multicollinearity problem between experience and its squared term. Once the experience squared term is included, both variables become statistically insignificant. It is thus excluded from the regression.

[5] Although for the net income per labourer equation, the coefficient for animal input is not significant.

Table 3.1.   *OLS estimation of household net income equation*

	Log (NHI)		Log (NHI/LABOUR)	
	Coeff.	*t*-ratio	Coeff.	*t*-ratio
Constant	6.284	23.10	6.402	21.83
Log (total household work-days)	0.319	9.65	0.230	4.83
Log (land) (Mu)	0.443	12.70	0.474	14.27
Log (animal ploughing and sowing) (hr)	− 0.015	− 2.08	− 0.011	− 1.55
Log (plastic film) (kg)	0.010	0.72	0.026	1.87
Log (farm manure) (kg)	− 0.007	− 1.69	− 0.007	− 1.60
Log (pesticides input) (jin)	0.033	2.15	0.036	2.35
Log (seeds input) (jin)	0.004	0.21	0.002	0.12
Log (tractor ploughing and sowing) (hrs)	0.031	2.66	0.036	3.06
Average years of schooling per labourer	0.036	4.39	0.045	5.50
Average potential work experience (year)	0.004	1.69	0.007	3.16
Agricultural work-days/total work-days	− 0.321	− 5.45	− 0.338	− 5.70
Total female labourers/total labourers	0.029	0.28	0.070	0.68
Dummy variable for 1995:	0.320	12.46	0.316	12.28
Jianxi	− 0.790	− 16.98	− 0.795	− 17.06
Jilin	− 0.943	− 14.48	− 1.017	− 14.59
Sichuan	− 0.885	− 17.27	− 0.855	− 16.98
Shandong	− 0.602	− 12.25	− 0.575	− 11.80
Adjusted R^2	0.50		0.49	
No. of observations	1,863		1,863	

Note: Jin = Chinese weight measure: 1 jin = 0.5 kg.
Source: Author's estimations.

animal ploughing and sowing only, the results again indicate that additional animal ploughing and sowing hours contribute negatively to household income (or income per labourer).[6] This may suggest that the number of animal ploughing and sowing hours may be an indirect measure of the quality of soil which is ploughed or sowed. The worse the quality of the land, the longer it will take to plough or sow. This, however, should not be the case for tractor ploughing and sowing.

The coefficient for the variable which measures agricultural work-days as a percentage of the total work-days is negative and significant. It indicates that the higher the share of agricultural work-days, the lower the household net income. In other words, agricultural activity is less productive in terms of generating income than non-agricultural activities.

By controlling for all these production inputs and other related variables, it is found that an average number of years of schooling and work experience contributes positively and significantly to household net income per labourer. An extra year of education and experience increases

---

[6] The estimated results are available upon request from the author.

net household income per labourer by 4.5 and 0.7 per cent, respectively. These results suggest that human capital variables do affect household income and that individual productivity is being rewarded as a result of the HRS.

In the pre-reform system, the age structure of household members affected household grain distribution significantly. Perhaps our labour experience variable is capturing this effect rather than a productivity effect.[7] One way to eliminate this possibility is to see if the age of household members matter in determining household income. A variable 'average age of *household member*' instead of 'average years of experience (or age) of *household labourers*' was used in the household net income and net income per labourer equations. It turns out to be insignificant in both cases.[8] This result suggests that the average work experience of a household labourer contributes positively to household income because it is a productivity-related variable and not a reflection of the old work point and grain allocation system.

As expected, under the HRS a household's gender composition does not affect household or individual net income. As mentioned earlier, under the commune system, women earned systematically lower work points than men. This would be reflected in the household income equation as a negative relationship between the female/male labourer ratio and household incomes: the greater the proportion of women in a household, the lower the household's income. Under the HRS, however, households try to allocate labourers in order to maximise their income, and this should expand the income earning opportunities of women. For example, some TVP textile manufacturing jobs hire a high percentage of women and provide them with a higher income in comparison to work on farms. In addition, rural women are in high demand as maids in cities and, once again, they are being paid more than for agricultural work. Thus, women are no longer being systematically disadvantaged in terms of income earning.

As a similar study for the pre-reform era is not available, it is hard to make comparisons. Nevertheless, Putterman's (1990) study of the pre-reform rural incentive system provides some insights. According to Putterman, pre-reform income distribution in rural production teams was essentially egalitarian. The data used in Putterman's study indicate that in the commune system the income distribution among production team members comprised two parts: grain and cash, with grain distribution

---

[7] This is because of the fact that, following Mincer (1958), the work experience variable is derived from the age variable using the formula: work experience = age − years of schooling − school starting age.   [8] The results are available upon request from the author.

accounting for 74 per cent of total distributed income. Given that grain distribution was based on food requirements which were calculated on the basis of the number of household members and their age and gender distribution, the dominance of the grain distribution in household income implies a distribution of income which is not related to individuals' or households' work efforts.[9]

The results obtained from this exercise strongly suggest that labour productivity and effort are directly rewarded under the new system. It is not surprising that reforms are generating large productivity gains.

Changes in labour supply behaviour

The work point system adopted in the pre-reform era discouraged individuals from supplying an efficient number of hours of labour and encouraged free-rider behaviour (see Burkett and Putterman 1993). How have the changes brought about by the HRS affected labour supply behaviour in the agricultural sector? Have the changes been as significant as implied by the results of the previous section?

Burkett and Putterman (1993) estimated models of labour supply under the old collective farming system. Their main findings were that wage rates[10] had no impact on the individuals' labour supply and that individuals tended to over-supply labour so as to maximise their work points and their share of the collective payment under the terms of the work point system.

After the introduction of the HRS, one would expect utility-maximising labour supply behaviour from the farmers. A neo-classical theory of household time allocation, for example, would suggest a positive relation between the market wage rate and labour supply up to a certain point, after which, when a household is rich enough, it can afford to 'buy' more leisure as wages increase. If this were to occur, one would observe a backward-bending labour supply in response to wage increases. However, does China's rural labour supply respond to market signals? Here labour supply behaviour is subjected to an empirical test. Following Burkett and Putterman (1993) the model is specified as follows:[11]

---

[9] In the author's experience, households often earned work points which were less than the value of distributed grain rations.

[10] The 'wage rate' here refers to the value of a work point.

[11] In their study Burkett and Putterman (1993) had four labour supply equations for the busy and slack seasons and minimum required (busy season) and maximum allowed (slack season) as well as maximum voluntary (busy season) and minimum voluntary (slack season) supply of working-days. In this study, the specification for voluntary supply of working-days is adopted owing to the fact that under the HRS labour supply is always voluntary and not restricted to the agricultural sector only.

$$LS_i = \alpha + \beta_1 W_i + \beta_2 W_i^2 + \beta_3 AGE_i + \beta_4 AGE_i^2 + \beta_5 FLR_i + \beta_6 LMR_i + \varepsilon_i \qquad (3.7)$$

where: subscript i represents the household

LS is labour supply

W is the wage rate

AGE is the average age of household labourers

FLR is household female labour as a proportion of total household labour

LMR is total household labour as a proportion of total household members[12]

ε is the error term.

The data set used is the same as in the previous section. As both labour supply and income variables were reported as household aggregates, the dependent variable, which measures labour supply, is defined as household average labour work-days. This variable is generated by dividing total household work-days by the number of labourers in the household. Wage rate data are not directly available from the survey. However, it is possible to derive the returns to the quantity and quality of labour as the proxy for wage rate. From the household net income per labourer equation (3.6) estimated in the last section, the returns to the quantity and quality of labour can be specified as:

$$Returns\ to\ labour = \frac{\partial(HNI^A)}{\partial(workday^{TA})} * (work\text{-}day^{TA}) + \frac{\partial HNI^A}{\partial EDU^A} * EDU^A$$

$$+ \frac{\partial HNI^A}{\partial exp^A} * EXP^A \qquad (3.8)$$

where $\dfrac{\partial(HNI^A)}{\partial(work\text{-}day^{TA})}$ is the marginal income of work-days per labourer

$\dfrac{\partial HNI^A}{\partial EDU^A}$ is the marginal income of years of schooling per labourer

$\dfrac{\partial HNI^A}{\partial EXP^A}$ is the marginal income of years of experience per labourer.

---

[12] In Burkett and Putterman (1993), the gender and the dependency ratio of an individual were also included. As the data available in this study is only at the household level, the variables FLR and LMR are used to replace the gender and dependency ratio, respectively.

From the results presented in table 3.1, one can derive:

$$\frac{\partial HNI^A}{\partial work\text{-}day^{TA}} * work\text{-}day^{TA} = \frac{\partial \ln(HNI^A)}{\partial \ln(work\text{-}day^{TA})} * HNI^A = 0.23 * HNI^A$$

$$\frac{\partial HNI^A}{\partial EDU^A} * EDU^A = \frac{\partial \ln(HNI^A)}{\partial(EDU^A)} * HNI^A * EDU^A = 0.045 * HNI^A * EDU^A$$

$$\frac{\partial HNI^A}{\partial EXP^A} * EXP^A = \frac{\partial \ln(HNI^A)}{\partial(EXP^A)} * HNI^A * EXP^A = 0.007 * HNI^A * EXP^A$$

This procedure is equivalent to the application of instrumental variables, which allow the estimation procedure to avoid an endogenecity problem arising from including the wage rate in the labour supply equation.[13] The estimated results of (3.7) are presented in table 3.2.[14]

The adjusted R^2 suggests that the model explains 55 per cent of labour supply variations among the households surveyed. The impact of wage rates on labour supply appears to be inverse-U-shaped. An increase in the daily wage rate by 1 yuan initially increases annual labour supply by 3

Table 3.2.   *Estimated labour supply equation (work-days per household labourer)*

	Coeff.	t-ratio
Constant	125.33	3.65
Daily wage	3.31	7.64
(Daily wage)^2	− 0.03	− 5.37
Average age per household labourer	6.88	4.39
(Average age per household labourer)^2	− 0.09	− 4.62
Household labourer/household member	− 8.15	− 1.28
Female labourer/household total labourer	− 5.47	− 0.54
Dummy variable for 1995:	− 9.91	− 3.86
Jilin	− 139.77	− 29.28
Jixi	− 5.58	− 1.11
Sichuan	11.57	2.43
Shandong	− 4.29	− 1.00
Adjusted R^2		0.55
No. of observations		1904

Source: Author's estimations.

[13] The drawback of this procedure, though, is that using generated regressors may create inconsistent estimates (Pagan 1984). However, as explained by Pagan (1984), when the hypothesis to be tested is $\beta = 0$, the OLS estimator of the variance of β is consistent and the t-statistics are valid.
[14] See the appendix (p. 33) for further explanation and summary statistics of the variables used in this section (tables 3A.1 and 3A.2).

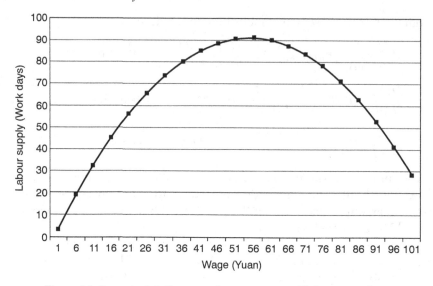

Figure 3.1 Impact of daily wage change on annual labour supply
Source: Author's calculation from results in table 3.2.

days. This response will gradually decline until the daily wage rate reaches a certain point ($W = 56$ yuan) after which a further increase in wages will result in less labour being supplied (when the income effect dominates). In this data set, the average wage rate is only around 8.2 yuan,[15] which is far from reaching the situation of a backward-bending labour supply curve (figure 3.1).

In addition to the impact of the wage rate, age also exhibits an inverse-U-shaped relationship with labour supply. Initially, a 1-year increase in age increases annual labour supply by 6.9 days. The rate of increase, however, decreases among older workers. After the age of 40, labour supply decreases. The female labour ratio and the labour/family member ratio have no effect on average household labour supply.

The most important finding, therefore, is that household labour supply behaviour has changed significantly after the rural economic reforms. According to Burkett and Putterman (1993), the wage rate had no effect on labour supply in pre-reform rural China. The findings in this study suggest that rural labour supply responded in a normal way to market signals – the wage rate exhibited an inverse-U-shaped relationship with labour supply. The signs for both age variables and the labour/family member

[15] See table 3A.2 (p. 35) for summary statistics of wage rates and figure 3A.1 (p. 34) for the distribution of the variable.

ratio are the same as in the Burkett and Putterman study. However, in their study, the variable *SEX* has a positive sign, suggesting that females supplied more labour-days than their male counterparts. This is, however, not the case for the post-reform era.

The analysis suggests that, since the beginning of the economic reform, the rural labour arrangement has gradually shifted towards a market-oriented system, one in which income is determined according to labour productivity and labour supply responds to market signals.

Appendix: description of the data

The data set used in this study is from a 1994–5 sample survey of about 1,000 rural households of China's five provinces, Guangdong, Jilin, Jiangxi, Sichuan and Shandong. This survey was jointly conducted by the Chinese Economy Research Unit, University of Adelaide, Australia, and the Ministry of Agriculture, China, as a part of an Australian Centre for International Agricultural Research (ACIAR) project on China's grain production, marketing and consumption.

The number of observations used in this study is the number of effective observations that allow a comparison between the data collected in 1994 and in 1995. There are 931 household observations actually used in the estimation of the model.

The derivation of each variable is explained as follows.

Dependent variable

Household net income (yuan): The income variable obtained from the survey data is household gross total income, which is equal to the household total sales *plus* earnings from outside activities. Household net income is the household gross total income *minus* the cost of renting inputs, deflated using 1994 rural CPIs for each region.

Household net income per labourer (yuan): Household net income divided by the number of household labourers.

Annual work-days per household labourer (*alwday*) (day): Household total working-days divided by the number of household labourers.

Independent variable

Labour (L) (person): Total household work-days.

Land (A) (Mu): Arable land contracted by the household.

Capital inputs: Animal ploughing and sowing hours; plastic film used for production (kg); farm manure used for production (kg); pesticides input (jin); seeds input (jin); tractor ploughing and sowing hours.[16]

Education (EDU) (year): Average years of schooling per household labourer.

Age (year): Average age of household labourers.

Experience (EXP) (year): Average potential years of labour market experience per household labourer, which is measured by the average age of household labourers *minus* 7 (the age children start school in China) *minus* average years of schooling per household labourer.

Rate of female labour (flr) (per cent): Total number of household female labourers divided by the total number of household labourers.

Rate of agricultural working-days (agrwday) (per cent): Household total agricultural working-days divided by the household total working-days.

Wage (Wage) (yuan): As defined in (3.8) (p. 30).

Household labourers as proportion of the total number of household members (LMR): Total household labourers divided by total household members.

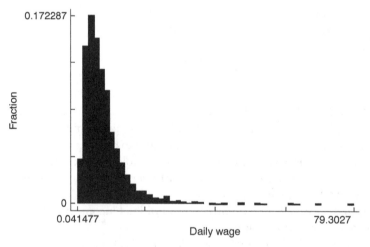

Figure 3A.1 Distribution of derived variable 'daily wage'

---

[16] In the net income per labourer equation, all the labour, land and capital inputs are divided by the number of household labourers.

Table 3A.1.   *Summary statistics of variables used in income equations*

	1994		1995	
	Mean	SD	Mean	SD
Net household income	08,820.08	10,079.05	11,087.84	11,883.92
Net household income per labourer	2,995.31	3,126.92	3,741.56	4,646.11
Total household work-days	752.04	401.70	735.11	390.50
Household work-days per labourer	238.83	81.62	234.47	77.42
Land (Mu)	9.26	9.30	9.17	9.80
Animal ploughing and sowing (hr)	50.67	105.29	61.43	124.22
Plastic film (kg)	4.06	8.25	3.74	7.22
Farm manure (kg)	13,633.74	17,618.54	13,748.35	22,758.34
Pesticides input (jin)	12.87	30.06	12.70	28.78
Seeds input (jin)	159.39	197.39	143.94	150.67
Tractor ploughing and sowing (hr)	5.36	18.15	8.97	44.71
Average years of schooling per labourer	6.48	1.93	6.59	1.94
Average potential work experience (year)	23.97	7.38	24.60	7.32
Agricultural work-days/total work-days	0.63	0.27	0.64	0.28
Total female labourers/total labourers	0.50	0.13	0.49	0.12
Dummy variable:				
Jianxi	0.24		0.24	
Jilin	0.15		0.16	
Sichuan	0.23		0.23	
Shandong	0.23		0.22	
Guangdong	0.15		0.14	
No. of observations	949		949	

Note: 1 Mu = 0.1647 acre; 1 jin = 0.5 kg.
Source: Author's calculations.

Table 3A.2.   *Summary statistics of variables used in labour supply equation*

	Mean	SD
Annual work-days per labourer	37.50	79.39
Daily wage	.26	8.22
(Daily wage)^2	35.74	518.04
Average age per household labourer	7.87	6.66
(Average age per household labourer)^2	1478.22	557.07
Household labourer/household member	.71	0.21
Female labourer/total labourer	.49	0.12

Source: Author's calculations.

4

Labour arrangements in the rural non-agricultural sector

The introduction of the HRS has clearly changed the incentive system in the agricultural sector. As a result of this reform and an increase in producer prices of grain products in 1979, China's grain output increased 3 per cent per annum, and farm family income increased 7.3 per cent per annum between 1978 and 1995. In addition, rural township (formerly commune), village (formerly brigade) and privately-owned enterprises have experienced extremely rapid growth, especially since 1983.[1]

The rural economy as a whole has undergone a two-pronged transformation. First, the better production incentives associated with the HRS caused a sharp rise in labour productivity which, in turn, created a large agricultural surplus. Second, the implicit surplus of agricultural labour which was a characteristic of the pre-reform era became explicit. Despite these changes, the regulations separating urban and rural economies did not change significantly, at least until the late 1980s.[2]

The combination of barriers to migrate to the cities and an agricultural production surplus led to industrialisation in the countryside. Hundreds of thousands of manufacturing, construction and other non-agricultural enterprises were set up, first in the southeast and coastal areas of China, and then all over the country. These enterprises absorbed surplus agricultural labour and raised the income of the rural population. By 1995, about 29 per cent of the total rural labour force was employed in the rural non-agriculture enterprises, while 56 per cent of the value of national industrial output was from the rural industrial sector (table 4.1).

Clearly, one of the most interesting changes brought about by the HRS has been the dramatic growth of the rural non-agricultural sector.

---

[1] The theoretical and empirical discussions of this chapter draw heavily on Meng (1996a).
[2] A labour force survey of 222 villages showed that the permanent migration of rural labour to urban areas accounted for only 1.75 per cent of the total labour force up to 1986 (Yu, 1989).

Table 4.1. *Share of rural industrial sector in rural and total economy, 1978–1995 (per cent)*

	Employment[a]		Gross industrial output value
	TVE[b]/rural total	Agri./rural total	TVE/National
1978	9.2	90.8	n.a.
1980	9.4	90.6	n.a.
1984	14.5	85.5	n.a.
1985	18.8	81.2	18.8
1986	20.9	79.1	21.6
1987	22.6	77.4	23.5
1988	23.8	76.2	24.9
1989	22.9	77.1	23.8
1990	22.1	77.9	25.3
1991	22.3	77.7	30.8
1992	24.2	75.8	36.8
1993	27.9	72.1	44.5
1994	26.9	73.1	42.0
1995	28.6	71.4	55.7

Notes: [a]The employment figures in the rural non-agricultural sector include only the TVEs before 1984. Thereafter, the figures include all rural non-agriculture employment.
[b]TVE = township and village-owned enterprises.
n.a. = Not available.
Source: SSB (various years b).

Reform of the rural non-agricultural labour market

After the introduction of the HRS, the production team, which had previously been the basic accounting unit in rural China, lost most of its administrative and economic functions. With production and income distribution decisions now made within families, it was impossible and meaningless for those who worked in enterprises to have their income distributed within their home production team (now called the group of villagers). Therefore, between 1978 and 1983 the income distribution system of commune and brigade enterprises was transformed from the work point system to a within-firm wage system. As a result, various wage systems appeared, for example, a within-firm work points system; a fixed cash wage, which took wage levels in state-owned enterprises as the point of reference (but normally paid a slightly lower wage); and a half-fixed cash wage, which was paid monthly *plus* half within-firm work points, paid at the end of the year.

1983 was a turning point for the township, village and privately-owned enterprise (TVP) sector. In this year the *production responsibility system* was introduced to most township and village-owned enterprises (TVE). This meant that TVEs had more power over managerial decision-making.

Privately-owned rural non-agricultural enterprises were encouraged, and the majority of commune and brigade enterprises (by 1984 they had changed to TVEs) switched to a monthly cash wage system. The cash wage system linked an individual's work effort and payment more directly than the work points system, providing more incentive for working hard. Most firms, for example, adopted a piece-rate wage system whenever possible. For those jobs which were impossible to monitor in this manner, a time rate wage was adopted, supplemented by a bonus system.

Managers of TVEs had decision-making power over wage determination from as early as 1985. In the World Bank 1986–7 survey (Byrd and Lin, 1990), for example, over 60 per cent of firms in the sample claimed that they had decision-making power over wage and bonus determination. Labour allocation in the TVE sector, on the other hand, moved rather slowly towards a market system. Immediately after the introduction of the HRS, the three levels of authorities (commune, brigade and production team, later changed to township, village and the group of villagers) lost their power over agricultural decision-making. However, most non-agricultural production was still organised by communes and brigades. As labour productivity in the non-agricultural sector was much higher than that in the agricultural sector, wages in the two sectors differed considerably, and there was thus always an excess supply of labour in the rural non-agricultural sector (see chapter 5). To solve this problem, townships or the villages assigned labour to the TVEs. The assignment system was similar to that of the pre-reform urban employment system, whereby a township or village authority decided who could work in a TVE enterprise and also how many new employees the TVE was allowed to hire. In effect, individual farmers were unable to find a job in the TVE sector by themselves, and firms were not allowed to hire or fire workers.

Up until 1985, this situation did not change much in most rural areas of China. According to a survey conducted by the World Bank in 1986–7 in four counties of rural China,[3] about 60 per cent of the sampled rural

---

[3] This survey was conducted jointly by the World Bank and the Institute of Economics of the Chinese Academy of Social Sciences in 1986–7. Four counties were involved in the survey: Wuxi county in Jiangsu province; Nanhai county in Guangdong province; Jieshou county in Anhui province; and Shangrao county in Jiangxi province. Five questionnaires were designed for the TVP sample survey: a Workers' Survey Questionnaire (WSQ) for TVP employees; an Enterprise Survey Questionnaire (ESQ) for management teams of sample firms; an Enterprise Director Questionnaire (EDQ) for directors of sample firms; an Enterprise Quantitative Questionnaire (EQQ), filled out by accountants of sample firms; and a Township Leader Questionnaire (TLQ). The total number of firms included in the survey is 121. The ESQ, EDQ and EQQ each sampled 121 firms. The WSQ was conducted in 46 firms of the total of 121 sample firms, and the total number of observations was 1,174. The main part of this study is based on the WSQ.

industrial sector employees reported that they were directly or indirectly assigned to their jobs by local authorities (Meng 1992). In addition to this rigid labour allocation process, labour mobility across townships and villages was also very limited. The same survey showed that about 70 per cent of rural industrial sector employees were from the same village or township, and that around 90 per cent were from the same county.

Nevertheless, there were some alterations in the rural industrial sector's recruitment system. The World Bank survey suggested that workers who were employed in 1978 had been mostly assigned to their jobs, while among those who were employed in 1985, 50 per cent had found their jobs through a market mechanism and only 17 per cent had been assigned by the authorities. This suggests that the importance of the market mechanisms in labour allocation had grown substantially since the introduction of the reforms (Gregory and Meng 1995).

Since 1985, these changes have continued to transform the rural labour market. Firms owned by townships or villages are becoming much more flexible in their hiring and firing of labour. A survey conducted by the Rural Economy Research Centre and the World Bank in 1991 provides information on 300 TVEs in 14 provinces (Xu, Jefferson and Rathja 1993). The findings there suggest that, by 1991, about 96 per cent of the 300 enterprises claimed to have direct (67 per cent) or indirect (29 per cent) decision-making power with respect to the recruitment of new employees, and 95 per cent with respect to dismissal of employees (72 per cent having direct and 23 per cent having indirect decision-making power).[4] This has been necessary in order for the TVEs to survive the increasing competition from private firms.

Table 4.2. *Ownership structure of TVP in terms of employment 1984–95*

	Total TVE employment (10,000 person)	Per cent of TVE	Per cent of other ownership employment
1984	5,208.1	72.5	23.5
1985	6,979.0	62.0	38.0
1990	9,264.8	49.6	50.4
1991	9,609.1	49.6	50.4
1992	10,581.1	48.7	51.3
1993	12,345.3	46.7	53.3
1994	12,018.2	49.1	50.9
1995	12,862.1	47.1	52.9

Source: SSB (various years b), tables 11–29.

[4] The figures presented here are from author's own calculations from the survey data.

Competition for labour comes from the increasing numbers of private-ly-owned, joint venture, and fully foreign-owned firms that have emerged in countryside and which can employ whoever they want. Table 4.2 shows the growth in employment and changes in the ownership structure of TVPs in terms of employment for the decade from the mid-1980s onward. Since the early 1990s, the TVEs have employed only about half of the total TVP labourers. Taken in conjunction with the dramatic changes in the employment system within TVEs, it can be seen that market recruitment mechanisms have gradually come to dominate the employment system in the rural non-agricultural sector, especially since the early 1990s

Theoretical considerations of wage determination

The main difference between the TVE labour market before 1985 and the theoretical construct analysed in conventional economic theory is clear-cut: neo-classical models assume that individual firms take market wages as given and choose the number of employees to maximise their profits, whereas under the TVE labour market system, firms do not have decision-making power over the number of employees and wages, instead of being a pre-determined variable, are endogenously set by the township and village enterprises.

The behaviour of firms in the TVE sector may partly be explained by the efficiency wage theory (for example, Stiglitz 1974; Solow 1979, 1985). This theory modifies the neo-classical labour market model by letting firms use the wage as a means of encouraging employees to stay with the firm to minimise training costs, or as a means of inducing greater effort from workers. This theory is usually used to explain the phenomenon of the simultaneous existence of unemployment and above-market-level wages.

The situation in the pre-1985 TVEs was, however, slightly different. In the TVE labour market, the attachment of a firm and employees was exogenous. Firms could not freely hire or fire employees. In addition, the only alternative employment opportunity for employees – agricultural employment – provided much lower income as labour productivity in the agricultural sector was lower than that in the rural industrial sector (see chapter 5).[5] Employees in the TVEs would therefore not choose to quit

[5] Stiglitz (1982) also points out that

> [E]fficiency wage considerations may be important in both the rural and urban sectors; but there is no reason that the efficiency-wage function should be the same in the two sectors (since the nature of the work performed is so different, as are the environmental factors which affect the effect of wages on productivity). Thus, the wages paid in the two sectors may differ markedly.

their jobs in order to obtain lower wages, given that the TVE firms paid employees according to their labour productivity. Although employees could choose to shirk given that they could not be fired, if shirking was detected, the workers' wage level could be decreased as managers had the right and incentive to do so.[6] On the other hand, TVE firms operated in a very competitive environment and were subject to fairly hard budget constraints. If the firms were not successful, both employees and managers would lose their jobs. Managers were thus motivated to operate efficiently by setting up an effective incentive system, and this implied that the firm had to pay its employees fairly. This situation had three major effects. First, it prevented firms from paying employees lower than their alternative wage, since workers would choose to quit from the TVEs. Second, firms were under pressure to set an effective incentive system and consequently would pay workers according to their productivity. Third, where firms paid their workers fairly, it was expected that the workers would respond by providing sufficient effort.

Under these circumstances, how would firms react in order to maximise their profit?[7] The firm's problem is to choose wage levels in order to discourage shirking, and to induce the level of effort from employees in order to maximise profit. This problem can be written as:

$$\max_{w} \pi = pf[e(w)\bar{L}, \qquad \bar{K}] - w\bar{L} - \bar{r}\bar{K} \tag{4.1}$$

where π is profit

p is price of output

w is wage rate

e is effort provided by each individual

L is labour input which is a constant in the short run

K is capital stock which in the short run is assumed to be a constant

r is rent for capital

$f[e(w)L, K]$ is the production function.

The first-order condition in this problem is:

$$pf_e = w_e \bar{L} \tag{4.2}$$

Here, f_e is the partial derivative of f with respect to e, or the marginal product of effort, and w_e is the partial derivative of w with respect to e, or the marginal wage of effort. The marginal cost of effort is represented by

---

[6] Monitoring is, therefore, extremely important for the TVE firms: they often choose a piece-rate payment system, as this is the cheapest and best monitoring mechanism.

[7] Byrd (1987) gives a detailed explanation when he assumes Chinese state-owned enterprises have an objective of profit-maximisation. His explanation is even more relevant to the TVE case.

$w_e \bar{L}$. The result of (4.2) therefore means that in order to maximise its profit the firm has to pay each individual a wage where the value of the marginal product of effort is equal to the marginal cost of effort.

Several points are evident from the above analysis. First, it is clear that the role of the wage in the TVE firm is to induce effort from each individual so as to maximise the firm's profit. Second, in order to achieve this, the firm must pay individuals a wage where the value of their marginal product of effort equals their marginal cost of effort. However, the above analysis is based on the rather strong assumption that individuals are homogeneous with respect to their provision of effort. If we relax this assumption by accepting the fact that individuals, in reality, are different in terms of their productive effort provision, it is obvious that individuals who provide different levels of effort will receive different wage rates, provided firms are able to monitor effort. Then, if an individual's productivity can be increased through the augmentation of human capital (for example, through education and labour market experience), individuals could expect to get the market rate of return to their investment in human capital.

More specifically, the following propositions may be stated:

- Labour market experience should have a significant impact on wage determination, as it has a direct impact on labour productivity. No matter what skill levels a job requires and keeping all other attributes equal, an experienced worker will be more productive than an inexperienced worker.
- The impact of education on wage determination depends on whether it affects labour productivity. In the case where the levels of technology and the required skills are low, education may not have a significant impact on labour productivity. It may therefore not affect individual wage determination in some parts of the TVE. On the contrary, when the level of technology is high it might be expected that education would be an important determinant of wages.

To sum up, according to the model described above there are two hypotheses to be tested: (1) Wage levels are likely to be determined by labour productivity in the TVEs; (2) human capital theory should be applicable to wage determination in the TVEs.

Testing wage determination

To test the above propositions, this section uses data from Workers' Survey Questionnaire (WSQ) of the World Bank 1986–7 survey. The four counties – Wuxi, Jieshou, Shangrao and Nanhai – involved in the survey represent different levels of rural industrialisation and varying degrees of administrative control and ownership structures. These four types of development conditions, particularly from the point of view of rural industrialisation, should approximately represent the various situations in most areas of rural China.[8]

The data were taken from 49 of the 121 sample firms of the TVP sector.[9] There are 1,174 observations on individual employees, but owing to missing values the sample has been reduced to 1,060 observations. In this study, the analysis is confined to a sample of male workers. The sample size ranged from 400 to 529, depending on the exact set of variables chosen for analysis.[10]

According to many applications of the human capital model, schooling and work experience, including general labour market and firm-specific skills, are the factors that have the most significant impact on individual wages. In an application across areas that differ appreciably in terms of economic development, there is also expected to be a regional element to wage determination. The basic human capital model can, therefore, be specified as follows:

Model 1

$$\ln(w) = a + b_1 S + b_2 FT + b_3 FT^2 + b_4 OJ + b_5 OJ^2 + b_6 RE + u$$

where w is daily wage

S is years of schooling

FT is firm-specific tenure

FT^2 is the squared term of firm-specific tenure

OJ is other job experience

OJ^2 is the squared term of other job experience

RE is a vector of regional dummies

u is a random-error term.

This model can be generalised in a number of ways. When the data were collected most TVP firms had existed for less than 10 years and most employees were farmers before they were employed by the firm. Model 2 is therefore specified to capture the relationship between the wage level and agricultural and non-agricultural experience.

[8] For detailed information on the characteristics of each region, see Byrd and Lin (1990b).

[9] The sample includes TVE as well as a very small number of privately-owned enterprises. The extent of community (township or village) control varies by region and enterprise, as does the level of economic development. A fuller discussion of the project can be found in Byrd and Lin (1990b).

[10] Detailed explanations and summary statistics of variables used in the study are presented in table 4A.2 (p. 56).

Model 2

$$\ln(w) = a + b_1 S + b_2 FT + b_3 FT^2 + b_4 ONAJ + b_5 ONAJ^2 + b_6 AEXP + b_7 AEXP^2 + b_8 RE + v$$

where $ONAJ$ is other non-agricultural experience
       $ONAJ^2$ is the squared term of other non-agricultural experience
       $AEXP$ is agricultural experience
       $AEXP^2$ is the squared term of agricultural experience
       v is a random-error term.

Finally, it is generally argued that wages in different types of work may incorporate a compensating differential that accommodates peculiar disamenities associated with that work. Accordingly, the wage-generating function is often expanded to include variables for the type of work undertaken. Reflecting this, both models are also estimated with a set of dummy variables for occupations. The total number of employees is divided into staff and workers. 'Staff' refers to those who are engaged in managerial and technical work, while 'workers' refers to those who are engaged in manual work. The occupation variable has staff coded as 1 and workers as 0.

To test the applicability of the human capital model in TVP wage determination, the above models are estimated for total male employees in the first instance, and then separately for the two occupational groups – namely, the staff and workers groups (tables 4.3 and 4.4).

The salient features of these results can be discussed in relation to the impacts of experience and schooling on wages.

Experience

The results show that experience is an important determinant of wages. Other job experience (total experience *minus* firm tenure) and firm tenure are statistically significant and are associated with a rate of return of about 2.5–3 per cent for each additional year of experience over most of the first decade of work. This is similar to the pattern of experience effects reported in studies of Western labour markets (for example, Polachek and Siebert 1993). When other job experience is further disaggregated into agricultural experience and non-agricultural experience (see model 2 of table 4.3), the estimates of the coefficients appear very similar across the experience variables. This suggests that the source of labour market experience is largely irrelevant, though the result is a little surprising in that one might not expect a close relationship between experience in agricultural and non-agricultural jobs. However, when the total male sample is disaggregated into workers and staff sub-groups the situation becomes clearer (table 4.4).

Table 4.3.   *OLS results of models of wage determination, China's TVP sector, 1985*

	Model 1		Model 2[a]	
	Without ocp	With ocp	Without ocp	With ocp
	$n = 529$	$n = 525$	$n = 457$	$n = 454$
Constant	1.016	1.089	1.068	1.154
	(10.69)[b]	(11.44)	(9.89)	(10.87)
Schooling	0.011	−0.0002	0.007	−0.007
	(1.63)	(−0.003)	(0.85)	(−0.81)
Firm-specific tenure (FT)[c]				
FT	0.028	0.021	0.032	0.024
	(2.80)	(2.15)	(2.91)	(2.19)
$(FT)^2$	−0.0007	−0.0006	−0.0009	−0.0007
	(1.93)	(−1.61)	(−2.15)	(−1.77)
Other job exp. (OJ)				
OJ	0.029	0.027	n.a.	n.a.
	(5.48)	(5.12)		
$(OJ)^2$	−0.0006	−0.0006	n.a.	n.a.
	(−3.83)	(−3.89)		
Other non-agri. exp. $(ONAJ)$				
ONAJ	n.a.	n.a.	0.023	0.019
			(3.76)	(3.12)
$(ONAJ)^2$	n.a.	n.a.	−0.0005	−0.0004
			(−2.91)	(−2.65)
Agri. exp. $(AEXP)$				
AEXP	n.a.	n.a.	0.025	0.022
			(3.18)	(2.89)
$(AEXP)^2$	n.a.	n.a.	−0.0005	−0.0005
			(−2.02)	(−1.94)
Occupational dummy	n.a.	0.144	n.a.	0.177
		(3.53)		(4.13)
County dummies:				
Jieshou	−0.274	−0.265	−0.309	−0.293
	(−6.28)	(−6.16)	(−6.36)	(−6.19)
Shangrao	−0.441	−0.427	−0.495	−0.472
	(−8.19)	(−7.72)	(−8.77)	(−8.10)
Nanhai	0.529	0.524	0.481	0.478
	(7.70)	(7.54)	(6.61)	(6.56)
Breusch–Pagan[d] chi-squared	47.02 (8)	55.44 (9)	47.64 (10)	51.72 (11)
Adjusted R^2	0.34	0.37	0.34	0.36

Notes: [a]By deleting observations with negative values of work experience in the residual categories, the sample size for model 2 is reduced by about 15 per cent.
[b]*t*'-statistics in parentheses.
[c]*FT* is firm tenure; *AEXP* is agricultural experience; *OJ* is other labour market experience, excluding firm tenure; *ONAJ* is other non-agricultural experience.
[d]Breusch–Pagan χ^2-tests for heteroscedasticity; the degrees of freedom for the χ^2 statistics are presented in parentheses.
n.a. = The variable is not applicable in this specification.
ocp = Occupation.

Table 4.4.　*OLS results of models of wage determination, by occupational groups[a]*

	Model 1		Model 2	
	Workers	Staff	Workers	Staff
	$n = 271$	$n = 262$	$n = 230$	$n = 230$
Constant	0.967	1.466	1.012	1.494
	(7.56)[b]	(9.96)	(7.23)	(9.22)
Schooling	−0.009	−0.009	−0.014	−0.003
	(−0.08)	(−0.87)	(−1.09)	(−0.29)
Firm-specific tenure (FT)[c]				
FT	0.049	0.0002	0.057	−0.002
	(3.47)	(0.02)	(3.86)	(−0.13)
$(FT)^2$	−0.0017	0.0001	−0.002	0.0002
	(−2.91)	(0.23)	(−3.39)	(0.32)
Other job exp. (OJ)				
OJ	0.015	0.031	n.a.	n.a.
	(1.89)	(4.66)		
$(OJ)^2$	−0.0002	−0.0007	n.a.	n.a.
	(−0.77)	(−3.96)		
Other non-agri. exp. ($ONAJ$)				
$ONAJ$	n.a.	n.a.	0.024	0.014
			(2.82)	(1.66)
$(ONAJ)^2$	n.a.	n.a.	−0.0005	−0.0004
			(−1.92)	(−1.20)
Agri. exp. ($AEXP$)				
$AEXP$	n.a.	n.a.	0.012	0.026
			(1.03)	(2.92)
$(AEXP)^2$	n.a.	n.a.	−0.0002	−0.0007
			(−0.35)	(−2.36)
County dummies:				
Jieshou	−0.219	−0.299	−0.212	−0.347
	(−3.70)	(−4.96)	(−3.21)	(−5.35)
Shangrao	−0.222	−0.648	−0.256	−0.694
	(−2.87)	(−7.80)	(−2.96)	(−8.07)
Nanhai	0.821	0.211	0.774	0.190
	(8.22)	(2.93)	(7.35)	(2.44)
Breusch-Pagan[d] chi-squared[e]	36.31 (8)	7.05 (8)	29.96 (10)	9.21 (10)
Adjusted R^2	0.41	0.33	0.40	0.35

Notes: [a]In this table, the results for the workers' group (both model 1 and model 2) are corrected for heteroscedasticity (using White's consistent covariance matrix). There is no heteroscedasticity problem for the staff group. The 't'-statistics presented in the table for the staff group use the OLS covariance matrix.
[b]'t'-statistics in parentheses.
[c]FT is firm tenure; $AEXP$ is agricultural experience; OJ is other labour market experience, excluding firm tenure; $ONAJ$ is other non-agricultural experience.
[d]Breusch–Pagan χ^2 tests for heteroscedasticity; the degrees of freedom for the χ^2 statistics are presented in parentheses.
[e]The critical chi-squared value at the 5 per cent significance level for $n = 8$ is $\chi^2 = 15.51$; for $n = 10$, $\chi^2 = 18.31$.
n.a. = The variable is not applicable in this specification.

For workers, firm tenure and other non-agricultural experience are statistically significant, with firm tenure having the greater impact on wage determination. Farm experience has a statistically insignificant effect on the wage. These results accord well with human capital theory. As an individual's experience in the firm or in other non-agricultural jobs increases, their labour productivity is expected to increase; consequently, their wage should increase.

For staff, however, the most important source of experience seems to be agricultural employment. Other non-agricultural experience ranks second and firm tenure seems unimportant. These are very surprising results. Two conjectures are offered to explain these results. First, as noted previously, most employees were assigned to their positions. Moreover, the community authority normally assigned leaders of the production team or brigade to be the management staff of the firm. The rank and starting wages in the firm, therefore, reflected the length of the time that individuals had been agricultural leaders. This might account for the strong relationship between agricultural experience and wages for staff. Once they have become staff members and have gained experience in one firm, they are often assigned to a new firm to a higher level. If the wage levels set for staff depended on firm tenure (either in the old or the new firm), they would be reluctant to move. Hence, there is no strong link between firm tenure and earnings, but there is such a link between other non-agricultural job experience and earnings. Second, management skills learned in agricultural and other non-agricultural sectors are easily transferred to management in an enterprise.

Education

Most studies of Western labour markets have shown education to be a key determinant of income distribution (Psacharopoulos 1985). The most unusual result arising from the analysis of the male labour market in the TVEs is the insignificant effect of education on individual wage determination. The poor performance of the education variable is a characteristic of both the analysis of the total male sample (table 4.3) and of the analysis based on data disaggregated into workers and staff groups (table 4.4). The return to education is, at most, 1 per cent for the total male sample and appears to be negative for the disaggregated data. Does this unusual result reflect a labour productivity effect or is it due to socially determined rules of payment?

Normally, productivity of effort is very hard to measure as the cost of monitoring is too high. However, monitoring costs are relatively low for

Table 4.5.   *Wage determination for piece-rate and time-rate employees*

	Model 1		Model 2	
	Piece-rate $n = 166$	Time-rate $n = 363$	Piece-rate $n = 147$	Time-rate $n = 310$
Constant	1.041	1.011	1.038	1.012
	(7.12)[a]	(8.20)	(6.78)	(7.42)
Schooling	0.010	0.013	0.009	0.010
	(0.91)	(1.54)	(0.58)	(0.91)
Other job exp. (*OJ*)				
OJ	0.026	0.033	n.a.	n.a.
	(2.53)	(5.38)		
$(OJ)^2$	− 0.0006	− 0.0006	n.a.	n.a.
	(− 2.19)	(− 3.65)		
Firm-specific tenure (*FT*)[b]				
FT	0.045	0.019	0.05	0.024
	(2.84)	(1.42)	(3.1)	(1.56)
$(FT)^2$	− 0.0012	− 0.0004	− 0.001	− 0.0006
	(− 1.66)	(− 0.89)	(− 2.0)	(− 1.19)
Other non-agri. exp. (*ONAJ*)				
ONAJ	n.a.	n.a.	0.026	0.025
			(2.45)	(3.39)
$(ONAJ)^2$	n.a.	n.a.	− 0.001	− 0.0005
			(− 2.7)	(− 2.50)
Agricultural exp. (*AEXP*)				
AEXP	n.a.	n.a.	0.031	0.027
			(2.14)	(2.87)
$(AEXP)^2$	n.a.	n.a.	− 0.001	− 0.0006
			(− 1.64)	(− 1.83)
County dummies:				
Jieshou	− 0.339	(− 0.261	(− 0.356	(− 0.287
	(− 5.01)	(− 4.60)	(− 5.30)	(− 4.60)
Shangrao	− 0.381	− 0.591	− 0.441	− 0.621
	(− 5.10)	(− 8.18)	(− 5.40)	(− 8.40)
Nanhai	0.524	0.521	0.488	0.471
	(4.01)	(6.60)	(3.61)	(5.57)
Breusch–Pagan[c] chi-squared[d]	44.60 (8)	25.03 (8)	49.3 (10)	27.9 (10)
Adjusted R^2	0.36	0.34	0.36	0.34

Notes: [a]'*t*'-statistics in parentheses.
[b]*FT* is firm tenure; *AEXP* is agricultural experience; *OJ* is other labour market experience, excluding firm tenure; *ONAJ* is other non-agricultural experience.
[c]Breusch–Pagan χ^2 tests for heteroscedasticity; the degrees of freedom for the χ^2 statistics are presented in parentheses.
[d]The critical χ^2 values for $n = 8$ and $n = 10$ at the 5 per cent significance level are the same as shown for table 4.3. In this table, the standard errors in all four regressions are corrected for heteroscedasticity.
n.a. = The variable is not applicable in this specification.

some kinds of production, where the quantity and quality of output can be counted by the piece. In this case, productivity of effort can be directly related to the items produced and, hence, to the piece-rate payment.

In the sample used for this study, 40 per cent of employees were paid by piece-rate and their earnings can thus be considered as a direct measure of labour productivity. If we group the data into those paid by piece-rate and those paid by time, and compare the results, it may be possible to test if employees in the TVEs are paid according to their labour productivity.

Models 1 and 2 are estimated separately for piece-rate and time-rate male employees, and the results are presented in table 4.5. Statistical tests revealed that the processes of wage determination for the two groups were the same.[11] The results suggest that, once again, schooling is statistically insignificant for both groups, a result that holds no matter which specification of experience is adopted. As piece-rate earnings are a direct measure of productivity, it appears that education does not affect labour productivity in the TVEs.

From the perspective of the evidence associated with the wage–education relationship in Western labour markets, the results for the TVEs are, once again, a puzzle. Perhaps, many jobs in the TVE firms are unskilled and productivity would be the same for all workers in these jobs, regardless of their levels of education. Hence, it would be expected that education would not be an important factor in wage determination.

Impact of change of the employment system on wage determination

An analysis of the institutional changes to employment in the TVE sector may also provide further understanding of the role of education in TVE wage determination. As mentioned on p. 39 above, one of the important changes in the employment system in the TVE sector between 1978 and 1985 was that a much larger fraction of employees found their jobs through their own effort rather than through assignment.

To test how such a change affects wage determination, the sample was disaggregated into market (those who found their jobs through their own efforts) and non-market (those who were assigned to their jobs) groups, and wage equations were estimated for the two groups separately (table 4.6). The most interesting result here is that education is significant for the

[11] *F*-tests were conducted to see whether the wage structures were the same for the piece-rate and time-rate groups. For model 1 $F(9,529) = 1.40$ and for model 2 $F(11,457) = 1.22$. These are both less than the respective critical value of $F(9,\infty) = 1.88$ and $F(11,\infty) = 1.83$, so the null hypothesis of no structural change for both models cannot be rejected.

Table 4.6. *Wage determination for market- and non-market-oriented employees*[a]

	Model 1			Model 2		
	Market $n=182$	Non-market $n=229$	Difference $n=411$	Market $n=153$	Non-market $n=206$	Difference $n=359$
Constant	0.689 (4.24)[b]	1.910 (8.90)	−0.603 (−2.69)	0.634 (3.23)	1.416 (9.15)	−0.782 (−3.13)
Schooling	0.039 (3.13)	−0.007 (−0.68)	0.046 (2.80)	0.041 (2.64)	−0.007 (−0.61)	0.048 (2.46)
Other job exp. (OJ)						
OJ	0.038 (3.13)	0.029 (3.56)	0.009 (0.63)			
$(OJ)^2$	−0.0007 (−1.79)	−0.0008 (−3.20)	0.0003 (0.08)			
Firm-specific tenure (FT)[c]						
FT	0.039 (2.05)	0.007 (0.51)	0.031 (1.31)	0.046 (2.04)	−0.005 (−0.29)	0.051 (1.83)
$(FT)^2$	−0.0007 (−0.86)	−0.0003 (−0.47)	−0.0004 (−0.45)	−0.0008 (−0.94)	0.0001 (0.17)	−0.0009 (−0.86)
Other non-agri. exp. (ONAJ)						
ONAJ				0.057 (3.47)	0.020 (1.62)	0.036 (1.76)
$(ONAJ)^2$				−0.002 (−2.30)	−0.0009 (−1.59)	−0.0009 (−0.94)
Agri. exp. (AEXP)						
AEXP				0.029 (2.14)	0.022 (2.23)	0.006 (0.39)
$(AEXP)^2$				−0.0003 (−0.63)	−0.0007 (−2.23)	0.0005 (0.89)

County dummies:					
JS	−0.263	−0.185	−0.078	−0.300	−0.234	−0.067
	(−3.61)	(−3.12)	(−0.84)	(−3.64)	(−3.92)	(−0.66)
SR	−0.382	−0.496	0.113	−0.465	−0.524	0.059
	(−3.12)	(−6.97)	(0.89)	(−3.96)	(−7.33)	(0.43)
NH	0.323	0.690	−0.368	0.169	0.671	−0.503
	(2.78)	(6.72)	(−2.28)	(1.27)	(6.35)	(−2.96)
Breusch–Pagan[a] chi-squared	6.93 (8)	23.9 (8)	31.9 (17)	18.5 (10)	22.1 (10)	40.9 (21)
Adjusted R^2	0.30	0.39	0.37	0.35	0.40	0.39

Notes: [a]The results listed in the columns of differences are the interaction terms between a dummy variable for the market and non-market groups and all other variables in a pooled data analysis.

[b]t-statistics in parentheses.

[c]FT is firm tenure; $AEXP$ is agricultural experience, excluding firm tenure; OJ is other labour market experience, excluding firm tenure; $ONAJ$ is other non-agricultural experience.

[d]Breusch–Pagan χ^2-tests for heteroscedasticity; the degrees of freedom for the χ^2 statistics are presented in parentheses.

n.a. = The variable is not applicable in this specification.

market group but insignificant for the non-market group. Specifically, the coefficient of schooling for the market group is 0.039 with a *t*-statistic of 3.13, while for the non-market group it is − 0.007 with a *t*-statistic of − 0.68. However, even the returns to education for the market group, at around 4 per cent, are considerably lower than the 7–10 per cent reported for the United States (Psacharopoulos 1985).

Why is education significant for the 'market' group but not for the 'non-market' group? Does this reflect labour productivity effects? To examine this question, both the market and non-market groups are sub-divided into piece-rate and time-rate groups and human capital wage equations estimated for each sub-sample. The results from this experiment indicate that education is a significant determinant of wages for both piece-rate and time-rate employees within the market group, while it is uniformly insignificant for employees in the non-market group.

Hence, it is not the method of payment that leads to the difference between the impact of education for the market and non-market groups. Rather, it must be something to do with the underlying nature or philosophy of these two models of obtaining employment. One reason why education might have a significant impact on labour productivity in the market group but not in the non-market group might be that the underlying technological processes of the work undertaken by each group are different. It may be that people involved in using more sophisticated technology need to be more highly educated in comparison to those who undertake simpler jobs.

To further develop this explanation, assume that there are two different kinds of firms, one employing high technology and the other low technology. Before economic reform, most of the TVE firms probably used low technology. Some firms might have used high technology but were not allowed to choose the better educated employees they required. The gradual liberalisation of the TVE labour market has, therefore, allowed high-technology firms to hire more appropriately skilled employees. And most importantly, because firms were allowed to choose the quality of their employees, more new firms may then have started to use high technology. The education levels of employees has, therefore, had a significant impact on the labour productivity of these high-technology firms. In turn, such productivity is rewarded.

Firms whose technology was relatively low, however, remained with the old recruitment system. They also paid their employees according to labour productivity although education did not increase labour productivity in the low-skilled jobs that predominated in these firms.[12]

This speculation seems to be reinforced by the steeper tenure–earnings

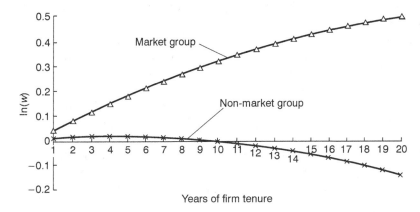

Figure 4.1 Comparison of tenure–earnings profiles between the market and non-market groups
Source: Author's calculation from table 4.6.

profile for the market group compared with the non-market group (figure 4.1). Economic theory regards the slope of tenure–earnings profile as an indicator of the technology level adopted. When higher technology is adopted, a firm's investment in on-the-job-training will be higher than a firm which adopts a lower level of technology. If workers who were trained quit the job, firms have to re-invest in new recruits and the investment they put in for the quitters will be lost. To reduce quitters, therefore, a firm with high technology will tend to pay a premium to encourage employees to remain. Thus, we observe a steeper tenure–earnings profile for those who work in a firm with a high technology level (for example, Salop and Salop 1976; Tan 1980; Hashimoto and Raisian 1985; Mincer and Higuchi 1988).

The steeper tenure–earnings profile for the market group compared with the non-market group suggests that firm-specific training is more important for the former than for the latter. This, in turn, suggests that the underlying technological level for the market group may be higher than for the non-market group.

Although by 1985 the TVE labour markets had features that diverged from those defined in neo-classical theory, the human capital model can

---

[12] The argument here suggests that technology alone is insufficient in the sense that it requires a certain economic environment in order to take effect. This argument could have been tested by linking technology to educational requirement and different institutional settings had a variable relating to the firms' technology levels been available.

still be used to explain the emerging wage determination patterns to a certain extent.

Things have been changing rapidly in the TVP sector since 1985. As mentioned on p. 39, by 1995 the number of employees in the TVEs accounted only for less than 50 per cent of total TVP employment. Furthermore, within TVEs, the employment system has moved further towards a market-oriented system. It can be speculated that the wage determination process may also have changed. Unfortunately, data are not available for empirical evaluation of this proposition.

The next question that arises is whether the wage levels in the rural agricultural and non-agricultural sectors have been converging, given the rather perfect labour mobility between the two sectors. This is examined in chapter 5.

Appendix: description of the data

The variables used in this study are created from responses to the *Workers' Survey Questionnaire* (WSQ), one of five questionnaires used in the *Township, Village, and Privately-Owned Enterprises Sample Survey*.

Income

The WSQ asked: 'What was your yearly income in 1985?', 'How many months did you work in 1985?' and 'How many days did you work per week?'. The daily income variable was obtained by the following formula: *yearly income*/[*days* × 4.345 × *months*], where 4.345 = (365/12)/7.

Years of schooling

Schooling data are defined in seven levels. Each level of education corresponds to the years of schooling indicated in table 4A.1.

Labour market experience

Firm tenure (*FT*) and total non-agricultural job experience are reported in the questionnaire. Total experience is measured as age *minus* years of schooling *minus* 7. As there is a high degree of multicollinearity between total experience and firm tenure, the total experience variable is divided

Table 4A.1. *Years of schooling corresponding to education level*

Level of education	Years of schooling
Illiteracy	0
4 years' primary	4
6 years' primary	6
Junior high school	9
Senior high school	12
3 years' degree from correspondence school	15
University and above	16

into firm tenure and other job experience (*OJ*), which is measured as total experience *minus* firm tenure (see table 4A.3 and 4A.4).

Occupations

There are six categories of occupation reported in the WSQ. These are workers, shift leaders (SL), operational personnel (OP), technical personnel (TP), ordinary staff (OS) and middle-level staff (MS). In the regressions, the category of workers is used as the base for the occupational dummies.

Regional dummies

There are four counties included in the survey: Wuxi, Jieshou, Shangrao and Nanhai. Wuxi is used as the base for the regional dummies.

Table 4A.2. *Summary statistics of variables*

Variables	Total Mean	SD[b]	Wuxi Mean	SD	Jieshou Mean	SD	Nanhai Mean	SD	Shangrao Mean	SD[b]
YW[a]	1,455	948.3	1,660	749.2	907.5	407.7	2,499	1,447	852.3	266.5
DW	4.5	2.88	4.8	2.1	3.2	1.4	7.7	4.4	2.8	0.95
LDW	1.35	0.54	1.5	0.45	1.07	0.4	1.9	0.6	0.99	0.35
EDU	8.8	2.9	8.5	2.8	9.5	2.6	7.5	2.8	8.7	2.8
AGE	30.9	10.0	33.8	9.5	27.8	7.8	29.5	10.5	33.8	11.3
TEXP	15.2	10.6	18.3	10.0	11.3	8.3	15.1	11.5	18.7	12.8
OJ	9.4	9.6	12.1	9.7	6.9	7.6	9.3	9.9	9.5	9.3
FT	5.8	5.1	6.1	4.8	4.4	3.9	5.8	6.3	9.2	6.8
AEXP	5.6	7.5	7.6	7.7	3.9	6.0	6.2	8.7	5.2	5.9
ONAJ	3.9	6.6	4.5	7.1	3.0	5.1	3.1	5.4	4.3	6.6

Notes: [a]YW is yearly wage; DW is daily wage; LDW is daily wage in log form; EDU is years of schooling; TEXP is total experience; FT is firm tenure; AEXP is agricultural experience; OJ is other labour market experience, excluding firm tenure; ONAJ is other non-agricultural experience.
[b]SD is standard deviation.
These abbreviations will be used in tables 4A.3 and 4A.4.

Table 4A.3. *Statistical characteristics of main variable for workers and staff*

	Total		Workers		Staff	
	Mean	SD	Mean	SD	Mean	SD
YW	1,455	948.3	1,325	1,046	1,610	865
DW	4.5	2.88	4.2	3.2	4.8	2.4
LDW	1.35	0.54	1.24	0.6	1.47	0.5
EDU	8.8	2.9	8.0	2.8	9.7	2.8
AGE	30.9	10.0	27.8	9.1	34.3	9.7
TEXP	15.2	10.6	12.8	10.1	17.6	10.7
OJ	9.4	9.6	7.8	8.3	11.0	10.3
FT	5.8	5.1	5.1	4.8	6.7	5.5
AEXP	5.6	7.5	5.0	6.7	6.0	8.1
ONAJ	3.9	6.6	2.8	5.3	5.0	7.5

Table 4A.4. *Statistical characteristics for market and non-market groups*

	Market		Non-market	
	Mean	SD	Mean	SD
YW	1,305	675	1,745	1,151
DW	4.2	2.0	5.1	3.4
LDW	1.3	0.5	1.5	0.6
EDU	9.0	3.0	8.1	2.7
AGE	30.0	9.0	33.0	10.0
TEXP	14.4	9.7	18.0	10.5
OJ	9.3	8.8	10.8	9.5
FT	5.2	4.6	7.2	5.8
ONAJ	3.6	6.6	4.1	5.9
AEXP	5.8	7.3	6.8	7.9

5

The wage gap between the rural agricultural and non-agricultural sectors

Although rural labour arrangements have gradually moved towards a market-oriented system and real wages have increased substantially during the economic reforms, one puzzling feature has been that all the available data suggest a persistent and widening wage gap between the rural agricultural and non-agricultural sectors. As mentioned in chapter 4, the rural non-agricultural sector comprises two parts: TVEs and privately-owned, joint venture and wholly foreign-owned enterprises. As data for the latter are not available, figure 5.1 presents the change in the wage level in the TVEs and the agriculture sector.[1] It shows not only a wage gap between the two sectors, but also a widening of this gap over the period 1984–94.

It is important to understand the causes of the widening wage gap, because if firms are efficient there should be an equality between the wage and the value of the marginal productivity of labour. Hence, a wage gap across sectors implies a marginal productivity gap across sectors. Consequently, if labour was reallocated to the high marginal productivity areas (TVEs) from the low labour productivity areas (agriculture) there would be an output gain without the need to utilise more resources. Data presented in figure 5.1 suggest that the size of this potential gain is increasing and, in terms of the reallocation of labour across sectors, the efficiency of the rural labour market seems not to be improving; indeed, it appears to be worsening.

Unfortunately, as wage data for 'other' ownership (private, foreign-owned and joint ventures) enterprises are not available, it is hard to estimate the size and direction of the wage gap between the rural agricultural and 'other' ownership non-agricultural sectors. However, it is possible to comment indirectly on the wage gap by focusing on the gap of marginal productivity between the two sectors. A study by Wang (1997) suggests that when both TVEs and other types of rural industrial enter-

---

[1] Data for non-TV-owned enterprises are not available.

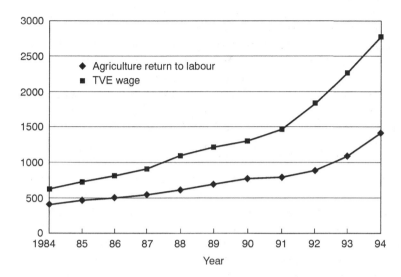

Figure 5.1 Wage gap between agricultural and TVE sectors, 1984–1994
(yuan)
Note: Wage rate for the TVE sector includes only TVEs.
Source: SSB (various years b) and author's calculations; for detailed
calculation methodology, see appendix B (p. 75).

prises are considered, there was a persistent marginal productivity of
labour (MPL) gap between the agricultural and non-agricultural sectors
during the period 1980–92. Although the gap fell slightly during the
period 1980–8 (the ratio of MPL in the non-agricultural sector to that in the
agricultural sector changed from 2.55 times in 1980 to 2.29 times in 1988), it
started to widen again after 1989 (the ratio of MPL changed from 2.48
times in 1989 to 3.68 times in 1992).

Both the wage data presented in figure 5.1 and the marginal productivity of labour data analysed by Wang (1997) thus indicate that the gap
between the agricultural and non-agricultural sectors in the rural labour
market has been large and has increased. Why have the wage levels and
MPL across the two sectors not equalised after the labour arrangements in
the rural economy shifted towards a market system?

Understanding the wage gap

Existing theories for interpreting the existence of a wage gap between the
modern and traditional sectors in a dual economy cannot satisfactorily

explain the widening wage gap evident between China's rural agricultural and non-agricultural sectors.

Neo-classical theory suggests that in a flexible labour market, when the wage level reflects the value of the MPL, wages between the two sectors should be equalised, taking into account the cost of moving from one to the other. This is because labour flows from a low MPL sector, where it is paid less, to a high MPL sector, where it is paid more, thus lowering MPL in the high productivity sector and raising MPL in the low productivity sector. The 'equal wage' outcome of this theory, however, can eventuate only when the following assumptions hold. First, wages have to reflect the MPL. Second, there should be no restrictions on labour flows between the two sectors. Third, no differences can exist in living expenses or costs of searching and transferring between two sectors. Fourth, the comparison should be made for jobs which require the same type of labour and are equally desired by workers. Finally, there should be no institutional arrangements (such as the implementation of an effective minimum wage in one sector but not the other) which may prevent the adjustment of wages.

Any violation of the above assumptions may cause the wage levels between the two sectors to differ. For example, development economics often explains a wage gap between the modern and traditional sectors by a difference in the cost of living, the high cost of job searching and differences in the institutional settings of the two sectors (Lewis 1954; Harris and Todaro 1970; Todaro 1971; Myint 1971).

The usual explanations of the wage gap do not seem to fit the unusual conditions prevailing in China. Lewis (1954) argues that capitalist wages must be somewhat higher than subsistence earnings in order to compensate labour for the cost of moving from one sector to the other, and to induce labour to leave the traditional life of the subsistence sector. In addition, the higher cost of living in the urban area also affects the wage gap between the two sectors. However, unlike in the normal dual economy, rural non-agricultural enterprises are located within the rural township or village thus there are hardly any significant costs involved in farmers moving. Further, as most TVE workers still live with their families after they have gained a non-farming job, their living costs are exactly the same as those of other family members. Hence, there is no need for a real wage difference.

Todaro (1971) argues that taking into account the costs of transferring and the existing unemployment in the cities, the urban wage must be higher than rural earnings in real terms to attract farmers to migrate to the cities. But in rural China if there is a probability that TVP workers become unemployed, they can move back to their family farms without incurring any significant cost.

Both Harris and Todaro (1970) and Myint (1971) suggest that the minimum wage regulation and trade union movement may be the causes for the wage gap between traditional and modern sectors. Nevertheless, China does not have minimum wage regulations for rural enterprises and unions in the TVPs, if any exist, have not yet played any important role in the employment system or wage determination.

Why is the wage gap widening?

One might hypothesise that the obstacles to labour flowing from the agricultural to non-agricultural sectors are the cause for the existence of wage gap between the two sectors. However, this does not seem to be the explanation for a increasing wage gap. Since economic reforms have been gradually reducing these obstacles, a narrowing rather than widening wage gap should be expected.

Another explanation might be the obstacles restricting farmers moving from less developed to more developed regions. Wang (1997) argues that although there have been few administrative restrictions on labour migration between rural regions, the local township and village governments in relatively developed rural regions, where the rural non-agricultural sector expanded very rapidly, have refused to accept migrants from less developed rural regions. The reason for such a restriction is that one of the most important objectives of local government is to maximise the *per capita* income of the region. If migration is allowed, migrants will come to share local income; this, in turn, will reduce *per capita* income within the region. This immobility of labour between agriculture-dominated and non-agriculture-dominated regions, therefore, may have generated the large wage gap between the agricultural and non-agricultural sectors in rural China as a whole.

However, this argument is still unsatisfactory. It might explain the existence of the gap in marginal productivity between the two sectors, but once again it cannot explain why the gap has been *widening*, given the fact that the restriction on labour mobility across rural regions has been gradually reduced over last decade or so. Furthermore, it is common knowledge that in most developed regions local governments use revenue obtained from the non-agricultural sector to subsidise wages for agricultural sector employees. This seems to suggest that although income levels in agricultural and non-agricultural sectors within relatively developed rural regions are closer than those in the less developed regions, the actual

MPL gap between the two sectors in the more developed regions is much greater than the income gap. The question thus still remains as to why MPLs in the two sectors have not been converging, even in the rich regions.

Perhaps widening wage gap can be explained by technological dualism. The term 'technological dualism' has been developed in the literature to characterise the use of different production technologies in the advanced and traditional sectors (Higgins 1968; Eckaus 1955). While output can be produced with a wide range of combinations of labour and capital in the traditional agricultural sector, technical substitutability in the modern sector is limited.

In the short run, if the non-agricultural sector adopts technology which has a very limited substitutability between labour and capital, there may be a very limited chance for labour to flow from the agricultural to the non-agricultural sector even if MPL in the latter is higher than that in the former. More importantly, in the long run, if relative factor prices change so that firms choose to adopt labour-saving technology, further increases in capital input will still not necessarily increase labour demand in the non-agricultural sector. This, therefore, limits the labour flow from the low- to the high-productivity sector that would otherwise increase labour productivity in the agricultural sector and equalise MPLs in the two sectors.

A theoretical model for the widening wage gap

To investigate the possibility of 'technological dualism', first consider two extreme cases of technologies in terms of factor substitutability: one with perfect substitutability, and one with zero substitutability (fixed coefficients). In the case where both sectors have technologies with perfectly substitutable factors of productions, labour may flow continuously from the low-MPL sector to the high-MPL sector, thereby substituting for capital in the high-MPL sector. In turn, this will lower the MPL in the high-MPL sector and increase MPL in the low-MPL sector, consequently equalising the MPL in the two sectors. Perfect substitutability, however, hardly exists in reality, particularly for the modern sector in a dual economy as described in Higgins' study (1968).

Suppose now that the rural non-agricultural sector adopts a zero or limited substitution technology whereby the combination of the inputs is relatively fixed when producing a certain level of output. In a modern production process, once the input combination is chosen, it is normally difficult to change it in the short term. Thus, the MPL in the short run is discontinuous. Figure 5.2 presents the zero substitutability case, where the

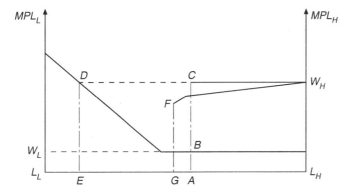

Figure 5.2 MPL in a dual economy

MPL_L and MPL_H axes represent MPL in the low-MPL and high-MPL sectors, respectively; while L_L and L_H represent labour demand in the low-MPL and high-MPL sectors, respectively. As the technical substitution of factors is relatively fixed in the high-MPL sector, the marginal productivity of labour curve for this sector is presented as W_HCAL_L, which suggests that with currently available capital,[2] the MPL for the amount of labour L_HA is W_HL_H, and any increment in labour employment will reduce the MPL to zero.[3]

Suppose labour employment increased from L_1 to L_2 in figure 5.3. Unless the capital stock increases from K_1 to K_2, output will not change at all and the MPL will drop to zero. Thus, profit-maximising firms will definitely not choose to absorb more labour from the agricultural sector when capital input is fixed in the short run. Because of the fixed or limited substitution technology, the amount of labour that the high-MPL sector can absorb is fixed (at L_HA, figure 5.2) or within a limited range. The MPL in the two sectors thus remains different ($MPL_H > MPL_L$) as long as capital input is held constant.

However, in the long run, if the relative factor price is held constant and the supply of capital increases from K_1 to K_2, output will increase from Y_1 to Y_2 (see figure 5.3) and MPL_H will remain constant at the level of W_HL_H (refer to figure 5.2). If the capital supply is large enough, MPL_H and MPL_L

---

[2] This analysis assumes that capital is infinitively divisible. Suppose that one originally has 10 units of capital and the fixed capital/labour ratio is 1/2. Up to 20 units of labour input, the MPL will be fixed. However, after 20 units of labour input, there is no more available capital. Any extra labour input, therefore, will produce zero output and, hence, the MPL will be equal to zero.

[3] In the case of limited substitutability, the MPL_H may be represented by W_HFG in figure 5.2.

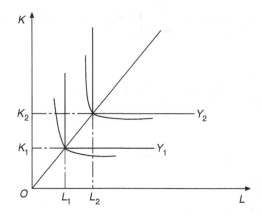

Figure 5.3 Production expansion under the assumption of fixed
(or limited) substitution

would intersect at point D, and the low-MPL sector would absorb the
amount of labour equal to $L_L E$ while the high-MPL sector would absorb
$L_H E$. The MPL in the two sectors will thus eventually converge.

The question, then, is whether the relative factor price is held constant in
the rural non-agricultural sector. If the relative price of capital/labour
decreases, the non-agricultural firms will adopt labour-saving technologies. This, in turn, suggests that an increase in capital input does not
necessarily increase labour demand in the high-MPL sector. Figure 5.4
depicts this situation. In the long run, when capital input increases from K_1
to K_2, the output will increase to Y'_2 given that the relative price of capital
and labour remain constant at the slope of AB. The non-agricultural sector
can thus absorb $L_1 L'_2$ more units of labour from the agricultural sector.
This, however, will not be the case if the relative factor price changes, say,
from AB to AC. In this case, firms will adopt labour-saving technology
which will result in an increase in output from Y_1 to Y_2 without any
increase in labour demand at all.

Empirical tests

In this section, the hypotheses postulated in the last section are tested. To
test whether the rural non-agricultural sector in China adopted limited
substitution technology, an adjusted version of the Adam *et al.* (ACMS)
(1961) approach is adopted.

The ACMS (1961) relation is defined as:

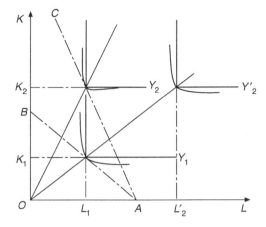

Figure 5.4 Impact of labour-saving technology on employment

$$\ln\left(\frac{Y}{L}\right) = \beta_0 + \beta_1 \ln W \tag{5.1}$$

where β_1 is the estimate of elasticity of substitution between labour and capital. This relationship is derived as followed. The MPL for the CES production function takes the form:

$$\partial Y/\partial L = \mu(1 - \delta)\beta_0^{\frac{\rho}{\mu}} Y^{\left(1 + \frac{\rho}{\mu}\right)} L^{-(\rho + 1)} \tag{5.2}$$

In the case of constant returns to scale, $\mu = 1$,

$$\partial Y/\partial L = (1 - \delta)\beta_0^{\rho} Y^{(1 + \rho)} L^{-(1 + \rho)} = C(Y/L)^{(1 + \rho)} \tag{5,3}$$

where $C = (1 - \delta)\beta_0^{\rho}$

Rearranging the equation and assuming the MPL is equal to the real wage, one can derive $\ln(Y/L) = \ln C + (1/(1 + \rho))^* \ln W$. Where $\mu \neq 1$, that is, non-constant returns to scale, the above condition can be written as:

$$\ln(Y/L) = \ln C + \mu/(\mu + \rho)\ln W - (1 - \mu/(\mu + \rho))(1 - \mu)\ln L \tag{5.4}$$

where: $\beta_1 = \mu/(\mu + \rho)$
$\beta_2 = -(1 - \beta_1)(1 - \mu)$
$\sigma = \beta_1/(1 + \beta_2)$

According to Griliches and Ringstad (1971), it is better to estimate the elasticity of substitution from the ACMS relation than to calculate it from the estimation of a production function. The reason is that in the ACMS

Table 5.1. *Summary statistics of variables, 1984–1990*

	Real output (yuan)		Real capital (yuan)		Labour (person)		Real average wage (yuan)	
	Mean	SD	Mean	SD	Mean	SD	Mean	SD
1984	247,319.94	492,487.30	70,384.89	92,341.75	262.7	286.1	80.59	60.63
1985	334,466.36	703,435.89	93,693.63	133,151.98	295.0	327.6	82.68	58.16
1986	355,625.75	725,375.72	127,790.03	241,719.92	324.1	384.1	85.65	102.85
1987	455,327.72	1,073,168.60	167,493.95	355,203.28	334.7	423.3	84.44	55.38
1988	495,389.56	1,100,580.60	132,103.47	269,489.71	325.4	395.2	115.03	476.82
1989	529,009.03	1,356,331.30	142,818.23	295,173.30	320.1	392.8	106.71	442.43
1990	469,742.83	944,016.60	130,704.01	224,488.54	323.4	428.0	83.14	52.72
Total	413,837.00	958,906.85	125,886.25	250,340.41	312.8	380.8	92.97	277.56

Source: Author's calculation from the RDCC and World Bank 1984–90 data.

relation, σ enters into the estimation as a first-order parameter and hence 'has a much better chance of being estimated with some precision' (Griliches and Ringstad 1971). The disadvantages of this form come from the specific assumptions required, such as the assumption of constant returns to scale and an equality of the MPL and the real wage. The first assumption can be relaxed by estimating (5.4) rather than (5.1). The second assumption generally holds in the case of China's rural non-agricultural sector, as has been argued in chapter 4 and as will be further discussed later in this chapter. It is thus reasonable to apply the ACMS relation in this study.

The data used to estimate the above equations are from a survey conducted by the Rural Development Centre of China (RDCC) and the World Bank on 300 TVEs over the period 1984–90. The survey covers 11 provinces of China. The variables used are all at the firm level.[4] Table 5.1 presents summary statistics of the variables used here. The data show a steady growth of the TVEs in terms of both output and inputs until 1989. The decline of the growth over the period 1989–90 was mainly caused by the contractionary macroeconomic policy implemented by the Chinese government.

The data set is in panel format, which takes the form:

$$Y_{it} = \alpha + X_{it}\beta + v_i + \varepsilon_{it} \tag{5.5}$$

where v_i is the firm-specific residual, which differs among firms but, for any particular firm, its value is constant. ε_{it} is the residual with the usual properties. It is clear from (5.5) that if an OLS estimation is used, it must assume that $v_i = 0$. On the other hand, although both fixed-effect and random-effect models assume v_i is not equal to zero, the random-effect model has a rather strong assumption that v_i is uncorrelated with $\bar{X}_i$. Thus, before estimating (5.1) and (5.2), two tests – namely, the Breusch–Pagan Lagrangian Multiplier-test for $v_i = 0$ and the Hausman specification-test for v_i being uncorrelated with $\bar{X}_i$ – are conducted. The test results suggest that a fixed-effects model is the more suitable one.[5]

Further, the fixed-effects model has many advantages over cross-sectional OLS estimation. One of them deserves particular attention. As the fixed-effects model is equivalent to adding firm dummy variables into the regression, the estimated results take into account some basic observable and unobservable characteristics of the firms – for example, different

---

[4] For a detailed explanation of the variables, see appendix A (p. 74).
[5] For (5.2), the Breusch–Pagan Lagrangian Multiplier-test gives $\chi^2(1) = 2388.31$ and the Hausman specification-test gives $\chi^2(1) = 64.48$. For (5.3), the χ^2s for the Breusch–Pagan Lagrangian Multiplier-test and the Hausman specification-test are 2357.14 and 18.74, respectively. These results all suggest that the null hypotheses can be rejected.

Table 5.2.   *Estimation of substitutability according to the ACMS relation*

	Constant return		Non-constant return	
	Coeff.	*t*-ratio	Coeff.	*t*-ratio
Constant	9.92	60.40	4.74	20.43
Ln(W)	0.39	10.15	0.52	16.90
Ln(L)			0.88	27.09
Dummy for 1985	0.32	6.58	0.15	3.86
Dummy for 1986	0.40	8.12	0.16	3.99
Dummy for 1987	0.46	9.36	0.23	5.65
Dummy for 1988	0.52	10.98	0.35	9.11
Dummy for 1989	0.55	11.59	0.40	10.36
Dummy for 1990	0.46	9.72	0.32	8.29
No. observations	1,635 ($n = 299$)		1,635 ($n = 299$)	
R^2 (within)	0.18		0.47	

industry, locality, ownership, quality of management and quality of inputs.

The estimated results for (5.1) and (5.4) are reported in table 5.2.[6] The estimated coefficients suggest that the elasticity of substitution for the rural non-agricultural sector over the period 1984–90 is less than unity. If constant returns to scale are assumed, σ is estimated to be equal to 0.39, whereas if non-constant returns to scale are assumed, σ is calculated to be equal to 0.52. Both estimates seem to indicate that the rural non-agricultural sector adopted technology with rather limited factor substitutability over the period 1984–90.

Next, the hypothesis that in the long run the rural non-agricultural sector adopted labour-saving technology is tested. As mentioned in the last section, if the relative factor price of capital/labour decreases over time, firms are more likely to choose labour-saving technology. In other words, to test this hypothesis, one needs to show that the marginal rate of technical substitution (MRTS) $-\partial L/\partial K = MPK/MPL$, has declined over time.

To calculate MPL and MPK, a Translog production function is estimated owing to the flexibility of such a functional form. The functional form is specified in (5.6):

---

[6] There may be some concern about correlation between ln(L) and ln(W). This, however, is not a problem for the data set used in this study. Simple tests are conducted by estimating ln(W) against ln(L) and other time dummy variables and ln(L) against ln(W) and other time dummy variables. The results suggest that although ln(W) and ln(L) are statistically important determinants of each other, adjusted R^2s for the two regressions are 0.02 and 0.05, suggesting that multicollinearity should not be a concern.

$$\ln(Y) = \beta_0 + \beta_1 \ln L + \beta_2 \ln(K) + \beta_3 1/2[\ln(L)]^2$$
$$+ \beta_4 1/2[\ln(K)]^2 + \beta_5 \ln(K)\ln(L) + \varepsilon \tag{5.6}$$

A set of F-tests is conducted to decide if the Translog is the proper functional form to use. The test results suggest that Translog is preferable to a Cobb–Douglas production function. The cross-term in the Translog estimation, however, is not significantly different from zero, suggesting that the production function does not have the property of additivity. It is thus dropped from the final estimation.[7]

The estimated results for the three production functions are reported in table 5.3 and the F-tests for functional form are presented in table 5D.1 (p. 78).

Table 5.4 presents the calculated MPL and MPK and the ratio of MPK over MPL from the estimated results shown in table 5.3. The calculated results suggest that over the period studied, the marginal rate of technical substitution between capital and labour has been declining. This situation is clearly depicted in figure 5.5, where apart from 1988, the MRTS for the 300 firms has shown a declining trend. The peak at the trend line (1988) was mainly due to a sharp increase in MPK at that time. Figure 5C.1 (p. 77) also shows the similar trend of MRTS calculated from CES production function.

If we assume that relative factor prices equate with the relative marginal products, the above results seem to suggest that the relative price of capital to labour in the rural non-agricultural sector has been declining. In other words, the price of capital for China's rural non-agricultural sector has gradually become lower relative to the price of labour. This result is consistent with Wang's (1997) finding.

Further, this study suggests that the capital/labour ratio in the rural non-agricultural sector should have increased considerably owing to the relatively cheaper capital. Table 5.5 presents the change in the capital/labour ratio in the rural TV-owned non-agricultural enterprises. It shows that for the period 1978–94, the net value of fixed assets in the TV-owned non-agricultural sector increased at an average rate of 22 per cent per annum. In contrast, the average change in employment was rather slow,

---

[7] A Taylor series approximation of the a CES production function is also estimated, which is specified as:

$$\ln(Y) = \beta_0 + \beta_1 \ln L + \beta_2 \ln(K) + \beta_3 (\ln(K/L))^2 + \varepsilon$$

Nevertheless, the estimation of a CES production function requires normalisation of all the inputs and output units, and the estimated coefficients without such a normalisation are not unique. This study will thus focus on the results from the Translog production function. Results for CES production function are reported in tables 5C.1 and 5C.2 (pp. 76–7).

Table 5.3.   *Fixed-effect estimation of production functions*

	Translog		Final		Cobb–Douglas	
	Coeff.	t-ratio	Coeff.	t-ratio	Coeff.	t-ratio
Constant	8.11	11.96	8.33	13.97	7.25	40.28
Ln(L)	0.03	0.13	0.05	0.24	0.69	19.34
Ln(K)	−0.12	−1.01	−0.13	−1.10	0.22	10.21
Ln²(L)	0.13	3.24	0.12	3.31		
Ln²(K)	0.04	2.60	0.03	2.82		
Ln(L)*Ln(K)	−0.01	−0.70				
Dummy for 1985	0.14	3.39	0.15	3.43	0.14	3.36
Dummy for 1986	0.12	2.81	0.12	2.87	0.13	2.90
Dummy for 1987	0.19	4.27	0.19	4.31	0.20	4.52
Dummy for 1988	0.30	7.07	0.30	7.14	0.31	7.35
Dummy for 1989	0.29	6.87	0.29	6.94	0.31	7.20
Dummy for 1990	0.22	5.30	0.22	5.35	0.24	5.67
No. of observations	1,633 ($n = 300$)		1,633 ($n = 300$)		1,633 ($n = 300$)	
Adjusted R^2 (within)	0.4169		0.4167		0.4062	

Table 5.4.   *Changes in* MPK, MPL *and the* MRTS, *1984–1990*

	MPL (Translog) (1)	MPK (Translog) (2)	MPK/MPL (Translog) (3)
1984	1,093.63	1,142.9	1.045052
1985	1314.454	1,117.722	0.850332
1986	1333.598	1,087.999	0.815837
1987	1549.752	1,070.017	0.690444
1988	1866.222	1,672.35	0.896115
1989	1916.086	1,124.916	0.587091
1990	1699.569	1,088.565	0.640495

Source: Author's calculations according to table 5.3.

being only 0.7 per cent per annum. This leaves a rapid increase in the capital/labour ratio from 643 yuan per person in 1978 to 11,781 yuan per person in 1994. The average annual increase of this ratio is 17 per cent. From this analysis, it is obvious that capital-intensive technology has been adopted in the rural non-agricultural sector, which is consistent with the finding that the MPK/MPL ratio has been declining in this sector.

Why do TVEs not pay wages lower than the MPL?

The above analyses are conducted based on the assumption that the TVE firms pay wages according to the MPL. Although it is rather clear from the

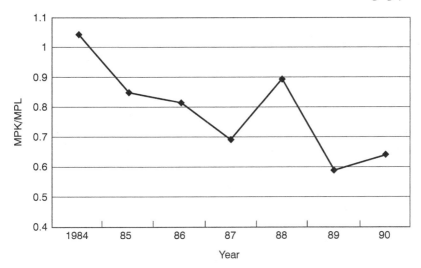

Figure 5.5 Change in relative price of capital and labour (MPK/MPL)
Source: Table 5.4, column (3).

investigation carried out in chapter 4 that this is what is actually happening, one might still ask the question as to why the TVEs do not pay wages which are lower than the rural non-agricultural MPL but higher than agricultural wages when there is a plentiful supply of labour.

Two factors may prevent this from happening. First, if there is a competitive labour market whereby the TVEs are not the only buyers in the rural labour market (a firm faces an elastic labour supply curve), they will be forced to pay their workers according to the MPL; otherwise, workers would work for other firms that pay wages equal to the MPL. In this situation, firms that pay workers a wage lower than the MPL would be forced to operate at a level which is lower than the profit-maximisation level. Second, if demand for labour in the agricultural and rural non-agricultural sectors is not homogeneous in terms of quality, and the supply of highly qualified labour to the rural non-agricultural sector is limited (the labour supply curve is elastic), firms have to pay workers a wage which is equal to their MPL.

Both situations can be depicted by figure 5.6, where a firm is assumed to have a kinked labour demand curve $DabD$ owing to lack of substitutability of capital and labour inputs (as discussed earlier). When the firm faces a perfectly elastic labour supply curve (SS) with a demand for labour at the amount of OL_1, it can set a wage rate anywhere in between W and W'. However, when the firm faces a less elastic labour supply curve (SS'),

Table 5.5.   Change in employment, capital and the capital/labour ratio in TV-owned non-agricultural sector, 1978–1994

	Employment (10,000 persons)		Net value of fixed assets (10,000,000 yuan)		Capital/labour ratio (yuan/person)	
	Value	% change	Value	% change	Value	% change
1978	2,826.56		181.80		643.18	
1979	2,909.34	2.93	226.10	24.37	777.15	20.83
1980	2,999.67	3.10	266.00	17.65	886.76	14.10
1981	2,969.56	–1.00	304.00	14.29	1,023.72	15.44
1982	3,112.91	4.83	342.40	12.63	1,099.94	7.44
1983	3,234.64	3.91	373.00	8.94	1,153.14	4.84
1984	3,982.17	23.11	445.70	19.49	1,119.24	–2.94
1985	4,327.10	8.66	589.70	32.31	1,362.81	21.76
1986	4,541.30	4.95	743.20	26.03	1,636.54	20.09
1987	4,718.30	3.90	959.80	29.14	2,034.21	24.30
1988	4,893.90	3.72	1,234.50	28.62	2,522.53	24.01
1989	4,720.20	–3.55	1,486.20	20.39	3,148.60	24.82
1990	4,592.40	–2.71	1,668.70	12.28	3,633.61	15.40
1991	4,767.00	3.80	1,959.30	17.41	4,110.13	13.11
1992	5,148.80	8.01	2,585.90	31.98	5,022.34	22.19
1993	5,767.70	12.02	3,768.04	45.71	6,533.00	30.08
1994	5,898.80	2.27	5,196.20	37.90	8,808.91	34.84
1995	6,060.50	2.74	7,139.80	37.4	11,780.88	33.7
Average annual rate of increase (per cent)		0.7		22.4		17.2

Source: SSB (various years a).

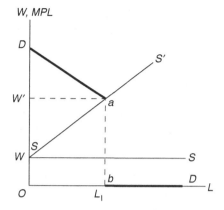

Figure 5.6 Impact of labour supply on wage settings

either because of the job opportunities that exist elsewhere for rural labour or because the skilled labour supply is limited, the wage rate can only be set at W' to ensure maximum profits.

The two factors discussed above have both been influential in China's rural non-agricultural sector, especially since the second half of the 1980s. As mentioned in chapter 4, employment in TVEs accounted for 74 per cent of the total rural non-agricultural employment in 1984. This figure declined to 47 per cent in 1995. Such a dramatic decline in the share of TVE employment suggests that employment opportunities have been increasing elsewhere within the rural non-agricultural sector. In addition, since the late 1980s, increasing numbers of rural residents have moved to the cities to find temporary jobs, suggesting an increase in job opportunities outside the rural non-agricultural sector (see chapter 9). Both of these facts indicate that the monopsony power of rural TVEs in rural labour markets has been dramatically reduced. This indicates that the elasticity of the labour supply curve for the rural TVEs has reduced.

Furthermore, as table 5.5 shows, the capital/labour ratio for the TVEs has increased rapidly, especially since the second half of the 1980s. This change must have been accompanied by an increase in the demand for skilled labour. However, the skilled labour supply did not change much. In 1988, new rural high school graduates accounted for about 2.1 per cent of the total rural labour force, and among them 0.16 per cent were new senior high school graduates. These figures changed to 2.3 and 0.1 per cent, respectively, in 1995. The absolute value of new senior high school graduates actually reduced from 640,500 to 446,500.[8] Such a change suggests that while the TVEs' demand for labour shifted from unskilled to skilled labour, the supply for the latter is rather limited.

Conclusions

It has been found that, apart from some institutional restrictions, the type of technology adopted in the rural non-agricultural sector – and, more importantly, the change in the relative factor prices in that sector – have contributed significantly to the widening wage gap between the two sectors. The findings indicate that the capital price in the rural non-agricultural sector has been too low relative to the price of labour. This prevented rural non-agricultural firms from adopting the more labour-intensive technology that would absorb the relatively abundant supply of labour in the agricultural sector and eventually to increase the MPL in the agricultural sector and equalise the price of labour between the two sectors.

Appendix A: description of the data

The variables used in this study are:

Output: Gross value of output reported at the 1980 (GVO80) price level. For some observations, only the gross value of output at current price (GVO) is reported. In those cases, the average price index is used to deflate the value. The average price index is obtained by dividing GVO by GVO80.

Capital: The data on the net value of fixed assets is reported in the survey questionnaire. This is deflated by industrial products' producer price indices reported in the *China Statistical Yearbook 1995*. The price in 1980 is set to be equal to 100.

Labour: Firm-level average annual employment for each year.

Wage: The data on the firm-level total wage bill is reported in the survey. The firm-level average nominal wage is obtained by dividing the total wage bill by firm-level average annual employment. This is then deflated by the overall consumer price index reported in the *China Statistical Yearbook 1995* to obtain the average real wage. Again, 1980 is set to be 100.

[8] See SSB (various years a) for reference.

Appendix B: calculations for wage levels in the agricultural sector

Average wages in the rural TV-owned non-agricultural sector were calculated using data from the *China Statistical Yearbook* by dividing the total wage bill by the number of employees in the TVEs. However, an agricultural wage or labour income is not readily available from the *China Statistical Yearbook*. Only the net income per household member from agricultural or household activities (NI_P) is reported in this source. This average net income, however, includes returns to other factors such as capital (NIL_K) and land (NIL_T), in addition to that of labour (NIL_L).

Two steps are involved in separating the labour income per agricultural worker from the net income per person data. The first is to calculate the net income per labourer (NIL), which is calculated by applying the following formula.

$$NIL = \frac{NI_P * POP_R}{AGW} \tag{5B.1}$$

where NI_P is net income per rural person obtained from the *China Statistical Yearbook*;
POP_R is the rural population
AGW is agricultural workers, which is equal to total rural labour *minus* rural non-agricultural workers.

The second is to separate the returns to agricultural labour income (NIL_L) from the total net income per agricultural labourer (NIL). If one knows the share of labour in the total net income, one is able to obtain the value for the share of labour by multiplying total net income per agricultural labourer and the parameter of the share of labour in total net income.

There are several studies in the literature which suggest different values of the share of labour in total net income for the Chinese agricultural sector. The study by McMillan, Whalley and Zhu (1989), covering the period of the first stage of agricultural reform in China (1978–84), indicated 0.59 as the share of labour income in total net income. Lin's study (1992), covering a longer period (1970–87), suggests a much lower share of 0.15. The estimated coefficient, 0.42, in Wang's study (1997), covering the period 1980–92, falls between the other two.

In the diagram presented in the text (figure 5.1, p. 59), Wang's estimation was adopted as the period of his study is most relevant to the present work. Table 5B.1 presents the data on agricultural wages calculated according to the three different parameters.

Table 5B.1.   *Agricultural returns to labour and TVE wages, 1984–1994*

| | Agricultural returns to labour | | | |
	Wang's estimation	McMillan *et al.*'s estimation	Lin's estimation	TVE wage
1984	409.01	574.56	146.07	622.00
1985	468.57	658.23	167.35	726.00
1986	503.43	707.20	179.80	810.00
1987	551.46	774.68	196.95	910.00
1988	627.85	881.98	224.23	1,106.00
1989	702.81	987.28	251.00	1,230.00
1990	788.66	1,107.88	281.66	1,321.00
1991	804.56	1,130.22	287.34	1,482.00
1992	903.51	1,269.21	322.68	1,858.88
1993	1,107.90	1,556.33	395.68	2,295.37
1994	1,438.16	2,020.27	513.63	2,798.03

Appendix C: CES production function estimation

Table 5C.1.   *Fixed-effects estimation of CES production function*

	Coefficient	*t*-ratio
Constant	7.25	40.38
Ln(L)	0.61	13.64
Ln(K)	0.31	8.22
$(Ln(K)/(L))^2$	0.02	3.02
Dummy for 1985	0.14	3.30
Dummy for 1986	0.12	2.77
Dummy for 1987	0.19	4.34
Dummy for 1988	0.30	7.12
Dummy for 1989	0.29	6.91
Dummy for 1990	0.23	5.43
No. of observations	1,633 ($n = 300$)	
R^2	0.4102	

Table 5C.2. *Change in MPK/MPL ratio using CES production function esti-mation, 1984–1990*

	MPL	MPK	MPK/MPL
1984	531.2599	1,233.735	2.322282
1985	627.7004	1,168.486	1.861535
1986	631.1092	998.789	1.582592
1987	731.9152	1,041.727	1.423289
1988	918.893	1,418.789	1.54402
1989	927.7453	1,311.401	1.413535
1990	833.966	1,273.367	1.526882

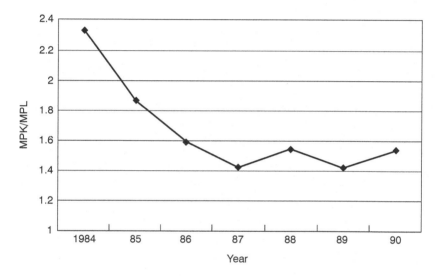

Figure 5C.1 Change in MPK/MPL ratio using CES production function estimates, 1984–1990

Appendix D

Table 5D.1.   F-*tests for functional forms*

Tested hypothesis	Degrees of freedom	Optional F-statistic	Critical value of F-statistic	Test outcome
Cobb-Douglas function $\beta_3 = \beta_4 = \beta_5 = 0$	3, 1,633	8.75	$F_{0.01}(3, \infty) = 3.78$	Rejected
Additivity $\beta_5 = 0$	1, 1,633	0.56	$F_{0.01}(1, \infty) = 6.63$	Not rejected

Source: Author's estimation results.

Part 2

Urban labour market reforms

Economic reform in China's urban sector began late, proceeded slowly and, on the whole, has been an erratic affair. Before reform, the state sector accounted for about 79 per cent of total urban employment and 78 per cent of the gross value of industrial output (SSB, various years a).[1] The rest of the economy mainly comprised the collective sector with a virtually non-existent urban private sector. Both the state and urban collective sectors were, more or less, controlled by the centrally planned system.[2] This system not only decided on what was produced, by whom and the uses to which it was put, but also how it was to be produced. The price level of both outputs and inputs were centrally determined. Enterprises could negotiate with central or local planning committees, but their influence was slight. The changes began with the decentralising of production decision-making, introduction of incentive schemes, reduction of centrally controlled output sales and the partial liberalisation of the price system. Firms were gradually granted most of the production decision-making power and the goods market was the first to be operated in a flexible market environment.

While the goods market was progressively liberalised, factor market reform was implemented much later, at a much slower pace and has not been as successful as the reform of product markets. This is particularly true for labour market reform. Most of the issues that slowed labour market reform arose in response to the complication associated with the ownership structure of enterprises and the political sensitivity of some of the reforms (see White 1988; Korzec 1992; Takahara 1992).

---

[1] State-owned enterprises (SOEs) are those which are owned by the central or local governments. The urban collective enterprises are owned by a city or a district authority. The private sector includes urban private enterprises, joint ventures, foreign-owned enterprises and the urban self-employed. Joint ventures are owned jointly by domestic and foreign owners, and the foreign-owned enterprises are owned fully by foreigners.

[2] Labour, in particular, was allocated to the collective enterprises in the same way as for the state sector, except that only those who had politically inferior personal characteristics or family background were likely to be assigned to jobs in the collective sector.

6

Urban labour market reform and wage determination

Urban labour market reform has been synonymous with reforming employment and wage determination systems in the state and collective sectors.[1]

It was argued in chapter 2 that although both employment and wage determination systems were inefficient in the pre-reform era, the essential problem with pre-reform urban labour arrangements was the lack of labour mobility, which prevented a proper incentive system from being established. This chapter discusses the progress and limitations of labour market reform measures, investigated mainly through an examination of changes in individual wage determination patterns over the period 1980–7.

Labour market reforms in the 1980s

It has been argued by most Chinese economists and policy-makers that the weaknesses of the pre-reform labour arrangements in China were two-fold. On the one hand, the lifetime employment system encouraged over-staffing, shirking and low productivity. On the other hand, the wage grade system valued 'formal' qualification – such as education and years of experience – too heavily, while ignoring individuals' real labour productivity. Hence, individuals were paid according to their qualifications and age rather than in relation to their actual labour productivity (Shan 1991).

Consequently, since the beginning of the 1980s, labour market reform has focused on the above two dimensions. The attempt to change lifetime employment was made by gradually introducing a labour contract system. The experimental rules of the labour contract system were first introduced in 1983 to cover new entrants to the state and collective sectors. As a result, 160,000 new workers were covered by the new contract system by the end of 1984. In 1986, the 'Temporary Regulations on the Use of

---

[1] This chapter draws heavily on Meng and Kidd (1997).

Table 6.1.   *Change of coverage of contractual employment, state sector, 1985–1995*

	Total state employment	Contractual employment	Per cent of contract workers
1985	8,990	332	3.7
1990	10,346	1,372	13.3
1991	10,664	1,589	14.9
1992	10,889	2,058	18.9
1993	10,920	2,396	21.9
1994	11,214	2,853	25.4
1995	11,261	4,396	39.0

Source: SSB (various years a).

Labour Contracts in State-Run Enterprises' were promulgated by the State Council. The extent of contract system coverage expanded quickly, reaching 7,260,000 (or approximately 8 per cent of employees in the state-owned sector) by the end of 1986 (Korzec 1992). Since the late 1980s, the coverage of contractual employment for new entrants to the state sector has increased even more rapidly, from about 4 per cent of total employment in 1985 to 13 per cent in 1990 and further to 39 per cent in 1995 (see table 6.1).

The labour contract system represents a relatively flexible labour allocation mechanism in comparison to the rigid pre-reform system. The contract system allows firms to select and hire suitable individuals, and from the late 1980s firms began to use examinations and conduct interviews to aid the selection and recruitment process (Research Group on Reform in Employment System 1991). However, in comparison to a free labour market, the flexibility of the contract system was still limited in several ways. First, the proportion of employees who were covered was small, especially in the beginning, because it was restricted to new entrants. Second, as Korzec (1992) has pointed out, there remained severe restrictions on geographical mobility. Third, although employees had the right to resign, quitting a job for personal reasons – for example, a better job offer – was not permitted (Korzec 1992). Fourth, even with contract workers, the contract normally led to continuous employment and, thus, did not provide employers with a flexible hiring and firing device.[2] Finally, although management had greater control over recruitment, they were still bound by the state labour plans and could not dismiss employees on the grounds of over-staffing until the early 1990s (Korzec 1992).

Since the early 1990s, managers of SOEs have been given further decision-making power over recruitment. A survey conducted by the China

[2] Information gathered from author's interviews with enterprise employees in Beijing, China.

Economic System Reform Commission in 1992 of 933 SOEs suggests that about 69 per cent of the sample firms had direct or indirect decision-making power over recruitment and about 86 per cent over dismissal. Another survey conducted by the Institute of Economics at the Chinese Academy of Social Sciences shows that, by 1995, among 752 SOEs surveyed, more than 70 per cent claimed to have direct control over employment and dismissal.

While a high proportion of SOEs claimed to have the right to dismiss workers, very few chose to do so even if they had serious over-staffing problems, unless they were facing serious financial problems and the threat of closure. However, the main reason for this reluctance to dismiss may not be because managers were prevented from doing so, but because they chose not to. This, as Walder (1989) claims, may be owing to the fact that an SOE is 'a socio–political community' whose managers are leaders of that community. They are responsible for that community's welfare and they are judged by both their superiors and subordinates on their effectiveness in all areas concerning community welfare, including employment, 'not just on meeting production and financial plans' (Walder 1989).[3]

The second dimension involved reforming the wage-setting system. Here, the emphasis was placed on introducing incentives to work and encouraging efficiency. Two major reform steps were implemented.

- First, the enterprise's total wage quota system, which was centrally fixed, was changed to a 'floating' total wage bill system. The new system relates the enterprise's total wage bill to its profitability. Enterprises were allowed to retain a certain percentage of their profits for welfare provision and bonuses. Initially, there was a ceiling for bonuses paid, which was set at a level of no more than 5 per cent of the total payroll. This ceiling, however, was gradually lifted.

- Second, attempts were made to link the wages of individuals to their labour productivity within firms. Various versions of this reform appeared in different regions and industries. The 'wage plus bonus' system was the most frequently adopted. However, as in most cases monitoring labour productivity is very costly, the bonus eventually became an extra component of wages, with bonuses equally distributed among employees. Over the reform period, the importance of bonus

[3] This is similar to the case of the labour managed firms. Although such firms have power over recruitment and dismissal, their objectives restrict them from firing employees as they are also owners of the firms. See, for example, Ward (1958); Domar (1966); Vanek (1970); Stephen (1984).

payments increased significantly. Table 6.2 suggests that while the share of the basic wage decreased, the bonus share increased from 2.4 per cent of the total wage in 1978 to 23.3 per cent in 1993.[4]

Impact of reforms on wage determination

The labour market reforms implemented in the 1980s were probably not very effective in terms of increasing labour mobility, as only new entrants were covered by the contract system, and even then the old rules of hiring and firing were still in place to some extent. It is interesting to see, therefore, whether the reform of the wage determination system has had any impact in promoting an appropriate incentive structure for workers. This is investigated by comparing the individual wage determination pattern before and after labour market reform.

The data used for this chapter are from a sample survey conducted in 1989 by The Institute of Quantitative Economics, The Chinese Academy of Social Sciences. The data were originally collected for a joint research project involving Li Jingwen, D. Jorgenson and M. Kuroda that aimed to examine productivity and international competitiveness in China, Japan and the United States. The data set is a firm-based employee panel survey for the period 1981–7. Approximately 120,000 survey questionnaires were

Table 6.2.   *Changes in the composition of the total wages, state sector, 1978–1995*

	Average nominal wage p.a. (yuan)	Per cent of basic wage[a]	Per cent of bonus	Per cent of subsidies	Per cent of other components
1978	644	85.7	2.4	6.5	5.4
1980	803	72.4	9.7	14.1	3.8
1985	1,213	64.6	14.5	18.5	2.4
1990	2,284	55.7	19.1	21.8	3.4
1991	2,477	55.4	20.0	22.1	2.5
1992	2,878	51.7	22.2	23.8	2.4
1993	3,532	46.6	23.3	25.1	5.1
1994	4,797	n.a.	17.9	24.5	n.a.
1995	5,625	55.6	16.8	23.0	4.6

Notes: [a]Real basic wage is nominal basic wage deflated by CPI, where 1978 is set to be equal to 100.
n.a. = not available.
Sources: SSB (various years a and b).

[4] 1994 seems to be a turning point when the share of basic wage starts to increase again.

distributed to various firms among 30 industries. The overall response rate was 40 per cent.[5]

The survey information of particular interest relates to the age, education, gender, wage, occupation and industry of individuals. In this study the analysis is restricted to male respondents, and avoids the well known problems associated with using Mincer's measure[6] of potential experience to proxy female labour market experience. The major focus of this chapter is an examination of the changing pattern of wage determination between 1981 and 1987. With this purpose in mind, the sample is restricted to individuals employed in either 1981 or 1987.[7]

The wage variable is the monthly wage, which is deflated according to the urban CPI, with 1981 set at 100. On average, real wages increased by 27 per cent between 1981 and 1987. Given the nature of the firm-based employee panel data set, an individual's industry is, by definition, fixed over time. Given the tendency for workers to remain in the same job, attrition in the sample is very low. The limited turnover, combined with limited employment expansion, explains the small difference in the sample size across the period. It is also not surprising, given the nature of the data, that there are only minor changes in the level of education over time. Also, as expected, labour market experience, as proxied by Mincer's measure, increases by approximately 6 years. In terms of occupation, there is some evidence of career advancement over the period, with a 5 per cent increase in managerial staff, a 0.4 per cent rise in technicians and a corresponding decrease in middle-level staff.

Separate human capital-based wage equations are estimated for 1981 and 1987. The specification includes four educational dummy variables ('primary school and below' is adopted as the base category), potential experience in level and quadratic form, three occupational dummy variables (the 'manual workers' group is used as the default) and 29 industrial affiliation variables (the food processing industry is used as the default). The coefficient estimates for each year, together with associated *t*-statistics, are included in columns (1)–(4) of table 6.3.

Pre-reform wage determination pattern

As an approximation, 1981 is interpreted as being representative of the pre-reform period. The 1981 results illustrate a relationship between

---

[5] This rate fell to around 31 per cent after removing invalid sample observations.
[6] Mincer's approach (Mincer, 1974) is to measure total experience, *TEXP*, by $TEXP = A - S - 7$, where A is age, S the years of schooling and 7 the number of years before schooling begins.
[7] See Meng and Kidd (1997) for basic statistics of all variables used in the empirical analysis.

Table 6.3. *Wage equation, 1981 and 1987[a]*

	1981		1987		Difference	
	Coefficient (1)	t-ratio (2)	Coefficient (3)	t-ratio (4)	Coefficient (5)	t-ratio (6)
Constant	3.3746	422.47	3.4378	412.23	0.0633	5.45
Bachelor	0.2905	43.24	0.3130	52.35	0.0226	2.52
Semi-bachelor[b]	0.2222	39.03	0.2221	42.36	−0.0001	−0.01
Senior secondary	0.1143	27.82	0.1165	30.85	0.0021	0.38
Junior secondary	0.0666	20.09	0.0553	18.21	−0.0113	−2.51
Total experience	0.0273	69.18	0.0283	60.83	0.0010	1.59
(Total experience)^2	−0.0001	−9.88	−0.0002	−18.53	−0.0001	−5.08
Managers	0.1020	25.64	0.1233	38.18	0.0213	4.17
Middle-level staff	0.0280	7.37	0.0279	7.84	−0.0001	−0.02
Technicians	0.0210	4.75	0.0446	11.38	0.0237	4.02
Metal mining	0.0701	9.27	0.1702	24.58	0.1002	9.78
Coal mining	0.1509	20.12	0.1761	25.61	0.0252	2.48
Petroleum and gas mining	0.1311	15.57	0.2665	34.45	0.1354	11.85
Non-metal mining	0.1696	15.79	0.1199	12.13	−0.0497	−3.41
Construction	0.1363	16.80	0.1730	23.22	0.0367	3.33
Tobacco processing	−0.0298	−2.35	0.0228	1.96	0.0526	3.05
Textile	0.0013	0.16	0.0164	2.19	0.0151	1.37
Garments	−0.0097	−1.09	0.0636	7.83	0.0732	6.10
Timber processing	0.1974	18.13	0.1851	18.55	−0.0122	−0.83
Furniture	0.1066	12.04	0.0709	8.71	−0.0357	−2.97
Paper production	0.0079	0.96	0.0942	12.54	0.0863	7.78
Printing and pressing	0.0094	0.99	0.0877	10.06	0.0783	6.08
Chemical	0.0136	1.59	0.1113	14.20	0.0977	8.44
Petroleum processing	0.0681	8.38	0.1720	23.09	0.1039	9.44
Rubber and plastic	0.0438	5.08	0.1061	13.42	0.0624	5.34
Leather	0.0348	3.64	0.0704	8.02	0.0356	2.75
Ceramic	0.0925	11.88	0.0877	12.26	−0.0048	−0.46
Metal	0.1025	11.30	0.2533	30.55	0.1507	12.27

Metal processing	−0.0044	−0.30	−0.0468	−3.49	−0.0425	−2.14
Machinery	0.1307	11.20	0.2074	19.61	0.0766	4.87
Automobile	0.1020	9.77	0.1325	14.38	0.0305	2.19
Other transportation	0.0546	6.84	0.1124	15.40	0.0578	5.35
Percussive instrument	0.2230	3.35	0.0369	2.50	−0.1861	−2.83
Other manufacture	0.0467	4.01	0.0394	3.71	−0.0073	−0.46
Transportation	0.0298	2.51	0.0950	8.73	0.0652	4.04
Telecommunication	0.0983	7.78	0.2910	25.15	0.1928	11.26
Electricity	0.1235	15.37	0.1140	15.49	−0.0095	−0.87
Service	0.1056	10.67	0.1701	18.72	0.0645	4.81
Government	0.1249	12.51	0.1820	20.04	0.0572	4.24
No. of observations	25,259		25,731		50,990	
Adjusted R^2	0.68		0.68		0.73	

Notes: [a]Primary and below, manual workers and food processing are used as the 'norm' categories for each group of dummy variables. [b]'Semi-bachelor' includes 3-year technical degrees and degrees by correspondence via television.
Source: Author's estimation.

wages and human capital variables somewhat similar to that of a market economy. Specifically, all four educational dummy variables are positive and significant, and total experience appears to exhibit the traditional inverse-U-shape and is statistically significant.

However, these similarities are superficial. There are a number of important differences between wage determination in China's state sector and that of a market economy. First, studies of most industrialised and developing market economies have found that no matter how rich a data set is, or how many individual human capital and family background variables are included in the wage specification, adjusted R^2 values are in the order of 20–40 per cent (for example, Kao, Polachek and Wunnava 1994; Miller 1987; Kidd and Shannon 1996; Kidd and Meng 1994). In the current analysis for China, however, 64 per cent of the wage variation can be explained solely by education, experience and occupation.[8] This suggests that wages are set mainly according to these three personal characteristics and there is considerable uniformity of pay within each category.

Second, although the signs and statistical significance of the human capital variables (education and experience) for China are similar to those for most industrial economies, the magnitudes differ significantly. Table 6.4 provides a comparison of the rates of return to education and experience for China's state sector and a sample of other industrialised economies. China appears to have a lower rate of return to human capital relative to the other countries: 1 more year of education increased individual earnings by 2.5 per cent in China in 1981.[9] The US and UK studies report an increase in earnings of 5 and 7 per cent, respectively. Psacharopoulos (1994) also reported a much higher return to education in developing countries. For low-income countries, a 1-year increase in schooling increases earnings by 11.2 per cent, and for Asian countries (not including Japan) the figure is 9.6 per cent.

In terms of dummy variables for the educational categories, the only result in table 6.4 which is directly comparable across countries is for the bachelor degree and above. The estimated coefficient suggests that in China, individuals with a bachelor degree or above earn 29 per cent more than those with primary school education. The corresponding figure is 38 per cent for Australia, and 59 per cent for the United States. In

---

[8] Estimated results without industrial dummy variables are reported in table 6A.1 (p. 96).

[9] To put this figure in the context of the existing empirical literature, Byron and Manaloto (1990) report a 4 per cent rate of return to education in urban Nanjing, and Gregory and Meng (1995) report a 1 per cent increase in earnings for each additional year of schooling in China's rural industrial sector. These studies confirm the low return to education in China relative to other market economies.

Table 6.4. *Comparison of return to human capital, China and some industrial countries, 1981–1990*

	China				Aust. 1990	United States 1989	United Kingdom 1980
	1981	1987	1990[b]				
Experience	0.0273	0.0283	0.0213	Experience	0.039	0.037	0.028
(Experience)[2]	−0.0001	−0.0002	−0.0001	(Experience)[2]	−0.001	−0.0006	−0.0005
Years of sch.[a]	0.0246	0.0266	0.0042	Years of sch.	n.a.	0.05[c]	0.071
Bachelor and above	0.291	0.313	n.a.	Bachelor	0.349	0.586[d]	n.a.
College	0.222	0.222	n.a.	Certificate	0.173	0.356[d]	n.a.
Senior secondary	0.114	0.117	n.a.	Trade	0.132	0.244[d]	n.a.
Junior secondary	0.067	0.055	n.a.	Secondary	0.095	n.a.	n.a.

Notes: [a]To make the results comparable with other studies, the author estimated two wage equations, one with years of schooling, the other with educational dummy variables.
[b]Estimation for 1990 (see Shao 1992).
[c]The results are from Mincer and Higuchi (1988). The figure reported in Psacharopoulos' (1985) study is around 7–10 per cent in the United States.
[d]The three educational categories for the United States are bachelor and above, some college, and completed high school.
n.a. = Not available.
Source: Author's estimation for China and Australia (1994); the US results are from Borland, Vella and Woodbridge (1995); the UK results are from Miller (1987).

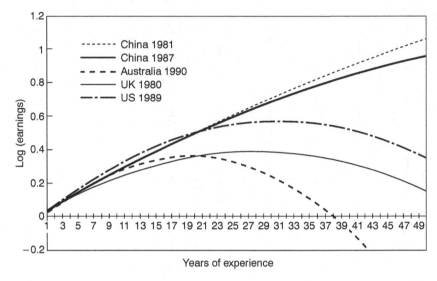

Figure 6.1 Comparison of experience–earnings profiles

general, although education is a statistically significant determinant of earnings, the rate of return is much lower than that in the market economies.

Figure 6.1 provides a comparison of experience–earnings profiles for China and Australia, the United States and the United Kingdom. The figure indicates that the relationship between experience and wage levels for the market economies is of the traditional concave shape, whereas the profile is upward-sloping for the entire working life in China's state sector. In market economies, the peak in earnings is reached when an individual (assuming that working life starts between the ages of 16 and 21) is in their middle 30s–middle 40s, suggesting that the experience profile exhibits a relationship between productivity and the wage, whereas for China, the experience profile rises continuously until retirement. It is difficult to rationalise the Chinese profile on the basis of standard human capital theory. China is not noted for high levels of innovation and adoption of technology, and it would seem unlikely that a worker's productivity increases over his/her entire life-span. This suggests that the profile is productivity-linked in market economies while it is more likely to be related to seniority in China.

One might argue that, although China's experience–earnings profile is different from those of Western industrialised and other market economies, it is similar to that of Japan. Figure 6.2 presents the comparison of

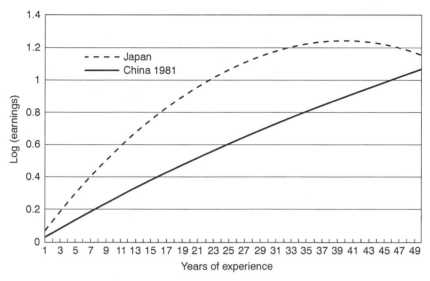

Figure 6.2 Comparison of experience–earnings profiles, Japan and China

the profiles for China and Japan.[10] Obviously, the peak earnings point for Japan (middle 50s–early 60s) is much later than that for the other industrialised countries. The close relationship between seniority and earnings and the prevalence of lifetime employment in Japanese firms are well documented (see Hashimoto and Raisian 1985; Mincer and Higuchi 1988).

Basic human capital theory provides a rationale for this relationship in Japan (Mincer and Higuchi 1988). In the past decade, Japan has had more rapid economic growth and technological change than Western industrialised countries. This has required greater and more continuous training and retraining of workers. The continuous investment in firm-specific skills leads to a close bond between workers and their firms. The joint investment of workers and firms in firm-specific training tends to curtail labour market turnover: lifetime employment is an institution which enables both the employer and employee to maximise the benefits from firm-specific skills. A steep tenure/experience–earnings profile is a tool which encourages a lifelong relationship between workers and firms.

---

[10] The Japanese profile is derived from results reported by Mincer and Higuchi (1988). This profile is for tenure rather than total labour market experience. Given the extent of labour immobility, total experience in China's state sector is reasonably comparable with firm tenure.

Lifetime employment is thus an endogenous variable for the Japanese economy and is encouraged by the existing system of wage determination. Japanese firms can freely hire and fire workers and there is no prohibition on an employee leaving the firm. In Japan, it appears that the wage determination system has evolved to keep workers with the firm, and it plays an important part in the lifetime tenure system. This, however, is completely different from the situation in pre-reform China where there was no need for the wage system to play such a role. Workers were assigned to firms, and in general they could not leave to obtain another job; the wage system did not thus need to be designed in order to affect job tenure. In addition, the level of technological progress in China was lower than in most western industrial countries, not to mention Japan. Continuous training and retraining thus does not provide the rationale for the steep experience–earnings profile in China. In other words, the lifetime employment and steep tenure-earnings profile in Japan reflect a direct relationship between experience and earnings which, in turn, reflects a close relationship between labour productivity and earnings. The seemingly similar phenomenon in China illustrates a relationship between seniority and earnings, without necessarily suggesting a direct link with productivity.

Structural changes over 1981 and 1987

Have the labour market reforms changed the structure of wage determination in China's state sector towards a structure which is more like that which characterises market economies? An *F*-test was used to examine whether there is evidence of structural change in wage determination between 1981 and 1987. The test statistics suggest that the structure of wage determination in 1987 is different from that in 1981.[11]

The final two columns of table 6.3 attempt to highlight the significant changes in the wage structure over the period. The differences between coefficients for the two years are obtained by estimating a pooled regression with a sequence of interaction terms between a time dummy variable and all other variables. The reported differences between the two years are the coefficients for the interaction terms. The results suggest that the increase in the experience coefficient over the period is not statistically significant, though the change in the coefficient for the quadratic term is significant. Comparing the experience–earnings profiles between the two years, it is clear that the profile in 1987 has the same general shape as

[11] The value of the *F*-statistic is $F(39, \infty) = 256$ with a critical value of $F(39, \infty) = 1.30$, so the null hypothesis of no structural change over the period 1981–7 is resoundingly rejected.

in 1981, and is still very different from that for the selected industrialised countries (figure 6.1). This indicates that in 1987, the relationship
between individual income and labour market experience was still largely
seniority-related.

Although data for later years are not directly available, a study by Shao
(1992) provides some comparable information as to whether the experience–earnings profile has changed. Data used in her study were collected
by the Institute of Economics at the Chinese Academy of Social Sciences.
The survey was carried out in 57 SOEs in six cities. The sample size was
2,899 individual employees. Shao (1992) estimated a basic Mincer wage
equation for male employees. The specification and methodology used are
comparable to this study. According to her estimation, the experience–
earnings profile in 1990 was still characterised by a very strong seniority–
earnings relationship (see table 6.4, 1990 column and figure 6B.1, p. 97),
suggesting that little had changed in this regard up until 1990.

In terms of the rates of return to education qualifications, two of the four
dummy variable coefficients have not changed significantly over the period. Moreover, even though the returns for a bachelor degree increased
significantly, the rate of return is still much lower than that found in other
industrialised countries (see table 6.4).[12] On balance, returns to education
have not changed a great deal. The most significant change appears to be
in the pattern of the industry dummy variables over time – out of the 29
industry dummy variables included in the regression, 25 of them play a
significantly different role in wage determination in 1987 *vis-à-vis* 1981.

Unfortunately, the above analysis is unable to quantify the impact of
each particular group of variables on the overall changes in wage structure
over the period. Given the presence of multicollinearity between industry
affiliation and the other regressors in the model, no unique decomposition
of the explained sum of squares in a given year is possible. A number of
methods are employed in order to shed light on the relative contribution
of changes in industry and human capital coefficients over the period to
the explanation of the changes in the variation of wages in logarithmic
terms. Following Dickens and Katz (1987), one can derive a range for the
contribution of industry. The lower bound is given by assuming that
the common industry and other regressor effects are attributable solely
to the non-industry contribution. This bound is evaluated by examining
the increase in the explained variation following the addition of a set of

---

[12] This is true especially when years of schooling is used. In this case the rate of return to an
additional year of schooling is much lower in China's state sector, even in 1987, than that
in the United Kingdom and the United States. Shao's (1992) estimation shows even lower
returns to years of schooling in 1990.

Table 6.5.   *Correlation between coefficients, 1981–1987*

Variables	Correlation coefficients
Total human capital	0.9953
Industry dummy	0.5336

industry dummies to a regression that already includes the other set of regressors. The upper bound of the range is found by regressing log wage on the set of industry dummies only. In 1981, the bounds for the contribution of industry are given by 3.7–7.5 per cent, and in 1987 by 6–11 per cent. Thus, clearly, industry plays an important role in explaining the variation in log wages, and this role appears to have risen substantially over the period.

An alternative method of highlighting the impact of changes in the role of industry and human capital variables in explaining the variation in log wages is suggested by Krueger and Summers (1988). The issue is examined by estimating the correlation between estimated coefficients for 1981 and 1987 (table 6.5).[13]

The results suggest that there has been little change in terms of the rates of return to the human capital variables and occupation dummies in these years. The change in the pattern of industry wage differentials, however, appears large.

The change in the pattern of industrial wage differentials is an interesting result given the amount of evidence suggesting stability of the industry wage differentials for the United States and other Western countries over time (Krueger and Summers 1988; Slichter 1950; Preston 1995). Although it is difficult to attribute the changes in industrial wage structures directly to the reform process, it is interesting to inquire why the reforms might have contributed to the observed effect.

The economics literature rationalises the existence of inter-industry wage differentials via either competitive theory or efficiency wage (or rent-sharing) theories. Competitive theory mainly explains the existence but not the changes of the inter-industry wage differentials, whereas in this study we are interested in finding out the underlying cause of the

---

[13] The choice of default groups is clearly arbitrary but will affect the estimated coefficients. Two sets of correlation coefficients are estimated, one with the default groups representing the lowest earnings (primary school, workers and food processing industry) and the other for the highest earnings (bachelor degree, managers and government). The correlations are insensitive to the choice of defaults. The results reported in table 6.4 are the ones with the lowest default groups.

significant *change* in the pattern of industry wage differentials over such a short period of time.

Efficiency wage (or rent-sharing) theories explain industry wage differentials by suggesting that managers in high-paying industries may maximise objectives other than shareholders' wealth, or that some industries may benefit from sharing profits with employees by reducing turnover or encouraging high effort (Krueger and Summers 1987, 1988; Slichter 1950). Given that the major change in the wage-setting system in China's state industry sector over the reform period was the introduction of a profit-related bonus system, inter-firm/industry wage differentials may differ from the original pre-reform pattern, and the difference is more likely to be profit-related. Owing to a rather equal distribution of bonuses among all employees, the major change of the wage-setting system in the 1980s – the change in inter-industry wage differentials – is unlikely to play an important role in inducing more effort from workers.

In summary, the changes in the wage determination pattern did not move towards a more productivity-related system over the period 1981–7. Rather, the evidence suggests that most changes in the wage determination system may be traced to the introduction of a profit-related bonus scheme.

Failures of the urban labour market reforms

If the central aim of labour market reform was to increase worker incentives, the evidence of success is not overwhelming. Why, then, did the implementation of the labour market reform measures not increase worker incentives more and why did wage determination at the individual level still appear to be related to seniority, rather than productivity? Two possible conjectures may be offered.

First, as mentioned in chapter 2, the main problem concerning pre-reform labour arrangements in urban China was the immobility of labour. As monitoring labour productivity is too costly, shirking is widespread. No matter how the wage structure is redesigned, it will not reflect actual labour productivity. Hence, the essential issue for labour market reform in China is how to increase the degree of labour mobility.

Second, there are still invisible constraints on labour mobility in the state sector. Although enterprises have gradually been given power to recruit and dismiss, managers in the state sector are unwilling to use the power. SOEs are socio–political communities (see Walder 1989). Managers are not owners or shareholders. The state, being both the owner of the enterprises and the welfare provider, cannot behave as a real owner by claiming residual rights. This vacuum in residual rights claiming leads the enterprises to function like social welfare communities, in that managers need to satisfy their subordinates through increasing their earnings and protecting their various interests, thereby making their management task easier. As Walder correctly pointed out, 'if a manager is not a good one by his employees' estimate, the resulting lack of harmony can curb the performance of the firm, and damage the manager's career' (Walder 1989).

On the other hand, as SOEs carry out most of the social welfare functions, most employees (especially the older ones) are unwilling to leave the state sector. Thus, when managers are reluctant to fire workers and workers are reluctant to leave, a lack of labour mobility is a pre-determined result. Furthermore, as managers' objectives are constrained by their employees, to please employees they not only choose not to sack workers, but also try to maximise employees' income. As Walder (1989) indicated 'managerial complicity in a rapid and unchecked rise in labour compensation unrelated to gains in productivity has already been widely documented and described'. We observed that most of the structural change in wages therefore came from equal distribution of profit-related bonuses rather than from productivity-related factors.

To sum up, it may be reasonable to conclude that the lack of labour mobility and the attitude of the state enterprise managers towards employees are the major problems with the post-reform urban labour market situation in China. These, in turn, are probably caused by a much deeper problem with the current ownership structure of the state sector.

Appendix A

Table 6A.1.   *Regression results without industrial dummy variables, 1981 and 1987*

	1981		1987	
	Coefficient	t-ratio	Coefficient	t-ratio
Constant	3.4565	731.74	3.8956	618.92
Bachelor	0.2864	41.38	0.3078	48.48
Semi-bachelor	0.2070	35.09	0.2009	35.80
Senior secondary	0.0987	23.33	0.0970	24.15
Junior secondary	0.0511	14.93	0.0378	11.67
Total experience	0.0283	68.90	0.0301	60.33
(Total experience)^2	− 0.0001	− 12.16	− 0.0002	− 21.36
Managers	0.1115	26.89	0.1329	38.28
Middle-level staff	0.0330	8.37	0.0360	9.36
Technicians	0.0362	7.88	0.0649	15.38
Adjusted R^2	0.64		0.62	
No. of observations	25,259		25,731	

Appendix B

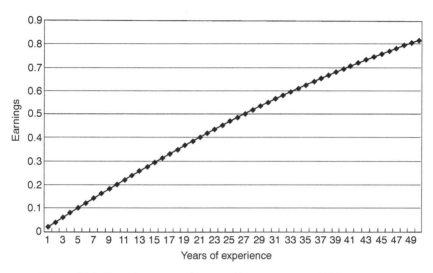

Figure 6B.1 Experience–earnings profile, state sector, 1990
(Shao's estimation)

Appendix C

Table 6C.1.　*Calculated coefficients (Suits' approach), 1981 and 1987*

	1981	1987
Constant	3.36287	3.7475
Primary	−0.1387	−0.1414
Bachelor	0.1517	0.1717
Semi-bachelor	0.0835	0.0807
Senior secondary	−0.0244	−0.0249
Junior secondary	−0.0721	−0.0861
Total experience	0.0273	0.0283
(Total experience)^2	−0.0001	−0.0002
Workers	−0.0377	−0.0489
Managers	0.0643	0.0743
Middle-level staff	−0.0098	−0.0211
Technicians	−0.0168	−0.0043
Food	−0.0777	−0.1194
Metal mining	−0.0076	0.0509
Coal mining	0.0732	0.0567
Petroleum and gas mining	0.0534	0.1472
Non-metal mining	0.0919	0.0005
Construction	0.0586	0.0536
Tobacco processing	−0.1075	−0.0965
Textile	−0.0764	−0.1030
Garments	−0.0874	−0.0558
Timber processing	0.1197	0.0658
Furniture	0.0289	−0.0485
Paper product	−0.0698	−0.0252
Printing and pressing	−0.0683	−0.0317
Chemical	−0.0641	−0.0081
Petroleum processing	−0.0096	0.0526
Rubber and plastic	−0.0339	−0.0133
Leather	−0.0429	−0.0490
Ceramic	0.0148	−0.0317
Metal	0.0248	0.1339
Metal processing	−0.0820	−0.1662
Machinery	0.0530	0.0880
Automobile	0.0243	0.0131
Other transportation	−0.0231	−0.0070
Percussive instrument	0.1453	−0.0824
Other manufacture	−0.0310	−0.0800
Transportation	−0.0479	−0.0243
Telecommunication	0.0206	0.1717
Electricity	0.0458	−0.0053
Service	0.0279	0.0507
Government	0.0472	0.0627

7

Ownership structure, labour compensation and labour demand

The labour market reforms introduced into the urban state sector have not resulted in a productivity-related wage determination system. It was conjectured in chapter 6 that this might be due to deep-rooted problems associated with the ownership structure within the urban state sector. In this chapter, this conjecture is tested by comparing the employment and labour compensation outcomes of firms with different ownership structures.[1]

Enterprise reforms and ownership structures

As a result of economic reforms, the share of the state and collective sectors in total urban employment had declined from 99 to 83 per cent by 1995. Over the same period, the employment share of the urban private sector increased from 0.2 to 16.4 per cent (SSB, various years b). Despite the changes, the state sector still clearly dominates urban employment.

Following the early success of agricultural reforms in the early 1980s the central and provincial governments made numerous attempts to reform the state-owned industrial sector. The main focus of the government's initial efforts to improve the managerial efficiency of the SOEs was to experiment by providing increased autonomy and financial incentives for managers.

Since the beginning of 1981 the *'economic responsibility system'* (ERS) has been gradually introduced to the SOEs. This system allows managers of the SOEs to draw up production plans and to sell their above-plan output to other enterprises at a market price. Most importantly, it allows the SOEs to retain a share of their profits. These profits can be used for employee welfare and bonuses, or for reinvestment.

However, despite the reforms the SOEs have not become more efficient.

---

[1] Portions of the discussion and part of the empirical results are drawn from Meng and Perkins 1996.

The reason is that risk-bearing and decision-making functions are performed by separate agents: the state bears the major financial risk while the managers of the SOEs make the decisions (see also Sicular 1994). This separation of functions enables managers of SOEs to pursue their own objectives.

Ownership normally comprises three functions: decision-making, risk-bearing and the provision of finance (Putterman 1993). It is widely accepted that the efficient way to operate an organisation is to have the same individuals who make the decisions bear the consequences of their decision-making. Under circumstances where risk-bearing and decision-making functions are separated, the state, being the major risk-bearer of the state firms, is unable to adequately monitor managerial decisions. So long as managers fulfil the targeted profit levels (and in some cases also certain output levels), they are basically free to do whatever they like in terms of production, wages and bonuses. State targets are often low. In addition, there is the 'soft-budget constraint' problem (Kornai 1980). Even when a SOE makes losses, the managers can sometimes obtain loans from the state-owned banks for the distribution of wages and bonuses.

If managers of the SOEs do not bear the full risk of their decisions, the question then becomes: 'What constitutes the objective function of managers?' One important component, according to Walder (1987, 1989), is to satisfy subordinates through increasing their earnings, thereby making the task of management easier. If a manager is not a good one by his employees' estimate, the resulting lack of harmony can curb the performance of the firm, and damage the manager's career (Walder 1989). This suggests that the managers of the SOEs tend to maximise the benefits of employees (see, for example Byrd 1992; Walder 1987, 1989; Sicular 1994). As a result they will tend not to dismiss workers when it is necessary and will not pay bonuses less than the level that other firms are paying. Given that state banks are at hand to help them out, some SOEs even pay high bonuses by borrowing money from banks when they are losing money. For these firms, so-called retained 'profit' is not related to their profitability in any way. This is why a non-productivity-related rapid increase in wages and other benefits has been a widespread phenomenon in the state sector (Walder 1987).

Table 7.1 presents the various ownership functions performed by different types of Chinese urban firms. The urban collective sector has roughly the same kind of management structure as the state sector. To some extent it is also supported by different levels of government. The major difference between the state and collective sectors lies in the financial strength of the level of government that supports them. Managers in the collective sector

Table 7.1. *The performance of ownership functions by different Chinese urban firms*

	Private	Urban collectives	SOEs
Provision of finance	Firm and/or financial institutions	Authorities or employees and/or financial institutions	State
Risk-bearing	Firm	Partial authority risk and *low* managerial risk	State
Decision-making	Firm	Managers	Managers

bear higher financial risks than those in the state sector. Given their management and ownership structures, it might be thought that the objective function of urban collective firms may also be to maximise income per worker (Smith 1995). However, as they are operating under harder budget constraints than SOEs, they cannot afford to maximise employee income regardless of the firm's economic performance.

Finally, private firms are basically capitalist, and operate in a competitive market to maximise profit. Firms are decision-makers and bear all financial risks.

These three types of firms form an interesting basis upon which the assumption of behavioural differences in labour compensation and employment determination across the different ownership structures can be tested empirically. The basic hypotheses may be stated as follows:

- Labour compensation is determined by labour productivity in the private sector, but is related to a firm's retained profit in the state and collective sectors.

- Managers in the state and collective sectors are reluctant to dismiss workers. As a result, over-staffing should be a serious problem in these sectors, but not in the private sector.

Model specifications and data description

To examine the impact of ownership structure on the firms' average labour compensation level, a semi-logarithmic average firm-level labour compensation equation[2] is specified as follows:

[2] It is conventional to use the semi-logarithmic form to estimate wage equations in empirical labour economic studies as the coefficients can be easily interpreted as the percentage impact of independent variables on dependent variables. In addition, it is not possible to take the logarithmic transformation for retained profit in observations where it is zero or negative.

$$\ln W = \alpha_0 + \beta_1 \frac{rt\pi}{L} + \beta_2 LP + \beta_3 region + \beta_4 industry + \beta_5 year + \varepsilon \qquad (7.1)$$

where ln W is average firm-level labour compensation in logarithmic form

$rt\pi/L$ is firm's retained profit per worker

LP is labour productivity, which is measured as value-added per worker

region is a group of regional dummy variables

industry is a group of industry dummy variables

year   is a group of year dummy variables

ε is an error term.

The two main independent variables are retained profit per worker and labour productivity. It is expected that in a profit-maximising firm, wages are determined by labour productivity, whereas in an income per employee-maximising firm, it may be retained profit per worker rather than labour productivity which contributes to the firm's average labour compensation level.

To test the impact of ownership on over-staffing among firms with different ownership structures, a labour demand function is specified as follows:

$$L = f(Y, W) \qquad (7.2)$$

where L is total labour employed

Y is total output

W is average labour compensation level.

Assuming Cobb–Douglas technology is used, to conduct an econometric test (7.2) can be written in a logarithmic form as:

$$\ln(L_i) = \alpha + \beta_1 \ln(Y_i) - \beta_2 \ln(W_i) + \varepsilon_i \qquad (7.3)$$

with ε_i being an error term. The coefficients β_1 and β_2 are referred to as the output and wage elasticities of labour, respectively. They measure the percentage change in employment in response to the percentage changes in output and wages.

Where enterprises are over-staffed, it is expected that the output elasticity of labour should be lower than the case where over-staffing is not a problem. This can be explained in two ways. On the one hand, if an enterprise decides not to fire workers when production is falling, it implies a reduction in production without a corresponding reduction in the labour force. By the same token, if an enterprise has excess labour, an increase in production will not bring forth a change in the labour force either. Thus, a low output elasticity of labour can be caused by over-staffing. On the other hand, the smaller wage elasticity of labour demand could also be an indicator of over-staffing. When over-staffing is present, changes in market wage rates will have less influence on a firm's employ-ment decisions. It is also possible, however, that the difference in the output and wage elasticity of labour demand is due to technological differences across firms. To control for this, a variable to measure the capital/labour ratio is included in (7.3).

The data used in this chapter cover all three sectors of Chinese industrial firms. This data set is from an enterprise survey conducted in 1993 jointly by the National Centre for Development Studies at the Australian Nation-al University and the Institute of Quantitative Economics at the Chinese Academy of Social Sciences. The survey was conducted in four coastal regions: Guangzhou, Xiaman, Shenzen and Shanghai. It includes two questionnaires: Manager's Qualitative Survey and Accountant's Quanti-tative Survey. The first questionnaire collected information for 1992 and the second for the years 1985, 1990–2.[3] The cities included in the survey are all in the coastal developed region where there is a high level of market competition from the non-state sector. There were 288 firms in the survey. By excluding missing or invalid values, the total sample of the study is 193–262 firms, approximately 589–855 observations, depending upon the variables used.[4] The state firms account for 61 per cent of the total valid sample. 19 per cent of valid firms were collectives and 20 per cent were private firms.

Table 7.2 presents the mean values and standard deviations of all variables used in this study for each year and ownership classification. There are several notable features of the data.

Over time, the sample firms' labour compensation levels, retained profit, value added *per capita*, capital/labour ratio and total output in-creased, while the average levels of employment decreased. The falling levels of employment may be due to the rising proportion of non-state firms in the sample in the early 1990s. The firm's total profit per worker, retained profit and total output decreased slightly between 1985 and 1990 owing to the general decline in output and profits as a result of the entry of many non-state firms which increased market competition.

Comparing firms with different ownership structures, it is found that workers in private firms had the highest income, and their productivity and profitability were also much higher than in the other two sectors.

---

[3] The data are in the form of an unbalanced panel.
[4] For a detailed description of the variables, see appendix A (p. 114).

Table 7.2. Descriptive statistics of variables used in the study, 1985–1992

	1985		1990		1991		1992	
	Mean	SD	Mean	SD	Mean	SD	Mean	SD
Monthly labour compensation	146	120	227	236	243	250	298	473
Total profit per worker	3,663	3,686	2,398	3,562	2,754	5,162	4,223	9,661
Total retained profit/labourer	1,301	2,929	1,118	2,396	1,617	4,815	1,812	5,255
Value added per worker	7,353	6,292	7,660	7,192	8,620	9,667	11,293	16,784
Average employment	1,537	1,890	1,392	1,878	1,237	1,667	1,268	1,875
Total output	5,050	10,756	4,683	11,196	5,081	12,171	5,759	14,884
Capital/labour	0.97	1.52	1.90	4.30	2.06	3.61	2.34	3.77

	State		Collective		Private	
	Mean	SD	Mean	SD	Mean	SD
Monthly labour compensation	239	264	146	76	394	577
Total profit per worker	2,808	3,527	1,508	2,322	6,714	12,979
Total retained profit/labourer	1,374	3,829	471	786	4,778	7,492
Value added per worker	8,288	6,191	4,812	4,624	15,442	22,872
Average employment	1,585	1,724	615	1,368	995	2,433
Total output	6,900	15,214	1,079	2,204	4,731	9,953
Capital/labour	1.56	2.31	0.59	0.81	3.59	6.09

Source: Author's calculations.

Profitability in the private sector is about twice that of the state and four times that of the collective sectors. Similarly, value added per worker in the private firms is more than twice that of the state sector and more than four times that of the collective sector.

Determination of labour compensation

The OLS estimates of (7.1) for the state, collective and private sectors separately are presented in table 7.3.

The explanatory power of the equation as measured by the adjusted R^2 is much higher for the private sector than for the state and collective sectors. A simple correlation between earnings and value added/labourer, and retained profit/labourer in the three ownership regimes was also calculated (see table 7.4). It is found that the high explanatory power for the private sector in table 7.3 can be largely explained by the fact that in this sector earnings are highly correlated with labour productivity, with the simple correlation coefficient being 0.86.

For the state sector, retained profit per labourer is the dominant determinant of wage variation among firms. Labour productivity – value added per labourer – seems to contribute little to wage variation in state firms.

The results for the collective sector, however, are very confusing in that opposite results are observed from those expected from the theoretical model. Variations in labour productivity have no impact on wage variation among firms, whereas profit per labourer affects a firm's average wage levels negatively. This may be caused by an omitted-variable problem. Although some variables which may affect earnings among different firms, such as industrial affiliation, regional allocation and time have been controlled for, firms may have other unobservable characteristics which are important in determining variations in earnings, such as firm size and technology used. Models with an omitted-variable problem will be estimated with a bias, which can sometimes change the sign of coefficients.

To overcome this problem, and to test the robustness of the estimated results, a feature of panel data is utilised. Recall the discussion of (5.5) (p. 67), where it is mentioned that in a panel data set two residuals, namely a unit-specific residual, v_i, and a normal residual, ε_i, are included. If an OLS estimation is used, it must assume that $v_i = 0$ and if a random-effects model is estimated, it must assume that v_i is not correlated with $\bar{X}_i$, which is a vector of mean value of regressors over time for each unit. The Breusch–Pagan Lagrangian Multiplier-test for $v_i = 0$ and Hausman

Table 7.3. *OLS estimates of the firm-level wage equation*

	State-owned firms		Collectives		Privately-owned firms	
	Coeff.	t-ratio	Coeff.	t-ratio	Coeff.	t-ratio
Constant	4.955	34.59***a	4.555	20.17***	4.941	23.09***
Value added/worker	0.017	0.34	0.080	0.80	0.128	5.60***
Retained profit/worker	0.001	10.40***	-0.002	-2.88***	0.000	1.95**a
Dummy for 1990	0.434	5.13***	0.397	3.09***	0.167	0.83
Dummy for 1991	0.469	5.52***	0.396	3.27***	0.336	1.69*
Dummy for 1992	0.508	5.91***	0.458	3.71***	0.389	1.92**
Industry dummy variables:						
Garment	-0.205	-1.73*a	0.462	2.6***	-0.192	-1.56
Electronic	-0.205	-2.32***	0.203	0.90	-0.178	-1.51
Machinery	-0.086	-0.55	-0.523	1.86*	n.a.	n.a.
Iron and steel	0.116	0.97	0.363	1.22	-0.004	-0.03
Heavy metal	-0.849	-3.46***	0.572	2.43***	0.722	3.44***
Other	-0.162	-1.68*	0.384	1.88*	0.080	0.63
Regional dummy variables:						
Shanghai	-0.086	-0.84	-0.200	-1.29	1.146	4.50***
Xiamen	-0.554	-3.68***	-0.650	-3.79***	-0.050	-0.48
Guangzhou	-0.155	-1.44	-0.442	-2.67***	0.052	0.43
No. of observations	366		101		54	
Adjusted R^2	0.33		0.27		0.86	

Note: a t-statistic values with *** are significant at the 1 per cent level; ** at the 5 per cent level; * at the 10 per cent level.
n.a. = Data for machinery sector are not available.
Source: Author's estimations.

Table 7.4. *Simple correlation coefficient between log average firm-level wage, profitability and productivity*

	Value added/ labour	Retained profit/ labour	Profit/ labour
State sector	0.12	0.44	−0.05
Collectives	0.28	−0.04	0.19
Joint venture and foreign-owned	0.86	0.51	0.41

Note: labour = per labourer.
Source: Author's calculations.

specification-test for v_i being uncorrelated with $\bar{X}_i$ are conducted. The test results suggest that for the data set used in this study, fixed-effects model is more appropriate.[5] Table 7.5 presents the results of the fixed-effects estimation.

Estimation of the fixed-effects model produces very different results for the collective sector, though the results for the SOEs and the private sector appear to be quite robust.[6] Once again, the R^2 for the private sector is much higher than for the other sectors. In both the SOEs and collective sectors profit-sharing was found to be a major positive determinant of wage variation.[7]

The results suggest that an increase of 1,000 yuan in *per capita* profit will increase the SOE workers' average earnings by 2 per cent,[8] and the average earnings in the collective sector by 40 per cent, while profitability contributes little to firms' average earnings in the private sector. In the private sector, it is labour productivity that matters. Every 1,000 yuan increase in value added per worker will increase wages by 2.1 per cent in the private sector. For the state enterprises and collectives, the effect is small and statistically insignificant.

These results appear to confirm that labour compensation in the SOEs and collectives is heavily determined by a firm's retained profits

---

[5] The Breusch–Pagan Lagrangian Multiplier-tests and Hausman specification-tests for the three estimations are reported in appendix C and table 7C.1 (pp. 117–18).

[6] To further test the robustness of our estimation, an equation where both dependent and independent variables were linear was also estimated. The results, which are presented in table 7D.1 (p. 119), confirmed the conclusions presented here.

[7] The fixed-effects estimation changed the impact of profitability on earnings from negative and significant (in OLS estimation) to positive and significant. Such a dramatic change may suggest a very flexible earnings determination system across firms.

[8] As the data for value added and profit are in 10,000 yuan and firms' average earnings are in yuan, the coefficients should be read with this measurement difference in mind.

Table 7.5.   *Fixed-effects estimations of wage equation*

	State		Collectives		Joint venture and foreign-owned	
	Coeff.	t-ratio	Coeff.	t-ratio	Coeff.	t-ratio
Constant	4.79	88.57***[a]	4.44	48.71***	4.86	30.13***
Value added/labourer	0.06	1.31	0.03	0.37	0.21	3.72***
Retained profit/labourer	0.20	3.03***	3.99	3.44***	−0.05	0.36
Dummy for 1990	0.36	7.85***	0.22	2.25**[a]	0.21	1.69
Dummy for 1991	0.44	9.39***	0.30	3.18***	0.32	2.64***
Dummy for 1992	0.48	10.34***	0.33	3.28***	0.33	2.73***
No. of observations		366		101		54
R^2 within		0.35		0.33		0.72

Note: [a]t-statistic values with *** are significant at the 1 per cent level; ** at the 5 per cent level.
Source: Author's estimations.

while in the private sector labour compensation is influenced by labour productivity.

Impact of bonuses on productivity

How, then, does this behavioural difference affect a firm's economic performance? Before investigating this issue, the studies on the performance of profit-sharing firms that have been undertaken over the last two decades are briefly reviewed. The empirical findings are inconclusive (see Weizman and Kruse 1990). While many studies find that profit-sharing enhances productivity (see, for example, Bhargava 1994; Cable and Wilson 1989, 1990; Kruse 1992), others find no statistically significant relationship between the two (see, for example, Florkowski 1988; Jones 1987). However, because the ownership structures of Chinese state and collective firms differs from the profit-sharing firms analysed in the other studies, it is likely that our analysis will produce different results.

The main difference between normal profit-sharing firms and Chinese SOEs and collectives is whether risk-bearing and decision-making are integrated. In the case of profit-sharing firms, they remain profit-maximisers and need to reward those who bear the financial risk. Hence, it is more likely that the firms only decide to share part of the profit with employees as an incentive to encourage employees to produce more profit (Blinder 1990). This, however, is not necessarily true in the Chinese case. For the state sector, the decision-makers are employees themselves and

they do not bear (or bear to only a limited degree) the financial consequences of their decisions. Thus, they have all the incentives to share out
profits regardless of the enterprise's financial performance. For the collectives, as the decision-makers have to bear a certain degree of financial risk,
financial performance should be of some concern, and it could be expected, therefore, that profit-sharing would be linked more closely to
labour productivity.

But to what degree is financial performance a concern for state and
collective firms when they determine the level of profit-sharing? To what
extent does profit-sharing increase productivity? These are, by and large,
empirical questions to which we now turn. Assuming profit-sharing aug-
ments labour productivity (see Kruse 1992) and following Yao (1995), a
CES production function is estimated to assist in understanding this issue.
The basic idea is to test if bonuses encourage an increase in labour
productivity. As the bonus paid may be an endogenous variable, a simultaneous equation system is estimated with value added per worker (*vadl*),
bonuses/wage ratio (*bwr*) and retained profit per worker (*rtπ/L*) as endogenous variables. The three equations in the system are defined as

$$\ln(vadl) = \alpha_1 + \beta_{11}\ln(K/L) + \beta_{12}[\ln(K/L)]^2 + \beta_{13}\ln L + \beta_{14}bwr + \beta_{15}Hedu$$
$$+ \beta_{16}Region + \beta_{17}Time + \beta_{18}Indu + \varepsilon$$
$$bwr = \alpha_2 + \beta_{21}rt\pi/L + \beta_{22}Region + \beta_{23}Time + \beta_{24}Indu + e$$
$$rt\pi/L = \alpha_3 + \beta_{31}(K/L) + \beta_{32}(Sale/L) + \beta_{33}Region + \beta_{34}Time + \beta_{35}Indu + v$$

where *vadl*   is value-added per employee
      K   is total capital stock
      L   is labour
      bwr is total bonuses per employee divided by total wage bill per
            employee
      Sale is total sale
      Hedu is the percentage of highly educated employees, which is
            defined as percentage of above-secondary graduates among
            all employees
      Region, *Time* and *Indu* are three vectors of dummy variables for
      region, time and industry, respectively
      ε, *e* and *v* are the residuals for the three equations.[9]

---

[9] According to Kruse (1992), the reason that bonus per labour and percentage of highly
educated employees are taken as non-logarithmic terms is that they are assumed to be
labour augmenting terms and hence are suggested to be approximated as in linear form. In
addition, retained profit per labourer cannot be taken as a logarithmic term because for
some observations it takes zero or negative values.

Table 7.6.   *Impact of bonus on labour productivity*

State sector	Value added		Bonus		Retained profit	
	Coeff.	t-ratios	Coeff.	t-ratios	Coeff.	t-ratios
Constant	0.231	0.49	−0.026	0.35	7.438	0.10
Bonus/wage ratio	3.270	1.92*[a]	n.a.	n.a.	n.a.	n.a.
Educated/total employees	0.129	0.59	n.a.	n.a.	n.a.	n.a.
Log(capital/labour)	−0.157	2.70***[a]	n.a.	n.a.	n.a.	n.a.
Log(capital/labour)²	0.014	0.34	n.a.	n.a.	n.a.	n.a.
Log(labour)	−0.006	0.07	n.a.	n.a.	n.a.	n.a.
Retained profit per labourer	n.a.	n.a.	0.001	1.37	n.a.	n.a.
Capital/labour	n.a.	n.a.	n.a.	n.a.	0.092	12.84***
Total sale/labour	n.a.	n.a.	n.a.	n.a.	0.002	0.48
No. of observations[b]			262			
System R^2			0.68			

Collective sector	Value added		Bonus		Retained profit	
	Coeff.	t-ratios	Coeff.	t-ratios	Coeff.	t-ratios
Constant	5.520	4.28***	0.143	1.28	18.845	0.75
Bonus/wage ratio	9.167	3.45***	n.a.	n.a.	n.a.	n.a.
Educated/total employees	2.483	2.56***	n.a.	n.a.	n.a.	n.a.
Log(capital/labour)	−0.388	2.12**[a]	n.a.	n.a.	n.a.	n.a.
Log(capital/labour)²	−0.031	0.28	n.a.	n.a.	n.a.	n.a.
Log(labour)	0.331	1.56	n.a.	n.a.	n.a.	n.a.
Retained profit per labourer	n.a.	n.a.	0.001	0.44	n.a.	n.a.
Capital/labour	n.a.	n.a.	n.a.	n.a.	0.025	4.77***
Total sale/labour	n.a.	n.a.	n.a.	n.a.	−0.001	0.02
No. of observations[b]			54			
System R^2			0.94			

Notes: [a] t-statistic values with *** are significant at the 1 per cent level; ** at the 5 per cent level; * at the 10 per cent level.
[b] The reason that the number of observations is different for the two sets of estimations is that the estimation for the fixed-effects model takes two steps. Hence, the model can predict for bonus per worker even though the variable has a missing value for some observations.
n.a. = Not applicable.
Source: Author's estimations.

The system is estimated for the state and collective sectors separately (table 7.6). The most interesting result revealed from table 7.6 is that although the bonus variable contributes positively to labour productivity in both the state and collective sectors, it is only marginally significant for the state sector. Further, the contribution of bonus to labour productivity is about triple for the collective sector compared to the state sector. This result suggests that with the same income-maximisation objective, firms with a relatively higher degree of integrated risk-bearing and decision-making (or harder-budget constraints) have profit-sharing behaviour more closely related to enhancing labour productivity than their counterparts with a low degree of integrated risk-bearing and decision-making (softer-budget constraints).[10]

Employment determination

To assess the over-staffing situation among firms with different ownership structures, (7.3) is estimated for the three sectors separately using a fixed-effects model. The results are reported in table 7.7.

All three equations seem to perform well, the R^2s are high and all the coefficients have the expected signs. However, both the output elasticity and the wage elasticity are much lower for the state and collective sectors than for the private sector. Every 10 per cent increase in output induces a 2.1, 1.8 and 3.3 per cent increase in labour for the state, collective and private sectors, respectively. The wage elasticity for the three sectors is 0.9, 0.2 and 2.1 per cent, respectively. The low output and wage elasticities of labour demand in the state and collective sectors imply that there is little need for labour to adjust to wage and output changes. This suggests that those sectors are not primarily focused on efficiency of labour use and the lack of labour response to output variation, for example, suggests an excess supply of labour.

More interestingly, when using the capital/labour ratio to control for technology differences it is found that the change in the capital/labour ratio has no impact on state sector employment while an increase in capital per worker reduces employment in the collective and private sector significantly. Intuitively, this suggests that when changing from a low to a high capital/labour ratio technology, *ceteris paribus*, firms in the state sector do not reduce their level of employment. In contrast, a 10 per cent increase in the capital/labour ratio will reduce employment by 15 per cent in the collective sector and by 20 per cent in the private sector.

These results seem to suggest that over-staffing is a problem for the state sector, while it is less of a problem for the collective sector, and even less of a problem for the private sector. To support this argument, table 7.8 provides information on the percentage of production workers, managerial workers and service workers in the total labour force in the three

---

[10] Studies by Groves *et al.* (1994) and Yao (1995) found a similar result which suggests that the incentive system did contribute positively to labour productivity in the state sector. However, in their studies, only the state sector is investigated. In this study, a comparison with the collective sector reveals an interesting insight that the degree of contribution of the incentive system to productivity in the two sectors is different.

Table 7.7. *Labour demand equation*

	State		Collective		Private	
	Coeff.	t-ratio	Coeff.	t-ratio	Coeff.	t-ratio
Constant	5.64	30.51***a	4.37	9.88***	4.52	10.64***
Log(total real output)	0.21	12.06***	0.18	3.63***	0.33	9.51***
Log(labour compensation)	−0.09	3.60***	−0.02	0.29	−0.21	2.78***
Log(capital/labour)	−0.03	1.60	−0.15	3.30***	−0.20	4.04***
No. of observations	456 (n = 131)		185 (n = 56)		214 (n = 75)	
R^2 between	0.75		0.68		0.69	

Notes: t-statistic values with *** are significant at the 1 per cent level.
Source: Author's estimations.

Table 7.8. *Descriptive statistics on over-staffing*

	State		Collective		Private	
	Mean	SD	Mean	SD	Mean	SD
Managerial/total labour (per cent)	12	7	10	5	10	0.06
Service worker/total labour (per cent)	8	5	4	5	2	0.03
Production worker/total labour (per cent)	69	19	79	18	81	0.18
Total dismissed/total labour (per cent)	6	11	7	10	16	0.62
Managers' view of over-staffing (per cent)	23	26	14	28	3	0.32

sectors. In addition, it also presents information obtained from the Manager's Qualitative Survey on what the managers of firms believe the extent (percentage) of over-staffing is in their own firms.

It is revealed in table 7.8 that the state sector had the highest (service worker/total labour) ratio and (manager/total labour) ratio, and the lowest (production worker/total labour) ratio. These data may suggest that the SOEs have surplus manpower. For example, on average, a private firm has 2 per cent service workers, while this figure is three times higher in the state sector.

The most informative figure from table 7.8 is the managers' estimate of their own over-staffing problem. The Manager's Qualitative Survey asks the manager whether there is an over-staffing problem, and if so or not, what he/she thinks is the optimal number of employees for the firm in that year (1992). The answer to this question is then subtracted from the firm's 1992 actual labour force and then divided by the firm's actual labour force to form a variable to measure the percentage of over-staffing. In the state

Table 7.9.   *Distribution of decision-making on dismissal*

	State		Collective		Private	
	Freq.	Per cent	Freq.	Per cent	Freq.	Per cent
Firm	111	78.2	46	78.0	76	95.0
Firm and authority	13	9.2	4	6.8	1	1.3
Share holders	0	0.0	0	0.0	1	1.3
Workers	13	9.2	9	15.3	0	0.0
Authority	5	3.5	0	0.0	2	2.5

sector, the average over-staffing was 23 per cent of workers, while this indicator was only 14 per cent in the collective sector and a relatively minor 3 per cent in the private sector.

Finally, dismissals as a percentage of the total labour force are lower in the state and collective sectors than in the private sector. This is not because firms are not allowed to fire workers. Table 7.9 provides information on decision-making on dismissals; it shows that almost 80 per cent of firms in the state and collective sectors had decision-making power over dismissals and another 7–9 per cent had partial decision-making power. This seems to indicate that lack of decision-making power is not the issue. It is the objective of maximising employees' benefits which prevents firms from firing over-staffed workers.

In summary, owing to lack of reform in the ownership structure, China's SOEs and urban collectives follow an objective of income per employee-maximisation rather than profit-maximisation. This is reflected in the fact that labour compensation in these sectors is determined by firms' profitability rather than labour productivity and that over-staffing is a serious problem for the state and collective sectors.

These findings are consistent with those of chapter 6. The findings from this chapter suggest that labour market reform in urban China has proved to be more difficult than product market reform. The success of labour market reform will require a major reform of ownership structure. However, to bring about such reform, there are some practical questions to be addressed, the most important one being how to redesign China's urban welfare system. Chapter 8 examines the issues involved.

Appendix A: description of the data

Wage: The dependent variable for the income equation is measured as a logarithmic transformation of a firm's average income level (firm's total wage bill/firm's total employment), where income is deflated by the urban CPI.

Productivity: Productivity is measured by firm's total value added (deflated by the industrial goods producer price index), divided by total number of employees.

Firm's retained profit per worker: Firm's retained profit is deflated by the industrial goods producer price index, divided by total employment in the firm.

Total output: Total output is measured by yuan and deflated by the industrial goods producer price index.

Capital/labour ratio: This ratio is defined as total capital, which is deflated by the industrial goods producer price index, divided by the total labour force.

Bonus per worker: Firm's total bonus bill deflated by the CPI, divided by total employment in the firm.

Regional dummy variables: There are three regional dummy variables in the study: Xiaman, Guangzhou and Shanghai; Shenzhen is used as the base case.

Time dummy variables: Four time dummy variables are used in this study; the year 1985 is used as the base year.

Industry dummy variables: Six industry dummy variables are used: Garment, Electronic Machinery, Iron and steel, Heavy metal and Other industries; the Textile industry is used as the omitted group.

Appendix B

Table 7B.1. *Robustness of impact of productivity on wage variation among private firms, OLS estimations*

	Coefficient	t-ratio		Coefficient	t-ratio
Constant	4.22	13.19	Constant	4.20	13.06
Value added/labour	0.16	4.89	Value added/labour	0.13	5.47
Profit/labour	-0.08	-1.49	Profit/total sale	-0.02	-0.20
Dummy for 1985	1.01	2.90	Dummy for 1985	1.01	2.87
Dummy for 1990	1.08	3.44	Dummy for 1990	1.08	3.43
Dummy for 1991	1.14	3.64	Dummy for 1991	1.16	3.66
Dummy for 1992	1.26	3.97	Dummy for 1992	1.26	3.96
Garment	0.04	0.32	Garment	0.06	0.59
Electronic	-0.22	-1.92	Electronic	-0.19	-1.69
Iron and steel	0.026	0.12	Iron and steel	0.04	0.20
Heavy metal	0.53	2.36	Heavy metal	0.56	2.50
Other	0.25	1.94	Other	0.27	2.17
Shanghai	0.21	1.83	Shanghai	0.21	1.81
Guangzhou	-0.26	-2.97	Guangzhou	-0.26	-2.98
Xiamen	0.11	0.64	Xiamen	0.11	0.62
Adjusted R^2	0.36		Adjusted R^2	0.35	
No. of observations	207		No. of observations	207	

Table 7B.2. Robustness of impact of productivity on wage variation among private firms, fixed-effects estimations

	Coefficient	t-ratio		Coefficient	t-ratio
Value added/labour	0.135	4.06	Value added/labour	0.109	3.78
Total profit/labour	−0.043	−1.32	Total profit/sale	0.058	1.01
Dummy for 1985	1.088	6.50	Dummy for 1985	1.087	6.47
Dummy for 1990	1.050	6.74	Dummy for 1990	1.052	6.74
Dummy for 1991	1.116	7.13	Dummy for 1991	1.121	7.15
Dummy for 1992	1.223	7.64	Dummy for 1992	1.220	7.60
Constant	4.242	28.51	Constant	4.248	28.46
within R^2	0.49		Overall R^2	0.49	
No. of observations	207		No. of observations	207	

Appendix C

Breusch–Pagan Lagrangian Multiplier-test for $v_i i = 0$:

State sector	$\chi^2 = 151.6{***}$	Prob $> chi^2 = 0.000$
Collectives	$\chi^2 = 7.55{***}$	Prob $> chi^2 = 0.006$
Private sector	$\chi^2 = 7.92{***}$	Prob $> chi^2 = 0.005$

Hausman specification-test:

State sector	$\chi^2 = 2.61$	Prob $> chi^2 = 0.856$
Collectives	$\chi^2 = 17.17{***}$	Prob $> chi^2 = 0.009$
Private sector	$\chi^2 = 4.04$	Prob $> chi^2 = 0.544$

Table 7C.1. *Coefficient difference between fixed- and random-effects estimations*

	State		Collectives		Private	
	Fixed	Random	Fixed	Random	Fixed	Random
Value added/labour	0.07	0.06	0.03	0.06	0.21	0.14
Retained profit/labour	0.20	0.32	3.06	0.02	−0.05	0.09
Dummy for 1985	0.42	0.40	0.23	0.24	n.a.	n.a.
Dummy for 1990	0.78	0.78	0.47	0.52	0.21	0.17
Dummy for 1991	0.86	0.85	0.54	0.57	0.32	0.29
Dummy for 1992	0.91	0.89	0.57	0.62	0.33	0.32

Note: n.a. = Not available.

Appendix D

Table 7D.1. *Estimation using average firm-level wage instead of log(w) as dependent variable*

	State		Collectives		Private	
	Coeff.	t-ratio	Coeff.	t-ratio	Coeff.	t-ratio
Constant	73.425	3.61	73.295	4.46	−37.49	−0.40
Value added/labour	10.034	0.64	1.055	0.07	119.71	3.64
Retained profit/labour	166.064	6.72	548.204	3.06	103.11	1.26
Dummy for 1985	55.198	2.54	21.007	1.23	n.a.	n.a.
Dummy for 1990	138.422	6.46	49.110	2.57	130.19	1.79
Dummy for 1991	153.812	7.05	49.030	2.68	154.38	2.17
Dummy for 1992	188.603	8.50	57.940	3.07	100.78	1.42
No. of observations	416		119		54	
R^2 within	0.34		0.26		0.73	
R^2 between	0.28		0.02		0.68	
R^2 overall	0.27		0.03		0.58	

Note: n.a. = Not available.

Appendix E

Table 7E.1.   *Over-time effect of wage determination, state sector, 1985–1992*

1985	Coefficient	t-ratio
Value added/labour	− 0.039	− 0.46
Retained profit/labour	1.106	6.65
Constant	4.709	52.96
1990		
Value added/labour	0.044	0.39
Retained profit/labour	2.052	7.53
Constant	4.998	48.05
1991		
Value added/labour	− 0.040	− 0.41
Retained profit/labour	0.716	5.20
Constant	5.234	51.69
1992		
Value added/labour	0.148	1.68
Retained profit/labour	0.597	4.64
Constant	5.116	46.78

8

Reforming social security

The economic reform process interrupted the cosy pre-reform social security system, whereby SOEs represented a lifetime of employment and welfare. SOEs are now expected to compete with the private sector in terms of efficiency and profitability. The various social welfare provisions to employees are now seen as a significant burden on production costs. For example, in 1993 retirees comprised 20 per cent of the total number of state sector employees. In some long-established SOEs, the ratio of retirees to total employment was 1:1 (World Bank 1996). Non-wage welfare benefits also added to the cost of running SOEs. In a case study of one SOE, the average yearly wage was 8,000 yuan, while the average amount of annual welfare expenditure per employee was an additional 12,000 yuan (see Mai and Perkins 1997). The issue of 'burdensome' social security provision goes hand-in-hand with encouraging labour mobility. Workers actually still prefer to stay with the already over-staffed state enterprises because they have job security and welfare. The private sector, on the other hand, does not offer either.

It is essential, therefore, that China establishes an external welfare system so as to reduce the financial burden of SOEs and facilitate labour mobility. The importance of social security reform has been recognised since the mid-1980s, but this issue has become urgent since a large number of SOEs were running at a loss in the early 1990s. Many reform measures have been implemented in a range of areas, although the actual instruments vary from region to region.

Even though China has started to reform its social security system in a piecemeal manner, the fundamental question still remains: what is the ideal welfare system for China? At present, the reforms are changing an entrenched internal social security into an external one. However, whether China should copy the Western style of welfare economy or an East Asian style of market arrangement is a crucial issue. The choice is, simply, whether China should adopt a social welfare system, a private welfare system, or a combination of both.

Reforms since the 1980s
_____

Unemployment benefits

The unemployment benefit system was first initiated in 1986 in a few large cities, such as Beijing and Shanghai. It now covers most urban areas in China. Generally speaking, eligibility for unemployment benefits is restricted to state sector employees who were dismissed because of mergers, bankruptcy, or planned redundancy of their enterprises (State Council of China [SCC] 1993). Eligibility varies from region to region. For example, in Shanghai, employees from any sector are entitled to obtain unemployment benefits (ADB and China's Ministry of Labour 1994).

In general, workers who have less than 5 years' tenure are eligible for unemployment benefits for a period of 12 months, whereas those who have more than 5 years' tenure qualify for a maximum of 2 years of benefits. In the first 12 months, the amount of unemployment benefit received is equivalent to 60–70 per cent of the worker's previous monthly basic wage. This benefit is reduced to 50 per cent of the monthly basic wage for the second 12 months. The level of the unemployment benefit is set so that it is less than the minimum wage and about 20–50 per cent higher than the poverty level (SCC 1993). If one considers that the basic wage accounted for only around 50 per cent of a state sector employee's total money income, with bonuses and other benefits accounting for the rest (SSB, various years b), then 60 per cent of the basic wage accounts for only 31 per cent of the normal income of an employee.[1] Unemployment benefits are provided by the enterprises. Each enterprise must pay 0.6–1 per cent of its total wage bill to the local Labour Bureau which, in turn, puts the funds into an unemployment benefit account at China's Industrial and Commercial Bank.

The reported number of people who obtained unemployment benefits has been very low, though the rate of increase since 1990 has been very high (table 8.1). There may be several reasons for this. First, most workers made redundant in the state sector were not dismissed, but laid off. They are, consequently, still considered to be employees and receiving living allowance from their former enterprises. They may thus not be entitled to receive any benefits. Second, both the enterprises and their redundant workers are not yet accustomed to the unemployment benefit system and, hence, may not have made good use of it.

_____

[1] 31 per cent of average income earned by a state sector employee was about 91 yuan per month in 1993, approximately US$11.

Table 8.1. *Change in number of unemployment benefit recipients, 1987–1995*

Year	No. of recipients	% increase last year = 100	% of total SOE empl.
1987–90	200,000	n.a.	n.a.
1991	105,000	110.0	0.10
1992	345,000	228.6	0.32
1993	1,030,000	198.6	0.94
1994	1,964,633	90.7	1.80
1995	2,613,130	33.0	2.40

Note: n.a. = Not available.
Source: SSB (various years a).

Housing

The provision of low-cost housing also remains a significant constraint on labour mobility. As a result of the highly subsidised housing scheme, demand for housing has always exceeded supply by a wide margin.[2] The loss of low-rental housing on quitting a current job is a deterrent to those who would otherwise consider working in the private sector. Even those who have not yet been able to rent an apartment may be affected as they may well have been on a waiting list for quite some time, and leaving a job will, therefore, often imply starting at the beginning of another queue.

Reforms began in the mid-1980s, starting with gradual rent increases to ease excess demand. However, as the high subsidies in the state sector corresponded to the low wages that had been set, a reduction in the subsidy had to bring about an increase in the wage level – or, in other words, a shift from an implicit to an explicit subsidy. One positive aspect of this type of reform was that those already receiving housing from an enterprise, as well as those still in the queue, all received the same amount of subsidy. Nevertheless, up to the present time, rental levels are still well below market equilibrium.

Rental reform, however, did not achieve the purpose of encouraging labour mobility. It was not until the early 1990s that employees were encouraged to buy the apartments which were rented to them. The basic rules and the setting of the selling price vary significantly from firm to firm, and from region to region. In general, however, prices are discounted considerably in comparison to the prevailing market price (in most cases,

[2] This situation was particularly acute in big cities such as Shanghai.

the housing price for the employees in the internal market is less than one-tenth of the market price). If an employee then wants to change jobs within 5 years after buying an apartment, they must sell the apartment back to the original enterprise at the purchase price. After this period, however, the worker is entitled to keep the house or sell it on the open market. Although still a constraint to job changes, this aspect of reform has made labour mobility much easier than before. At least for young employees, the 5-year restriction is not such a long period in relation to their total working life. It would be expected that, along with increases in income, more and more employees will be able to afford apartments internally supplied and that the price of enterprise housing will eventually increase so as to equalise the market demand and supply. Once the two-tier housing market disappears, housing will cease to be a serious constraint on labour mobility.

Medical care

The reforms in this area were initially aimed at reducing waste. As any kind of medical expense incurred by state employees was paid for by the state, the system of zero pricing for medical provisions encouraged over-utilisation: almost all households in urban China had 'small family pharmacies' of surplus medicines received. Most enterprises have now adopted a system whereby enterprises and employees share medical expenses. The amount contributed by employees varies. As in the case of housing reform, an equivalent amount of money subsidy has been paid to every state employee to compensate for the withdrawal of free medical care. By changing the implicit subsidy into an explicit one, the hope is that employees will not incur unnecessary medical expenses, especially as the money saved will contribute to their personal disposable income.

While these measures may be successful in decreasing waste, it still leaves medical care as a financial burden to firms and, at the same time, discourages labour mobility. A social medical insurance system has been recently introduced in many large cities. At this stage, it covers only the costs associated with serious illness. Basically, firms pay a premium which is equivalent to a certain percentage (varying from region to region) of their total wage bill and, in some areas, employees also contribute a certain percentage of their wages.

This reform directly addresses problems associated with the enterprise-based welfare system. On the one hand, the risk of an individual firm getting a large medical bill is shared by many firms in the region, which

Table 8.2. *Share of retirees in total employment, state sector, 1978–1995*

	No. of state retirees (1,000 persons)	Total state empl. (1,000 persons)	Retirees/total empl. (per cent)
1978	2,480	74,510	3.33
1980	6,380	80,190	7.96
1985	11,650	89,900	12.96
1990	17,240	103,460	16.66
1991	18,330	106,640	17.19
1992	19,720	108,890	18.11
1993	21,430	109,200	19.62
1994	22,490	112,140	20.06
1995	24,014	112,605	21.33

Source: SSB (various years a).

reduces the fluctuation of possible financial burdens on each individual firm. On the other hand, to a certain extent, socialised medical insurance reduces the employers' reluctance to lay off workers for fear of a potentially destabilising effect on society. At the same time, this reform will reduce employees' anxiety about dealing with serious illness if they leave the state sector, which should further enhance labour mobility. The coverage of medical insurance, and the number of regions which have introduced the system, however, is still very limited.

Pensions

Pensions have always been paid by state enterprises in China. Recently, however, as the proportion of the population who are retired accelerates, pensions have become an increasing burden. The figures presented in table 8.2 suggest that the number of retirees, as a percentage of total state employment, increased dramatically over the years 1978–95 and that, in the early 1990s, the problem became serious.

A regional, unified social pension fund was established in some cities during the early 1990s. The principle is that both firms and employees contribute to the pension fund. In Beijing, firms' contributions are equivalent to 19 per cent of the average monthly total wage bill and employees' contributions are equivalent to 5 per cent of their average monthly wage. Each individual has their own social security account number, and the money paid by each worker is deposited in the individual account. The firm's contributions, however, are only deposited in an individual's account when a firm reaches certain economic conditions set by the government, otherwise the firm's contributions remain in a general fund (Beijing

Bureau of Labour 1996). As mentioned above, the percentage of contributions made by enterprises and employees are different in other cities. For example, in Shanghai, firms' contributions are set at 25 per cent of the average monthly total wage bill and employees' contributions are initially set at 3 per cent of an individual's monthly wage (Economic Commission of Shanghai, Labour Bureau of Shanghai and Industrial Economic Union of Shanghai [ECS, LBS and IEUS] 1994). All enterprises in Shanghai participate in the superannuation scheme.

Reforming the pension system aims to enable retirees to be looked after by society, rather than by individual firms. The existing retirees, however, are not included in the unified pension system. One of the problems with a dual system like this is that when a firm becomes bankrupt the existing retirees will become a 'burden' on society.

In summary, China's social security reforms have only just started and it may take a long time for the emerging system to operate efficiently. More importantly, the reforms which have been implemented so far involve a number of problems which require serious consideration. The most important question is what kind of welfare system China should follow.

Should China become a welfare state?

It seems reasonable to say that the reform measures implemented so far are on the right track in terms of encouraging labour mobility. However, despite the fact that one of the reasons for the reform of the social security system was to reduce the level of financial pressure on SOEs, they are still shouldering the costs for most of the new social security devices. Firms are now obliged to pay for unemployment benefits, medical care insurance and pension contributions in addition to the existing implicit subsidies to employees. During the initial transition period, this may be unavoidable; but in the longer term, other sources for financing the welfare system must be considered.

This raises the question of what kind of welfare system is needed in China. There are two opposing choices: either society tries to look after each individual, or everybody looks after themselves. One may define the former choice as a social welfare system and the latter as a private welfare system. Most industrialised countries belong to the social welfare group, being so-called 'welfare states', whereas newly industrialised economies (NIEs) – such as Hong Kong, Taiwan, South Korea and Singapore – have adopted private welfare systems.

According to Barr (1992), welfare includes four broad areas: cash benefits, health care, education and food, housing and other welfare services.[3] Individual welfare is derived from four sources: the most important one is employment, from which individuals obtain their money income. A second source of welfare is private provision; a third is voluntary welfare, both within and outside the family; the last is that provided by the government.

In a welfare state, the government is the main provider of unemployment benefits, pensions, medical care and other kinds of welfare. The social welfare system in a welfare state functions as an income redistribution device to reduce inequalities in society. In most welfare states, progressive income tax and payroll tax are the main sources of funds for the government sponsored social security systems. Income redistribution, however, may prevent an economy from being efficient in many ways. For example, if a hardworking individual receives only half of what he/she earned after tax in the form of disposable income, while a lax individual earns a relatively higher disposable income, the former may be discouraged from working hard. Many cross-country studies have suggested that total income transfers (or government consumption) as a percentage of GDP have a negative and significant impact on GDP growth (see, for example, Garrett and Mitchell 1995; Birdsall, Ross and Sabot 1995; Clarke 1995). Thus, although a social welfare system aims at equality, the achievement of equality may be at the expense of economic efficiency.

Further, some social benefits may have negative effects on both social welfare and economic growth. For example, if unemployment benefits are set at too high a level, rational individuals may choose to work less; this will induce higher unemployment. Such an increase in unemployment implies that fewer people are getting cash benefits from contributing to economic growth, thus inducing income inequality and a slowdown of economic growth at the same time. Many studies have found that the provision of unemployment benefits and the inflexibility of the wage setting system in many OECD countries are important contributing factors to both the high unemployment rates and long spells of unemployment (see, for example, Karunaratne 1995; Ahn and Ugidos-Olazabal 1995; Ham and Rea 1987). An OECD cross-country study also found that the level of unemployment benefits contributes positively and significantly to the unemployment rate, and the causality goes only from the unemployment benefit to the unemployment rate (OECD 1994). These experiences suggest that social welfare systems may, in fact, not only reduce economic growth but also damage the overall welfare goals of a nation.

---

[3] While other forms of welfare are direct, education is actually an indirect form of welfare, in that individuals do not obtain money directly but through increasing their skills and hence their labour productivity.

Despite the efforts of their respective governments, income inequality has increased in the last decade or so in the United States, Australia and the United Kingdom (see Juhn, Murphy and Pierce 1993; Schmitt 1993; Borland 1996).[4] As a result of economic inefficiency and the rapid ageing of their populations, and correspondingly rapid growth of government expenditure on pensions, most welfare states have started to reform their social security system. This has involved the decentralisation of labour market wage-setting institutions and public expenditure cutbacks. The East Asian NIEs, on the other hand, have mainly adopted private welfare systems with decentralised labour markets. It is within these economies that high levels of economic growth, together with low levels of government intervention, low levels of government expenditure and low levels of unemployment were observed (Castles and Mitchell 1994).[5] In this regard, Hong Kong may serve as a good example.

There are virtually no government sponsored welfare schemes in Hong Kong, apart from two special schemes and government subsidies on education. The two special schemes are the so-called Public Assistance Scheme and the Special Needs Allowance scheme. The former was set up to help the poor to survive; the latter scheme specifically caters for the severely disabled and the elderly. In 1980, the two schemes comprised only about 3.2 per cent of the government budget (Chow 1981). For the majority of the population, pensions, medical expenses and unemployment benefits must all come from the individual's private savings: individuals must utilise market forces to support themselves. Some employer sponsored schemes are available; these are, however, entirely at the discretion of employers (see, for example, Chow 1981; Hong 1990; World Bank 1993b).

How does this system function in Hong Kong? Benefiting from the flexible labour market setting, Hong Kong, together with other East Asian NIEs, has experienced rapid economic growth for the last twenty years or so. Moreover, while the rest of the world suffered from high rates of unemployment, Hong Kong has, for a long period, recorded an unemployment rate of around 2 per cent. Even during the Asian financial crisis, the unemployment rate in Hong Kong remained below 5 per cent. Such

---

[4] Harding (1997) found that although the Gini coefficients for wage, salary and household gross income have increased, the Gini coefficient for disposable income has declined slightly in Australia over the period 1982–93.

[5] Although, the Asian financial crisis has brought some of these economies down, their unemployment records during this low-growth period are still to be envied by most of their OECD counterparts. For example, real GDP growth in Hong Kong in the first quarter of 1998 was − 2.8 per cent, while its unemployment rate was around 4.2 per cent (Census and Statistics Department, Hong Kong 1998).

Table 8.3. *Cross-country comparison of unemployment rates, 1984–1994*

Country	1984	1990	1991	1992	1993	1994
Canada	11.3	8.1	10.4	11.3	11.2	10.4
United States	7.5	5.6	6.8	7.5	6.9	6.1
France	9.7	8.9	9.4	10.3	11.7	12.3
Germany	7.9	6.2	6.7	7.7	8.9	9.6
United Kingdom	10.7	5.8	8.2	9.9	10.2	9.2
Australia	8.9	7.0	9.5	10.7	10.9	9.7
Sweden	3.1	1.6	3.0	5.3	8.2	8.0
Japan	2.7	2.1	2.1	2.2	2.5	2.9
Hong Kong	3.9	1.3	1.8	2.0	2.0	1.9
Singapore	2.7	1.7	1.9	2.7	2.7	2.6
South Korea	3.8	2.4	2.3	2.4	2.8	2.4
Taiwan	2.4	1.7	1.5	1.5	1.5	1.6

Sources: For OECD countries, the data are from (OECD (1996). For the NIEs, except Taiwan, the data are from UN (1995). Data for Taiwan are from Council for Economic Planning and Development Executive Yuan (CEPDEY) (various issues).

low unemployment rates are a common phenomenon in East Asian NIEs (see table 8.3). According to Barr (1992), full employment is the most important source of human welfare. This is not only because employment provides income, but also because employment creates occupational welfare. With a low level of unemployment, more people get a direct cash benefit while simultaneously contributing to a country's economic growth. In this regard, the East Asian NIEs have not only achieved a high level of welfare via the means of the market, but also, until the financial crisis of 1997–8, had not compromised their economic growth.

When income distribution is considered, Hong Kong and other East Asian NIEs have observed a decreasing income inequality over the last three decades. According to the World Bank (1993b), the Gini coefficient for Hong Kong decreased from around 0.42 to less than 0.39 during the 1970s and the 1980s. During the same period, the Gini coefficient movements for Korea, Singapore and Taiwan were from 0.39 to 0.34, from 0.46 to 0.41 and from 0.36 to 0.30, respectively (World Bank 1993b).

Efficiency and equality have been conflicting objectives in the area of policy-making in most economies. The East Asian NICs' experience seems to suggest that, at a certain stage of economic development, flexible labour market institutions and welfare systems may play very important roles in achieving both objectives at the same time. A country with a more flexible labour market setting and lower social welfare expenses may be able to encourage more work and effort and, at the same time, reduce the cost of production, thus becoming more competitive in the world market. Moreover, a private welfare system encourages private saving and investment, and hence growth. Economic growth, in turn, brings more jobs. If full employment is seen as one of the most important measures of welfare, then the East Asian region has, undoubtedly, achieved both growth and social welfare via a flexible labour market setting. In addition, the unique economic growth path of the East Asian NIEs may also contribute to their achievement in attaining both economic growth and equality. According to international trade theory, a country has a comparative advantage in a good which uses its relatively abundant factor intensively. Free trade will increase the relative price of that good and, thereby, increase the real income of the relatively abundant factor and reduce that of the relatively scarce factor. As all the NIEs were labour-abundant countries, the development of their labour-intensive exports not only enabled them to achieve high economic growth, but also increased the income of labourers relative to the owners of capital and, hence reduced income inequality.

Furthermore, investment in human capital has helped the East Asian NIEs' to achieve both growth and equality. All four NIEs' economies have invested considerably in primary and secondary school education over the period of their economic development. This is the result both of government policy influence and the East Asian cultural influence (see Ranis 1995). This is the only area of social welfare – the indirect welfare – in which all four NIEs had considerable government provision.[6]

The result of this investment in human capital has been twofold. On the one hand, it assisted economic growth in the East Asian NIEs. A cross-country study by Birdsall, Ross and Sabot (1995), for example, suggests that the 1-standard-deviation difference in enrolment rates translates into nearly a 1.5 percentage-point difference in the annual GDP *per capita* growth rate. This implies that a country with primary and secondary school enrolments half a standard deviation above the average in 1960 would have had a level of GDP *per capita* 40 per cent higher in 1985 than a country with 1960 enrolments half a standard deviation below the average, *ceteris paribus*. Ranis (1995) suggested that both Taiwan and Korea were able to count on a cheap and unskilled, yet efficient and literate labour force for their labour-intensive export-oriented growth.

On the other hand, education lowers inequality. A cross-country study by Birdsall and Sabot (1994) suggests the existence of a high correlation between basic education and lower levels of income inequality. As sugges-

---

[6] For example, expenditure on education in Taiwan rose from 2.1 per cent of GNP in 1955 to 4.6 per cent in 1970. While formal education in Taiwan is mainly funded by government, about half of vocational education was paid by the private enterprises. It should also be noted that in 1968 Taiwan changed its 6-year compulsory primary education to 9-year compulsory education. In Korea, the expenditure on education rose from 1.7 per cent of GNP in 1965 to 3.5 per cent in 1970.

ted by the World Bank (1993b), this correlation is partly caused by the fact that the increase in the skilled labour supply is faster than the increase in its demand, thereby eroding the scarcity rents that the educated earned. This then leads to a compression of the educational structure of wages. According to Birdsall, Ross and Sabot (1995), the gap in the rate of return to primary graduates and high school graduates during 1976 to 1985 in Korea changed from 47 to 29 per cent.

In summary, in stark contrast to most welfare states, the East Asian NIEs have simultaneously achieved rapid economic growth and a more equitable income distribution. This achievement may be attributed to their flexible labour market settings and private sector-dominated welfare systems.

China is at a crossroads. Having previously adopted an internal social welfare system, it should be extremely cautious when making a decision about the kind of welfare system it implements. In this regard, the long-run impact of different welfare systems on economic growth and social equality should be seriously considered.

Can China afford to become a welfare state?

Even without considering the long-run effects of different welfare systems on economic growth and social equality, one practical question is whether China can actually afford to become a welfare state. To look after its people in this manner, a nation must be rich and have a efficient taxation system. In order to redistribute wealth, part of a society must be wealthy enough to pay taxes so as to support the government's income redistribution plan. In 1997 China has a 58.2 billion yuan deficit, with more than 50 per cent of its state enterprises running losses and with a *per capita* GDP of 6,079 yuan (approx. US$730). The Chinese taxation system, especially its income tax system, is very inefficient. Given this situation, it is hard to imagine that the Chinese government would be able to find the extra money needed to finance a social welfare system which could look after everybody in every aspect.

The problem remains, however, that everybody in urban China has always been looked after by the state and has an expectation that this should continue. It may, therefore, take a considerable amount of time for individuals to adjust psychologically to a new situation, particularly one which is unlikely to be as generous or caring. The abrupt removal of all social security safety nets may cause social and political unrest. Hence, instead of abolishing the existing welfare system, the reforms have been aimed at restructuring this system so that enterprises are not directly responsible for it. This, however, does not solve the problem of who should carry the financial responsibility for the welfare system.

It may be more desirable if individuals were made more responsible for their own welfare during the process of social security reform. This will be possible given the anticipated increase in individual incomes. Such a system has been adopted by the more vigorous East Asian economies. In this regard, establishing a private insurance market, thereby introducing market competition into the system, may be very important for China to consider. In this section, the financial resources needed to support a government sponsored social welfare system which includes pensions and unemployment benefit, over the next 20–30 years are considered under different scenarios.

Pensions

The amount of money spent on pensions depends on the following factors: first, the size of the ageing population; second, whether the system covers the whole ageing population or only those who were once in the labour force; and, finally, how much to pay each potential pensioner. For the last 40 years in China only those who were once in the labour force were covered by the previous scheme. Hence, the participation rate is also a concern.

The size of the aged population in the next 30 years depends on the age structure of the current population and the mortality rate for each age group. Figure 8.1 presents the age structure of China's urban population in 1994.[7] The left of the pyramid represents females and the right represents males. Comparing the population pyramid for 1994 and the predicted one for 2024 (see figures 8.1 and 8.2), it is observed that if men retire at 60 and women retire at 55, in the next 30–40 years urban China will face a much greater pressure from an aged population than it does now, especially when people who were born in the 'baby boom' period (1950s–1960s) are turning 60 (for similar predictions, see West 1996).[8] This pre-

---

[7] Figures 8.1 and 8.2 are consistent with data obtained from China's population sample survey, which was conducted in 1994 by the State Statistical Bureau (SSB, various years b). The sample contains 0.063 per cent of the total population. The mortality rates for each age group are from the same source.

[8] The mortality rate for each 5-year age group is calculated according to the simple average of the mortality rate for each age group. In the sample there are only three age groups which are over 90 and the simple average of these three groups must be lower than the actual mortality rate for the group. Thus, the prediction presented in figure 8.2 may have over-estimated the surviving population in the group of 90 and above. Further, over time, the mortality rate will change, most likely in a downward direction, owing to improvements in medical knowledge and life-sustaining technology. In this study, however, it is assumed that the mortality rate will remain constant for the next 30 years; the prediction is thus rather conservative.

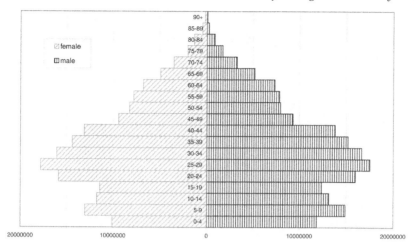

Figure 8.1 China's urban population pyramid, 1994

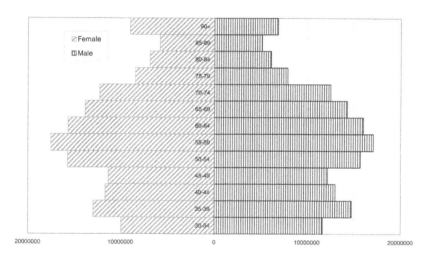

Figure 8.2 Prediction of China's ageing population in 2024

diction assumes that China's current population policy does not change, and that the mortality rate for each age group remains constant at the 1994 level. As indicated in figure 8.2 the aged population will account for about one-third of the total urban population in the year 2024. The size of the aged population, particularly of those at retirement age, gives the upper boundary of the possible pension coverage. The lower boundary depends

Table 8.4. *Prediction of pension payments, 1994–2024*

Year	Aged population (1,000 persons)	No. of retirees (1,000 persons)	Pension per retiree 5 per cent inflation (yuan)	Pension per retiree 10 per cent inflation (yuan)	Total pension payment, 5 per cent inflation (million yuan)	Total pension payment, 10 per cent inflation (million yuan)
1994	39,614	31,692	3,590	3,590	102,690	102,690
1999	9,653	47,723	4,582	5,781	218,665	275,885
2004	73,745	58,996	5,848	9,311	345,009	549,312
2009	91,319	73,055	7,463	14,996	545,209	1,095,531
2014	112,739	90,191	9,526	24,152	859,163	2,178,302
2019	135,047	108,037	12,157	38,897	1,313,412	4,202,334
2024	158,168	126,535	15,516	62,643	1,963,310	7,926,504

Source: Information for 1994 is from SSB (various years a), tables 10.1, 10.17 and SSB (various years b), tables 1.3, 2.2. The predictions are author's calculations.

on the size of the aged labour force. Traditionally, the Chinese government provided pensions only to those who were in the labour force; the actual pension coverage is thus determined by the labour force participation rate. Chinese official statistics, however, do not presently report the urban labour force participation rate.

There are two ways to calculate this participation rate, information on which is necessary for estimating the potential pension outlay.[9] One is to use 1994 population sample survey information, which provides detailed information on the potential labour force for women aged 15–55 and men aged 15–60. One could then use the actual number of economically active population provided by SSB (various years b) to calculate the labour force participation rate. Using this information, the calculated urban labour force participation rate is 89 per cent. The other possibility is to divide the current total number of urban retirees by the current urban population aged 55 and above for women and 60 and above for men, assuming that retirees were previously participants. This calculation gives a participation rate of 74 per cent. However, as the number of retirees in the private sector may be under-reported, this ratio may be under-estimated. The coverage rate used in this study is thus 80 per cent of the total urban ageing population, which is in between the two other figures.

The predictions of changes in the aged population, number of retirees and pensions payments over the period 1994–2024 are reported in table 8.4.[10] It is clear from the table that over the next 30 years the number of urban retirees in China will triple. In 1994, an amount of 102 billion yuan was paid in pensions throughout urban China, of which 86 billion yuan was paid by the state sector. The payment for the state sector alone accounted for about 2 per cent of China's GDP. In comparison to other East Asian fast-growing economies, China is already bearing an extremely heavy pension burden. According to the United Nations, during 1992–4 the total social welfare payment in Hong Kong, South Korea, Singapore and Japan accounted for only 1, 1.8, 0.5 and 2.5 per cent of GDP, respectively.[11]

Assuming no additional incremental pension payment will occur other than adjustments for inflation, the total pension payment in China will increase from 103 billion yuan in 1994 to 1,963 billion yuan (with annual inflation of 5 per cent) or 7,927 billion (with annual inflation of 10 per cent)

[9] For the detailed calculation, see table 8A.1 (p. 142).
[10] The prediction for the aged population provided here is a very conservative one compared to the prediction given by Zhang Wenfan, the chairman of the Chinese old people's association; at the 23rd international population conference. His figure suggests that in the year 2025 the aged population in China will reach 280 million.
[11] Author's own calculation according to data obtained from UN (1995).

in 2024. Further, when allowing for 5 per cent annual inflation and 5 per cent annual real GDP increase, the total pension payment *alone* will account for 2.8 per cent of China's GDP in 2024. This, however, is a conservative calculation, without considering any real increase in pensions. If one considers a 2 per cent per annum real pension increase along with a 5 per cent inflation rate, this ratio will rise to 4.8 per cent.[12] Such an outcome would impose a very large financial responsibility upon China. According to OECD predictions, the total pension expenditure for OECD countries will, on average, account for 2.1 per cent of GDP in the year 2020 (OECD 1996). With a much lower income *per capita*, China will probably carry the heaviest pension burden in the world if the Chinese government takes full responsibility for retirement pensions.

At the moment, most of the financial burden for pension payments is shouldered by the state enterprises. If the current reform only shifts the burden from the state enterprises to the government, then from the national viewpoint the problem is not solved. Indeed, if access to pensions is increased as a result of such a change the situation will worsen: government will be faced with two choices – high taxes or increasing government debt.

If, on the other hand, firms are forced to provide contributions at too high a level (for example, in Beijing it is 19 per cent of the monthly wage, and in Shanghai, it is 25 per cent of the monthly wage, which implies a 19 or 25 per cent increase in total wage costs), firms that join the scheme may lose whatever competitiveness they may have had. If all firms are forced to join the scheme, then a nation-wide increase in wages or inflation is inevitable. The direction of any intended reform in this area thus requires serious consideration. A systematic process of reform may take years to complete, yet there may only less than 30 years left before the problem of China's ageing population becomes serious.

A World Bank report (1996a) proposed a 'Three Pillars' system. The first of these pillars functions as a social security device which offers a 24 per cent replacement rate, assuming that individuals have 40 years of working life. The financing of this pillar is recommended to be provided by an employers' contribution of 9 per cent of the total wage bill. The second pillar could consist of a mandatory individual account which is funded by both employers and employees on a 50:50 basis. It is recommended that workers should contribute 8 per cent of their wage while employers

---

[12] In the 10 years 1985–95, China's real GDP growth was about 8.9 per cent p.a. (at 1980 prices) and the inflation rate was about 11 per cent p.a. It is a common belief that real GDP in China will not grow as fast as for the last decade; in this study a 5 per cent annual increase in real GDP and a 5 per cent annual increase in inflation are assumed for the next 30 years.

should contribute 4 per cent of their total wage bill. It is also suggested that the workers' contributions could be increased over time as their incomes increase. The third pillar should be entirely funded by individuals to provide supplementary pensions.

The problems that may be associated with this proposal are twofold. The first is that employers' contributions could increase labour costs considerably and might cause a loss of competitiveness and increased inflation. Second, the income redistribution device of the first pillar may induce less savings by individuals, as their expectations tell them that their futures are, more or less, secured. The World Bank (1996a) argues that, as individuals may be shortsighted, a basic social welfare system is needed. But, it is also possible that if individuals do not save even without the benefits of a government-provided security system then, with such added security, they may be even less inclined to safeguard their own futures. Further, when the pension fund is paid into individuals' accounts, they are made responsible for monitoring the efficient investment of the fund. However, if the pension contributions are paid into a social security pool, inefficient management of the fund will certainly occur as a result of public ownership.

More importantly, evidence from the OECD countries suggests that generous government pension schemes have induced a declining trend of the participation rate for men aged 55–64 in virtually all OECD countries except Japan, where such a scheme does not exist (see OECD 1996). Hong Kong's experience also suggests that when a government-provided pension scheme does not exist, people tend to work until they turn to 65, or even 70 (Tao 1981).

Considering all these factors, an income redistribution device portion of pension payments should not be taken on board without a great deal of caution. One possible scenario is to gradually reduce the share of the firms' compulsory contributions while increasing individuals' contributions (perhaps compulsory to a certain level). Individuals, however, need to be clearly informed about any possible changes to their pension plan over the next 20–30 years. Thus, as rational agents, individuals will be able to reshape their lifetime consumption and saving patterns. This will not only give society time to adjust and to reduce the financial burden presently borne by the firms or government, but it will also permit an increase in national savings which, in turn, will contribute to long-run economic growth.

Unemployment benefits

It was previously stated that many studies have found that the level of

unemployment benefits contributes positively to the level of unemployment. At the same time, experience from the NIEs indicates that without a
government-provided unemployment benefit system, none of the East
Asian NIEs have experienced the problem of high rates of unemployment.
Such a clear relationship indicates that the institutions associated with a
system of unemployment benefits play a vital role in determining incentives to find work on the one hand, and national savings, economic growth
– and, hence, labour demand – on the other. As one of the fastest-growing
Asian economies, China need not follow in the footsteps of the old industrialised countries to create a further problem for itself by establishing an
inappropriate system of unemployment benefits. China should learn from
the experiences of the East Asian NIEs in this regard to increase individual
contributions and employers' voluntary contributions to the unemployment security scheme.

However, China's state sector had about 10–30 per cent of surplus staff
in the late 1980s and early 1990s. Many studies have pointed out that
another 15–20 million workers will be made redundant before the turn of
the century (Zhou 1997).[13] As mentioned in chapters 6 and 7, the hidden
unemployment in the state sector is mainly due to its current ownership
structure. Although solving the over-staffing problem so as to achieve the
efficient allocation of labour depends on more radical reforms of the SOEs,
a transitory government unemployment benefit system may also be
necessary to assist in a smooth transition. Such a transitory scheme needs
to have strict eligibility criteria, as well as tight controls over the level and
the period of any benefit provision. The living allowance scheme introduced recently for redundant SOE workers may serve this purpose. It is
specifically designed to solve the over-staffing in the state sector with only
the employees dismissed or laid off being eligible for benefits. Redundant
workers are eligible for the living allowance provision for no more than 3
years and the level is set at no lower than the unemployment benefit
(Meng 1998). To ensure that this scheme is a transitory one only, new
entrants into the state sector should not be covered.

The current scheme is funded by the employers' contribution of only 1
per cent of the total wage bill. This is, by a long way, not an adequate level
of funding for the scheme. The 1 per cent of the total wage bill at the 1995
level is about 6.1 billion yuan. If the current 30 per cent of over-staffed
workers were all dismissed and required unemployment benefits from the
scheme, the total cost (not including administrative and training costs)
would be 65.8 billion yuan, which is 10 times the total employers' contri-

---

[13] The problem of state sector over-staffing will be discussed in detail in chapter 10.

Table 8.5. *Total amount of unemployment benefit for 30 per cent of state layoff workers, 1995*

Item	Value
Total state employees (1,000 persons)	112,610.0
Layoff workers (30 per cent of total) (1,000 persons)	33,783.0
Total state wage bill (billion yuan)	608.0
Total state bonus and subsidy bill	242.5
Total state basic wage bill	365.5
Average annual basic wage (yuan)	3,245.6
60 per cent of basic wage (unemp. benefit, yuan)	1,947.4
1 per cent employers' contribution of total wage bill (billion yuan)	6.1
Total unemp. benefit bill at 30 per cent of over-staffing rate (billion yuan)	65.8
Total unemp. benefit as per cent of total state wage bill (per cent)	10.8

Source: Author's calculations according to data obtained from SSB (various years b).

bution and 10.8 per cent of the state sector total wage bill (see table 8.5). The reason why the scheme has been working so far is that most retrenched workers from the state sector are currently paid within their old working units. If such an arrangement could be maintained until the surplus workers gradually find jobs somewhere else, the financial burden to the government budget might not be as serious as it appears. However, as enterprise reform proceeds, a large number of SOEs may go bankrupt.[14] This will put serious financial pressure on the current unemployment scheme.

More importantly, it needs to be stated that, as elsewhere in the world, unemployment may not be a transitory phenomenon in China. A permanent unemployment *insurance* scheme, which will cover all employees, thus needs to be introduced. According to the discussion in the previous section, such a scheme should not be financed by the government or involuntarily by the employers; rather, individuals should take the main responsibility to secure their own future. This will not only encourage individuals to create job opportunities for themselves, but also encourage individual saving, and hence encourage economic growth and further job creation. On the contrary, a government-financed scheme will discourage labour force participation and private saving and generate more unemployment.

The more serious problem is funding if China were to take up a government or employers sponsored unemployment benefit scheme. Table 8.6 presents a prediction of the total unemployment rate (not including state

[14] Currently about 50 per cent of SOEs are loss-makers (EAAU, 1997).

Table 8.6.   *Prediction of cost of unemployment benefits, 1999*

	1994	1999 (low)	1999 (high)
Potential labour force (1,000 persons)	192,740	231,050	231,050
Participation rate	0.897	0.897	0.897
Urban labour force (1,000 persons)	172,920	207,251.85	207,251.90
Total employment (1,000 persons)	16,816	196,747.20	190,525.30
Total unemployed (1,000 persons)	476	10,741.924	16,726.57
Unemployment rate (per cent)	2.8	5.2	8.1
Total wage (billion yuan)	665.64	1,012.9	1,012.9
Average wage (yuan)	3,958.373	5,149	5,150
Average basic wage (yuan)	1,979.186	2,574.5	2,575
Unemployment benefit (billion yuan)	n.a.	31.8	49.51
Administration cost (billion yuan)	n.a.	1.07	1.67
Total unemployment cost (billion yuan)	n.a.	32.87	51.18
Accounted for the total wage bill (per cent)	n.a.	3.2	5.1

Note: n.a. = Not available.

sector possible layoff workers), unemployment benefits and other costs, and the percentage of these costs in relation to the total urban wage bill in 1999, based on employment, unemployment and wage rate statistics for 1994. The potential labour force is also predicted according to population sample survey information and the urban labour force participation rate for 1994. There are two scenarios for the overall prediction for employment in 1999. The higher-boundary scenario is based on the assumption that during the period 1994–9 the annual economic growth rate and the rate of increase in urban total employment will be the same as for the period 1989–94 – namely 10 per cent and 2.63 per cent, respectively. However, China's economic growth may not continue at such a high level, especially now that Asian growth rates have slowed in response to the Asian crises; a lower-boundary scenario thus assumes an 8 per cent per annum economic growth rate, which yields a 2.1 per cent per annum employment growth, *ceteris paribus*.

This simple prediction yields an urban unemployment rate of 5–8 per cent by the year 1999. If it is further assumed that the nominal wage increases at 7 per cent p.a. (at 5 per cent inflation *plus* a 2 per cent real wage increase), the total wage bill will reach 1,012.9 billion yuan in the year 1999. To predict the cost of unemployment benefits, two more assumptions need to be made. First, it is assumed that, in 1999, half of the unemployed are in their first year (the relevant benefit being 65 per cent of the basic wage) and the other half are long-term unemployed (in their second year and hence receiving a benefit of 50 per cent of the basic wage).

Second, associated training and administration costs are assumed to be 100 yuan per person according to the assumption made by the Ministry of Labour. Following these assumptions, the predicted total cost of unemployment benefits will reach 33–51 billion yuan by the year 1999, which will account for about 3–5 per cent of the total wage bill at that time.

If the new unemployment insurance scheme were to make the government or employers mainly responsible for the financial support of the unemployment benefits, it would increase not only the supply price of labour, and hence induce further unemployment, but also increase total labour costs, thereby inducing macroeconomic instability. A private insurance scheme should thus be put into place.

To sum up, the answer to the question of whether China should become a welfare state is a very clear 'No'. This is so not only because China cannot afford to become a welfare state but, most importantly, because public policies for a welfare state may discourage economic growth and bring society more serious unemployment problems.

Appendix A

First method: According to the information provided in table 8A.1, the total urban working-age population in 1994 is 192.74 million and the total economically active population is 172.92 million (*China's Labour Statistical Yearbook, 1995*, table 1.5). This gives a participation rate of 89 per cent.

Second method: *China's Labour Statistical Yearbook, 1995*, table 10.1, provides the number of retirees in 1994 as 2.929 million and information provided in table 8A.1 gives 3.961 million as the total urban population aged 55 and above for women and 60 and above for men. This gives a participation rate of 74 per cent.

Table 8A.1. *0.063 per cent sample and total urban population, by age and sex, 1994*

1994 sample urban pop.	0.063 per cent sample					Total urban population		
	Males (persons) (1)	Females (persons) (2)	Per cent of total males (3)	Per cent of total females (4)	1994 total urban population (5)	Male (million persons) (6)	Female (million persons) (7)	
0–4	6,330	5,564	0.07	0.06	0–4	11.8163	10.08563	
5–9	7,976	7,175	0.09	0.08	5–9	14.88891	13.00582	
10–14	7,033	6,473	0.08	0.07	10–14	13.1286	11.73333	
15–19	6,611	6,301	0.07	0.07	15–19	12.34085	11.42156	
20–24	8,551	8,767	0.09	0.09	20–24	15.96228	15.89157	
25–29	9,365	9,829	0.10	0.11	25–29	17.48178	17.81661	
0–34	8,907	8,867	0.10	0.10	30–34	16.62683	16.07283	
35–39	8,131	7,928	0.09	0.09	35–39	15.17826	14.37075	
40–44	7,392	7,221	0.08	0.08	40–44	13.79875	13.0892	
45–49	4,972	5,181	0.05	0.06	45–49	9.281304	9.391379	
50–54	4,253	4,527	0.05	0.05	50–54	7.939137	8.205901	
55–59	4,199	4,289	0.04	0.05	55–59	7.838334	7.774488	
60–64	3,927	3,730	0.04	0.04	60–64	7.330588	6.761213	
65–69	2,762	2,718	0.03	0.03	65–69	5.155865	4.926803	
70–74	1,747	1,946	0.02	0.02	70–74	3.26115	3.527432	
75–79	909	1,132	0.01	0.01	75–79	1.696843	2.051928	
80–84	454	742	0.00	0.01	80–84	0.847488	1.344992	
85–89	122	262	0.00	0.00	85–89	0.227739	0.474916	
90+	30	114	0.00	0.00	90+	0.056001	0.206643	
Sub-total	93,671	92,766	1.00	1.00	Sub-total	174.857	168.153	
Total	383,568	368,862	0.51	0.49	Total urban population	343.01	343.01	

Sources: a Columns (1) and (2) are 0.063 per cent sample survey of 1994 urban population, which are from *China's Population Statistical Yearbook, 1995.*
b Columns (3) and (4) author's calculations from columns (1) and (2).
c Columns (6) and (7) author's calculations according to the total urban population in 1994, which is provided in SSB (various years a) and information presented in columns (3) and (4).

Part 3

Rural–urban migration

The segregation of China's rural and urban economies was in place for almost 40 years; it was not until the late 1980s that the restrictions on rural–urban migration were gradually eased. Economic reforms have released millions of rural labourers from agricultural production, who were originally absorbed by the TVP sector since migration was tightly controlled until the mid-1980s. However, the demand for rural labour in urban areas continued to increase during this period, partly in response to the rapid development of the *special economic zones* (SEZs), and partly owing to the demand for service providers in the cities.

The government has never made formal announcements about the relaxation of these restrictions. In practice, however, the controls were eased gradually in that rural residents were allowed to come to the city to work in some occupations. By the end of the 1980s and early 1990s the number of rural migrants working in the cities started to increase dramatically. In 1988, about 25 million migrants were working in the urban areas; this figure increased to 64 million in 1994 and to 80 million in 1995 (Centre for Rural Economic Research in the Ministry of Agriculture [CRER] 1996), which accounted for about 18 per cent of the total rural labour force or 34 per cent of the total urban labour force, respectively.[1] This massive movement of labour which brought cheap rural labour to urban China, has had, and continues to have, a tremendous impact on the Chinese economy.

---

[1] In formal Chinese statistical data, rural migrants are still accounted for as part of the rural labour force.

9

The impact of rural–urban migration

The surge of rural–urban migration is the most important change in China's labour market in the 1990s. After 40 years of segregation, the rural and urban economies began to be linked by massive labour mobility. Hundreds of thousands of rural workers, attracted by higher urban incomes, moved to the cities. The economic implications of this continuing exodus from the countryside to the cities are enormous.

The unique features of rural–urban migration in China

The features of China's rural–urban migration can be looked at in two different, overlapping, ways. The first relates to distortions caused by the segregation of the urban residents and rural migrants labour markets. The household registration system that has been in place in the cities for the past half-century has provided urban residents with generous subsidies and benefits that are not available to rural residents. Rural migrants cannot gain urban residency status by moving to the cities; they are thus ineligible for subsidies or benefits and not allowed to obtain permanent positions even if they are employed in the state-owned sector. Moreover, while urban residents are mainly employed under inflexible labour arrangements (chapters 2, 6, 7), wages for migrants are determined in the market and employment is mainly on the basis of either oral or written contracts.

The second feature of Chinese rural–urban migration arises from the various formal and informal restrictions that still hinder it. These restrictions include the still-existing (but not enforced) household registration system, the compulsory agricultural production quota and the fact that rural residents are not entitled to social welfare in urban areas.

The household registration system was enforced strictly before the late 1980s. Since then, enforcement has been gradually relaxed, but institutional barriers to migration remain effective in some ways. The impact of 40 years of rigid enforcement on urban and rural local government officials is not easily eliminated, and rural migrants often get rough treatment at both ends. For example, urban authorities require rural migrants to provide various statements from their home-town authorities to prove that they have been given permission to migrate. Sometimes, when there are local employment or political problems, the urban local governments may create substantial difficulties for rural migrants (see Wang and Wang 1995; Xiang 1996). In the countryside, township or village governments also often charge high fees for providing the necessary documents to migrants.

Agricultural production quotas have also significantly slowed the pace of rural–urban migration. As China is trying very hard to be self-sufficient in agricultural products, rural households are obliged to fulfil government agricultural production quotas. In most cases, the quota involves the delivery of farm products by a household that cannot be paid in cash. Thus, a certain percentage of rural labour has to work in the rural area to fulfil government quotas regardless of the differences in the marginal productivity of labour between rural and urban sectors.

In addition, as already discussed, rural migrants are not entitled to the social safety net provided in urban areas. This is especially important where children's education is concerned. Although free junior secondary education is provided in China, rural migrants are not entitled to it in urban areas. If the whole family migrates to an urban area, they have to pay extremely high fees to enable their children to go to school. Thus, those who are willing to take a risk and migrate are usually the young and those without children. Sooner or later even this group tends to return to their place of origin, as their land plays a special role as security in case of unemployment, sickness and old age.

Given these unique features of rural–urban migration, the role of migration on economic growth in China differs somewhat from that in other developing countries.

Does migration increase urban unemployment in China?

According to neo-classical economic theory, labour mobility from one sector to another will tend to equalise the marginal product of labour (MPL) across the sectors and, as a result, wages between the two sectors will also tend to be equalised. This will induce an efficiency gain for the whole economy (Williamson 1988).

Lewis (1954) and Ranis and Fei (1961) first formalised the two-sector model in the context of rural–urban migration. Their model assumes that in most developing countries the marginal productivity of labour in the rural sector is very low or equal to zero and rural–urban migration tends to narrow the wage gap between the rural and urban sectors. When the marginal product of labour is the same in both sectors the output of the economy will be maximised.

Todaro (1969) and Harris and Todaro (1970) developed a different model. In their model, there is a minimum wage in the urban sector, which is set above the market-clearing level and is assumed to be above the rural wage. Migrants move to the city for work and are prepared to be unemployed while waiting for a job at this higher wage. The minimum wage floor prevents full employment. Rural–urban migration, therefore, results in an increase in urban unemployment and, to a much lesser extent, a narrowing of the rural–urban wage gap compared to Lewis' and Ranis and Fei's model.

Fields (1975) pointed out that the Harris–Todaro model predicts an unemployment rate that is too high. He suggests that the problem with the Harris–Todaro model is the neglect of two important factors: the existence of an urban informal sector and the possibility of rural residents finding an urban job before they leave for the city. By incorporating these two factors, Fields' model predicts a much lower urban unemployment rate and indicates that rural–urban migration should bring about a greater narrowing of the rural–urban wage gap in comparison to the Harris–Todaro model.

Intuitively, it is easy to understand why Fields' model generates much less unemployment than the Harris–Todaro model. If most rural residents migrate only after they find a job in urban areas, everything else being equal, this kind of migration will not bring high unemployment to the urban economy. Further, if the role of the informal sector is taken into account and the degree of labour market flexibility in the informal sector is considered, even those who did not find a job before migration will have less chance of becoming unemployed.

The situation of rural–urban migration in China fits Fields' model better than the Harris–Todaro model. Many sample surveys suggest that around 70–80 per cent of rural migrants obtain a job offer via their relatives, fellow villagers or friends before migration (Meng 1996; Wu and Li 1997; Rural Economic Research Centre 1996). Three urban-based migrant surveys in Jinan, Dongguan, and Shanghai also indicate that less than 2 per cent of migrants in these areas are unemployed.

These surveys also indicate that rural migrants are mainly concentrated in those jobs considered to be inferior by urban residents, such as construction, services and self-employed businesses in the non-economic zones (Wu and Li 1997; Meng 1996b). A survey conducted by the Institute of Population Studies at the Chinese Academy of Social Sciences on 1,504 migrant workers in Jinan City, Shangdong province, suggests that about 42 per cent of migrants surveyed worked as construction workers, 15 per cent were employed in the service sector and another 13 per cent were self-employed (Meng 1996b). Another survey conducted by the Rural Development Research Institute finds that about 33 per cent of migrants surveyed worked on construction sites and about 31 per cent in the service sector (Han 1995). The difference between Fields' model and the Chinese case is that in Fields' model rural migrants are allowed to freely choose between urban formal and informal sector jobs, whereas in China, rural migrants cannot work as formal sector employees because of their residential status.

The segregation of the labour market for rural and urban workers has two implications: the types of jobs that can be undertaken by migrants or residents and the systematically high level of wages, subsidies and bonuses for urban residents.[1] To analyse the possible impact of rural–urban migration on employment, unemployment and wage levels in both rural and urban areas in China, a two-sector model is adopted.[2]

First, consider the case where there are two sectors, a rural sector and an urban informal sector. Assume that:

- the marginal productivity of labour is higher in the urban informal sector than in the rural sector

- both sectors are standardised market economies

- to a certain extent, institutional restrictions on rural–urban migration exist.

Without rural–urban migration, a large wage gap exists between the two sectors. If labourers are free to move, MPL and hence wages tend to be equalised in the two sectors. In the case of China, a restricted rural–urban migration will narrow the gap between the MPLs in the two sectors to a certain extent. But a wage gap between the two sectors will persist.

Second, consider an urban economy with two sectors, formal and informal. Assume:

- urban residents accept only jobs in the formal sector and migrants can be employed only in the informal sector

---

[1] Given the income-maximisation objective of enterprise managers in the state sector, the wages paid in this sector are higher than the MPL (see chapter 7 for a detailed discussion).

[2] Although a three-sector model is considered here (rural, urban formal and urban informal), the standard two-sector model can still be used as a tool for the analysis.

- the informal sector is a market sector, whereas firms in the formal sector pursue income per employee-maximisation

- at each level of labour demand, firms have to pay higher labour compensation in the formal sector than in the informal sector, where labour compensation is equal to the MPL in the informal sector

- without a loss of generality jobs in the formal and informal sectors are technically homogeneous, the only differences are the wage levels and the intensity of the work

- those employed in the formal sector work less intensively than in the informal sector, and only a fixed number of jobs is available in the formal sector

- workers are homogeneous in terms of skills, but differ in terms of residential status.

Figure 9.1 presents employment and wage levels in the urban formal and informal sectors. The Y axis represents wages or marginal productivity of labour in the urban formal and informal sectors, while the X axis indicates the quantity of labour demand. $D_m D_m$ is the real MPL curve for the urban formal and informal sectors. However, as the formal sector is paying employees higher wages than their MPL, the labour demand curve for the formal sector is $D_u D_u$. Because of differences in residential status, the labour supply curve for urban residents is $S_u S_u$ and the total urban labour supply is $S_t S_t$. The total labour demand curve for urban sectors is thus the kinked curve $D_u abD_m$, with the urban formal sector employing OL_{ub} amount of labour and the wage (or compensation) level for this sector being set at the point W_u.

The labour supply curve for the urban formal sector can be at the intersection of point a, but it can also be at any position to the right of point a. In the latter case, there will be open unemployment among urban residents. The reason for such unemployment is that the jobs in the urban informal sectors are considered as being low status, such as dirty, heavy labouring or dangerous jobs. Urban residents are unwilling to accept such jobs at the wage levels the market is prepared to pay. Open unemployment, however, has not been a serious problem in urban China. As hidden unemployment is not reported, the official open unemployment rate, which counts only urban residents, has been around 2–4 per cent for the last 10 years (SSB various years a).

As the market demand curve should be $D_m D_m$ rather than $D_u D_u$, the firms' real demand for the urban resident labourers at wage W_u is at $OL_{ub'}$,

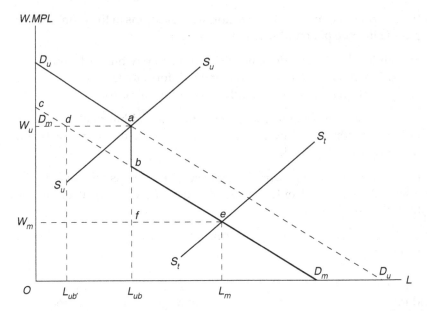

Figure 9.1 Employment, hidden unemployment and wages, urban formal and informal sectors

thus there is a hidden unemployment of $L_{ub}L_{ub'}$. Therefore, the urban formal sector produces $L_{ub}Ocd$ amount of product[3] and its employees are paid the amount of $L_{ub}OW_{u}a$. Whether this sector makes a profit or loss depends on the elasticity of demand and supply curves and the distance between D_uD_u and D_mD_m. Nevertheless, one thing is clear – firms in the formal sector make less profit than firms in the informal sector, which produces $L_{ub}L_meb$ amount of product and pays the amount $L_{ub}L_mef$ as wages.

Owing to various institutional and other kinds of barriers to entry,[4] labour flow from rural to urban informal sectors is limited to $L_mL_{ub'}$. The wage level for the urban informal sector is W_m.

Putting the three sectors into the same diagram, figure 9.2 presents the impact of rural–urban migration on employment and wages in the whole economy. The two Y axes represent rural and urban wages or the MPL, and the X axis measures labour input. The urban formal sector employs OuL_{ub} amount of labour and has $L_{ub'}L_{ub}$ hidden unemployment. If there is no restriction on rural–urban migration, the urban informal sector will employ L_eL_{ub} migrants and the rural sector employ OrL_e labour. However,

---

[3] As D_uD_u is not the marginal product curve for the state sector and the state sector real demand for labour is $OL_{ub'}$, *the amount of product produced in this sector is not* $L_{ub}OD_ua$.
[4] See the second feature of rural–urban migration in China on p. 154.

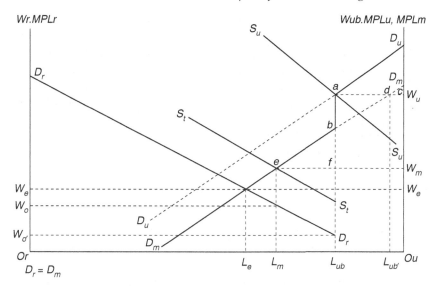

Figure 9.2 Three-sector model and rural–urban migration

this is not the case. Institutional barriers and search costs prevent rural labour from moving to the urban informal sector to the point L_e. Rural–urban migration stops at the point L_m. Employment and wages in the urban informal sector and rural sector are thus $L_m L_{ub}$ W_m and $Or L_m$, W_o, respectively. Hence, we have three different wage levels in the economy owing to institutional and other barriers.

In the case where rural–urban migration is strictly restricted and the urban wage level is set at W_u, the average urban wage level will be W_u and the average rural wage level will be $W_{o'}$. When migration is allowed at $L_m L_{ub}$ but an institutional barrier for migrants working in the formal sector exists, the average urban wage level will equal $\alpha W_u + (1 - \alpha)W_m$, where α is the fraction of urban residents in the total urban labour force. It is clear that $W_u > \alpha W_u + (1 - \alpha)W_m$, which implies that migration will reduce average urban labour costs. On the other hand, the average rural wage level will increase from $W_{o'}$ to W_o.

Because of the segmentation of urban labour markets between urban residents and rural migrants, rural–urban migration has little impact on urban hidden unemployment. The level of hidden unemployment, $L_{ub} L_{ub'}$, is the result of the institutional wage-setting and inflexibility of the employment system, which is not directly related to rural–urban migration.[5]

---

[5] A detailed discussion about hidden unemployment in the state sector is provided in chapter 10.

On the other hand, as rural migrants have no chance of obtaining the jobs held by the urban residents (beyond the point $L_{ub'}$), the wage level paid to the urban residents has no impact on rural migrants' expected urban wage. Rather, their expected wage is a function of the value of the marginal product for the urban informal sector and the probability of obtaining a job in such a sector. Given that about 80 per cent of migrants obtained a job before migration and the rest can normally find a job within a month or so after migration, the probability of getting a job is approximately equal to 1. Thus, the equilibrium condition of rural–urban migration should be:

$$W_r = \frac{W_m}{1+t}$$

where t represents the institutional barrier to entering the urban informal sector. The larger the barrier to entry, the larger the wage gap between the rural sector and the urban informal sector.

Migrants in the SEZs are mainly employed in the export-oriented manufacturing sector, the dominant sector in these kind of regional economies (Wang and Wang 1995; Meng 1996a). As most enterprises operating in these areas are privately owned, wage levels are determined in the market. With regard to figure 9.1, the situation in the SEZs can be represented by the informal sector labour demand curve. When this is compared to the situation in other cities, one can easily observe that labour costs in the SEZs are considerably lower than in the other cities, *ceteris paribus*. This may partly explain why economic growth in the SEZs has been more rapid than in other cities.

To sum up, the three-sector model outlined in this section suggests that given the institutional and other kinds of barriers, rural–urban migration in China has had little impact on urban unemployment. The main impact of rural–urban migration is that it reduces average urban labour costs and increases rural labour income. The degree of such impact, however, differs between SEZs other cities. The SEZs enjoy more benefits from rural–urban migration owing to the flexibility of their labour markets.

Empirical evidence

In this section evidence is provided to support the hypotheses postulated in the previous one – namely, that rural–urban migration contributes little to urban unemployment, results in a reduction in urban labour costs and increases in rural labour income. The main survey data sets used in this chapter include the Jinan Migrants' Survey conducted in 1995 by the

Institute of Population Studies at the Chinese Academy of Social Sciences, the Dongguan Migrants' Survey conducted in 1995 by the Sociology Department at Peking University, the Shanghai Floating Population Survey (FP) conducted in 1995 and the Shanghai Residents' and Floating Population Survey (RFP) conducted in early 1996 by the Institute of Population Studies at the Shanghai Academy of Social Sciences and the Chinese Grain Farm Household Survey conducted in 1994–5 by the Chinese Economics Research Centre at University of Adelaide and the Chinese Ministry of Agriculture.

Impact on the urban economy

According to various sources, rural–urban migration increased from around 20–80 million during the period 1988–95. The estimated number of migrants in 1995 ranges from a minimum of 40–50 million to a maximum of 80–100 million (see SSB, various years a; Xiang 1996; Zhou 1997). This huge increase appears to have had little impact on open urban unemployment. Since the late 1980s, China's official urban unemployment rate has changed little (see table 9.1). This is as expected from the model developed in the previous section. Owing to the segregation of urban resident and rural migrant labour markets, migration does not induce urban unemployment. As for rural migrants, the sample surveys mentioned above indicate an unemployment rate of less than 2 per cent.

Hidden unemployment in the state sector has always been a problem (chapters 7, 8). This does not appear to have been influenced by migration. The results from a survey[6] indicate that less than 12 per cent of rural migrants are employed in the state sector. These migrants accounted for 3.5 per cent of the total state sector employees in the sample. Even when migrants work in the state sector, their earnings are much lower than those of urban residents. The hourly earnings gap is about 55 per cent, suggesting that even in the same sector the labour demand curves for the two groups are different, as indicated in figure 9.2. The majority of the rural migrants (78 per cent) work in the private sector (see table 9.2).

To what extent, then, may rural–urban migration bring about a reduction in urban labour costs? The average earnings gap between the rural sector and the urban formal sector may provide an indication. Table 9.3 presents a comparison of average annual wages in the rural sector (both agricultural and TVE sectors) and the urban sector (state, collective and private sectors). It shows that in 1995 the average real wage in the rural

---

[6] Shanghai Residents' and Floating Population Survey (1996). See also chapter 11.

Table 9.1.   *Urban unemployment in China, 1985–1995*

	Urban unemployment (1,000 persons)	
	Level	Rate
1985	2,385	1.8
1988	2962	2.0
1990	3,832	2.5
1991	3,522	2.3
1992	3,639	2.3
1993	4,201	2.6
1994	4,764	2.8
1995	5,196	2.9

Source: SSB (various years b).

Table 9.2.   *Earnings and employment among migrants and urban residents, by sector, Shanghai, 1996*

	Urban residents			Rural migrants		
	Frequ. (Persons)	Per cent	Hourly earnings (yuan)	Frequ. (persons)	Per cent	Hourly earnings (yuan)
State	1,423	70.1	6.5	52	11.4	4.2
Collective	399	19.7	5.0	47	10.3	2.8
Private	208	10.2	6.2	359	78.4	2.7

Source: Author's calculations according to the Shanghai Residents' and Floating Population Survey (1996).

sector was about 45 per cent of the average for the urban sector. A large wage gap has thus been a significant factor in encouraging migration to the cities.

The wage gap between the rural and urban sectors suggests the potential for rural–urban migration to reduce urban labour costs. The actual effect, however, depends heavily on:

- the fraction of rural migrants in the total labour employed in the urban area

- the various forms (institutional, informational and financial) of restrictions on rural–urban migration

- the extent of rigidity of the urban resident labour market.

Table 9.3.   *Comparison of wage levels between rural and urban sectors, 1985–1995*

	Rural average annual labour earnings[a]		Urban average annual labour earnings	
	Nominal	Real[b]	Nominal	Real[b]
1985	517.04	517.04	1,148	1,148.00
1986	567.48	534.85	1,329	1,247.89
1987	632.41	561.14	1,459	1,276.47
1988	741.76	560.24	1,747	1,286.45
1989	823.43	521.49	1,935	1,207.87
1990	906.06	548.79	2,140	1,295.40
1991	955.62	565.79	2,340	1,370.02
1992	1134.3	641.57	2,711	1,492.02
1993	1439.15	716.00	3,371	1,617.56
1994	1804.16	727.48	4,538	1,754.83
1995	2381.77	817.35	5,500	1,816.38

Notes: [a]Rural average annual labour earnings is defined as the weighted average of the TVE annual earnings and the annual labour earnings in the agricultural sector. The definition of the latter is presented in chapter 5, appendix B and table 5B.1 (p. 76).
[b]The earnings for the rural sector are deflated by the rural CPI and for the urban sector earnings are deflated by the urban CPI.
Source: SSB (various years b).

These three factors can be expressed in terms of figure 9.2. If there were no barriers to entry for rural–urban migration, *ceteris paribus*, migration would proceed to the point where $D_rD_r = D_mD_m$ (or $MPL_r = MPL_m$) and the wage levels for the urban informal and rural sectors would converge to W_e. The average wage level in the urban sector would thus be equal to $\alpha W_u + (1-\alpha)W_e$, which is less than $\alpha W_u + (1-\alpha)W_m$. On the other hand, given W_u, W_m and W_r, the smaller the α the lower the $\alpha W_u + (1-\alpha)W_m$ as $W_u > W_m$. Finally, if the segregation of labour markets between urban residents and rural migrants did not exist, *ceteris paribus*, the urban wage levels would be equal to W_m, which is lower than $\alpha W_u + (1-\alpha)W_m$. Thus, the smaller the barrier to rural–urban migration, and the less rigid the urban formal sector, the lower the urban labour costs.

Table 9.4 presents wage differentials between urban residents and rural migrants provided by the Centre for Rural Economic Research in the Ministry of Agriculture (CRER). The wage gap between rural migrants and urban residents is large. CRER data suggest that rural migrants earn about 46 per cent of urban residents' wage (an hourly income of 1.68 yuan as opposed to 3.64 yuan). Similarly, the Shanghai Urban Residents' and Floating Population Survey indicates that while urban residents earn an

Table 9.4. *Comparison of average income between urban employees and migrants, 1995*

	Annually	Monthly	Hourly
Average wage for migrants from Sichuan	3,249.0	400.3	1.64
Average wage for migrants from Anhui[a]	2,725.1	420.5	1.72
Simple average of wage for migrants	2,987.1	410.4	1.68
Nat. average of urban employees' wage	5,500.0	458.3	2.70
Nat. average of urban empl. disposable income[b]	7,405.7	617.1	3.64

Notes: [a]The reason why migrants from Anhui earn less annually but more monthly and hourly in comparison to Sichuan's migrants is that they work a shorter period in a year compared to migrants from Sichuan.
[b]The 'disposable income' is the wage adjusted for housing, medicare and other subsidies provided to urban residents.
Sources: Centre for Rural Economic Research in the Ministry of Agriculture (CRER) (1996); SSB (various years a).

hourly wage of 6.21 yuan, rural migrants earn only 49 per cent of their earnings. These data not only suggest that the urban formal sector is very rigid, but also that given the rigidity of the urban formal sector, rural–urban migration is the only way to help to reduce urban labour cost.

Impact on rural development

Rural–urban migration not only functions as a brake on increases in urban labour costs, but can also contribute to rural development. The reallocation of the labour force from the countryside to the cities should increase labour productivity in the rural sector, thereby increasing labour income in rural areas. In addition, the remittances and new knowledge that rural migrants bring back to their home-towns could further increase rural income and stimulate economic growth in the countryside.

To test the contribution of out-migration on rural household income, this chapter uses the household net income model developed in chapter 3. The model specification is the same as (3.5) in chapter 3, except that labour input is disaggregated into the following three components: number of agricultural work-days, rural non-agricultural work-days and outside work-days (migration). The difference in the coefficients for these three variables indicates the importance of migration on household income relative to agricultural and rural non-agricultural activities. The estimated results are reported in table 9.5.[7]

The signs for most estimated coefficients are as to be expected and the adjusted R^2 is rather high for a cross-sectional estimation. The most

---

[7] Standard errors in this estimation are adjusted according to White (1980).

Table 9.5. *Estimated results for household net income equation*

	Log(*NHI*)	
	Coeff.	*t*-ratio
Constant	7.657	34.53
Log(total migration work-days)	0.044	8.19
Log(total rural non-agr. work-days)	0.036	6.18
Log(total agr. work-days)	0.032	1.23
Average years of schooling per labourer	0.040	4.45
Average labour years of experience	0.002	1.00
Log(land) (Mu)	0.476	10.97
Log(animal ploughing and sowing) (hrs)	−0.012	−1.79
Log(plastic film) (kg)	0.032	2.13
Log(farm manure) (kg)	−0.010	−2.34
Log(pesticides input) (jin)	0.025	1.40
Log(seeds input) (jin)	−0.006	−0.29
Log(tractor ploughing and sowing) (hr)	0.030	2.64
Household labourer/household member	0.173	2.64
Female labourer/total labourer	0.061	0.52
Dummy variable for 1995:	0.328	12.27
Jinxi	−0.841	−19.32
Jilin	−1.178	−14.90
Sichuan	−0.934	−18.16
Shandong	−0.649	−13.29
No. of observations	1,863	
Adjusted R^2	0.48	

interesting results for this chapter are the coefficients for the three kinds of labour input. Both out-migration-days and rural non-agricultural activity-days are statistically significant at the 1 per cent level. However, agricultural work-days do not seem to affect rural household net income significantly. The results presented in table 9.5 indicate that after controlling for all other variables, both out-migration and non-agricultural activity within rural areas contribute positively and significantly to total household income. A 1 per cent increase in out-migration-days induces a 4.4 per cent increase in household income, while a 1 per cent increase in rural non-agricultural work-days induces a 3.6 per cent increase in household income. On the other hand, agricultural work-days do not significantly affect net household income. These results confirm how important out-migration is in terms of increasing rural household net income.

To reinforce the importance of out-migration as a source of rural household income, table 9.6 summarises the percentage of remittance in the total income migrants earned using different survey data sets for migrants in Jinan and Dongguan. It suggests that about 30 per cent of migrants' incomes were sent back to their rural home-town.

Table 9.6. *Jinan and Dongguan, migrants' yearly remittances, 1995*

	Jinan			Dongguan		
	Total	Males	Females	Total	Males	Females
Yearly income (yuan)	6,235.2	6,683.6	5,122.7	9,511.1	11,167.3	7,251.2
Yearly remittance (yuan)	1,744.4	2,081.5	900.4	3,177.5	3,607.5	2,526.4
Remittance as per cent of income	28.0	31.1	17.6	33.4	32.3	34.8

Source: Author's calculations from survey data on Jinan and Dongguan migrants.

Table 9.7. *Income differentials between households with and without migrants*

	Household income (yuan)			Per capita net income (yuan)		
	A with migrants	B without migrants	A/B − 1	A with migrants	B without migrants	A/B − 1
Sichuan	9,408.7	6,468.3	45.4	1,638.3	1,041.5	57.3
Anhui	8,965.7	7,083.0	26.6	1,543.2	1,030.3	49.8

Source: CRER Report (1996).

The CRER Report (1996) also provides information on the importance of migration for rural household income. Among 2,820 households from rural Sichuan and Anhui, those with family member(s) who have migrated, on average, have *per capita* incomes 57 and 49 per cent higher than households without migrants (see table 9.7). This fact, however, may not be solely attributed to the remittances brought back by migrants. It may partly reflect the fact that migration eases the problem of agricultural surplus labour and so increases the *per capita* agricultural income of the members of the household who work on the farm. In addition, having worked in a city, migrants may bring home new ideas about other income-generating methods, together with the money and human capital acquired while working in the city. All of these factors may contribute to the higher income among the households with some members who have migrated.

Dismantling the barriers to migration

The theoretical model presented, which indicated that rural–urban migration would result in significant economic gains to both the rural and urban sectors, has been found consistent with the empirical evidence. In general, China's massive rural–urban migration can been seen to have increased its national economic efficiency.

However, the current rural–urban migration has taken place under a series of institutional constraints. In the urban areas, the segregation of urban resident and rural migrant labour markets and the inflexibility of the urban resident labour market restrict the full reduction of labour costs which rural–urban migration could have brought about. In the rural areas, the residual effects of the household registration system and the compulsory grain quota system have effectively confined migration to below the efficient allocation point where labour costs in the urban and rural sectors would have been equalised.

The main policy implication from this analysis is clear: further eliminating institutional constraints will generate a larger economic gain to the Chinese economy. However, the implementation of this policy could well lead to some adverse effects. For example, changing the compulsory grain quota system to a flexible cash quota system may affect China's grain self-sufficiency. And if urban labour markets were to become completely free, the hidden unemployment in the state sector might become open unemployment with potentially destabilising effects. The first of these concerns is beyond the scope of this book while the second is discussed in detail in chapter 11. Chapter 10 analyses a constraint for efficient allocation of the rural–urban migrant labourers – the insufficient information flows.

10

Regional wage differentials and information flows

From the analysis in chapter 9, it is clear that although rural–urban migration brings great benefits in terms of economic growth in both rural and urban China, there are problems preventing the efficient allocation of labour among different sectors and regions. An important constraint on the efficient allocation of rural migrants is insufficient information, reflected in the existence of a significant regional wage differential among regional migrant labour markets. Although there are no institutional barriers preventing migrants from entering different destinations, migrants earn considerably different wages in different urban cities.[1]

To enter a fully functioning labour market in China, job searches should be able to respond freely to demand and supply. However, the significant regional wage differentials indicate that migrants are not moving to higher-wage areas. Why is this, given that institutional barriers to the destination of migration have been dismantled? This chapter examines this question using data from two surveys on rural migrants in Jinan City (Shandong province) and Dongguan City (Guangdong province).

Background and data

Table 10.1 presents migrants' monthly earnings in six cities. It shows that the monthly wage gaps among the six regions are large, ranging from 4 to 50 per cent of the wage level in the highest wage region, Shenzhen.

Regional wage gaps could occur in the following situations:

- if there are restrictions on the destinations to which rural residents can migrate

- if the costs of migration to the various destinations are considerably different

- if living costs are considerably different

[1] Portions of this chapter draw heavily on Meng (1996b).

Table 10.1. *Earnings differentials between migrants, Jinan and Dongguan*

	Monthly wage (yuan)	Per cent of Shenzhen's monthly wage
Shenzhen[b]	822.2	100.0
Dongguan[a]	792.0	96.3
Shanghai[a]	590.4	71.8
Beijing[b]	529.5	64.4
Jinan[a]	520.0	63.2
Suzhou[b]	430.4	52.3
Wuhan[b]	412.1	50.1

Sources: [a]Author's calculations from Jinan, Dongguan and Shanghai surveys.
[b]Qu (1997).

- if migrants in different regions possess different skills and abilities

- if the information on job availability is restricted.

In addition to other supplementary information this chapter mainly uses two migrant surveys for Jinan and Dongguan migrants to examine the problem of wage differentials among regional migrant labour markets.

Dongguan is one of the newly developed cities in the Pearl River Delta in Guangdong province. The rapid economic growth in the Pearl River Delta is encouraged by the high levels of foreign direct investment (FDI) and rural–urban migration which is, in turn, induced by FDI in this region. Up until the early 1980s, Dongguan was a rural town with an agricultural base. The foreign investment that flowed into Guangdong in the mid-1980s changed the industrial structure and the economy of Dongguan dramatically.

The fast pace of growth and change in Dongguan can be illustrated by the example of Changan, one of Dongguan's townships. In the early 1980s, Changan had only three small state-owned industrial factories. The total value of social products[2] was about Y1 million in 1980. When foreign investment started to flow into Changan in 1985, the economy was transformed totally. By 1994, there were 1,200 foreign or joint venture industrial firms, 500 domestic-owned industrial firms and 5,800 family businesses in the town. The total value of social product increased to more than Y2 billion. Such a dramatic change is attributable not only to foreign investment, but also to rural–urban migration. In 1994, the total population of permanent residents in the township was 32,000, but the total labour force

---

[2] Chinese economic output was reported in terms of the value of social product.

Table 10.2.   *Levels of foreign investment and number of migrants, Dongguan,*
1982–1994

Year	Total migrants (1,000 persons)	Total foreign investment (US$ million)
1982	59	n.a.
1984	82	n.a.
1985	120[a]	n.a.
1987	179	500
1988	348[a]	1,200
1989	464[a]	1,000
1990	472	2,500
1992	656[a]	4,800
1994	1,398	7,300

Note: [a]Interview material provided by Dongguan Bureau of Labour.
n.a. = Not available.
Source: Wang and Wang (1995).

was more than 200,000 (Sun 1995), suggesting that more than 90 per cent of the Changan's workers were migrants.

Information on the levels of foreign investment and the size of migration in Dongguan over years 1982–94 is provided in table 10.2. The evidence confirms that economic growth in Dongguan is based on a combination of high levels of foreign investment and a ready supply of rural migrants.

The sources of economic growth in Dongguan can be contrasted with those of Jinan, the capital of Shandong province. Jinan is much larger than Dongguan in terms of population size. In 1994, when the total population in Jinan was 5.3 million, migrants numbered only about 100,500, or 2 per cent of the total population. The state dominates Jinan's economy; about 63 per cent of the labour force work in the state sector, as compared to fewer than 40 per cent in Dongguan. Total foreign investment in Jinan was about US$244 million in 1994, which accounted for about 3 per cent of what it is in Dongguan (US$7.3 billion).

The survey of Dongguan's rural–urban migrants was conducted by the Department of Sociology at Beijing University in early 1995, and covered a sample size of 292 migrants. The survey of migrants in Jinan was conducted by the Institute of Demography at the Chinese Academy of Social Science in July 1995. The sample size is 1,500. Because the questionnaires used in the two surveys are fairly similar, it is possible to choose approximate variables from both data sets to conduct a reasonably comparative study.

Table 10.3 presents basic statistics as well as the differences between Dongguan and Jinan for the main variables used in this study. There are a

Table 10.3. *Comparison of average migrant characteristics, Jinan and Dongguan*

Characteristic (1)	Jinan (2)	Dongguan (3)	Difference (4)
Current monthly wages	519.60	792.59	272.99
	353.27[a]	799.97	5.82
Age	25.60	25	−0.60
	7.73	6.24	−1.64
Years of schooling	8.80	9.2	0.40
	1.80	2.04	3.34
No. of children	0.70	0.71	0.01
	1.16	1.05	0.16
Married	0.44	0.39	−0.05
	0.50	0.49	−1.74
Male	0.71	0.58	−0.13
	0.45	0.49	−4.53
Farmer before migration	0.57	0.48	−0.09
	0.50	0.5	−3.07
Total experience	9.75	8.84	−0.91
	8.22	6.67	−2.33
City work experience	2.92	5.66	2.74
	2.68	4.89	9.56
Farm work experience	6.45	5.24	−1.21
	7.08	6.18	−3.34

Note: [a]Numbers in every second row for each variable are standard deviations (columns (2) and (3)) and *t*-statistics (column (4)).
Sources: Author's calculations from the two survey data sets.

number of similarities, particularly in demographic characteristics, between the migrants in Dongguan and those in Jinan. There are, however, a few significant differences as well. The average age for both groups of migrants is around 25, with males about 5 years older than females. The average years of schooling is slightly higher (0.4 year) for migrants in Dongguan than for those in Jinan. On average, about 40 per cent of migrants in each group were married and each migrant has fewer than one child (0.7). Migrants in Jinan have about 1 extra year of total work experience and a different composition of experience than their counterparts in Dongguan: migrants in Jinan have greater agricultural experience while migrants in Dongguan have greater city work experience. Another major difference is that the wage levels in Dongguan are about 50 per cent higher than in Jinan. Finally, a higher proportion of migrants are female in Dongguan than in Jinan.

Table 10.4.   *Regional wage and migration cost differentials*

	Monthly wage (1)	Migration cost (2)	Migration cost as per cent of wage ((2)/(1))
Shenzhen[b]	822.2	1,040.8	1.26
Dongguan[a]	792.0	514.6	0.65
Beijing[b]	529.5	830.9	1.40
Jinan[a]	520.0	322.5	0.62
Suzhou[b]	430.4	632.4	1.47
Wuhan[b]	412.1	502.3	1.22

Sources: [a]Author's calculations from Jinan and Dongguan surveys.
[b]Qu (1997).

Why do wages differ considerably across regions?

Could cost of migration be the major reason for the regional wage differentials? An investigation of total migration costs over migrant monthly wages suggests that the cost of migrating may be largely irrelevant (table 10.4). For example, although migrants in Dongguan earned 50 per cent more than their counterparts in Jinan, migration costs were approximately 63 per cent of the wage differential, which is similar to the case in Dongguan.

Another possible factor in the wage differentials could be that living costs in different regions vary widely. However, even comparing net income, which is total earnings *minus* total expenditures (taking into account regional inflation differentials), the difference between Dongguan and Jinan is still as large as 32 per cent (see table 10.5).

Given the fact that the difference in regional costs of living and migration costs do not appear to be very important, the wage differentials between regions must be caused by other factors. One approach to investigate these factors is to break down the wage differentials between regions into wage effects related to personal endowment and wage effects caused by the differences in the market evaluation of personal endowments (or by regional differences in the structure of the wage determination process).

To decompose the wage differentials between the Dongguan and Jinan migrant labour markets, the full distributional accounting approach developed by Juhn, Murphy and Pierce (1993) is employed. The wage equations for migrant *i* in Dongguan (*DG*) or Jinan (*JN*) are specified as:

$$\log w_{DG}^{i} = \beta_{DG} X_{DG}^{i} + \sigma_{DG} \theta_{DG}^{i} \tag{10.1}$$

$$\log w_{JN}^{i} = \beta_{JN} X_{JN}^{i} + \sigma_{JN} \theta_{JN}^{i} \tag{10.2}$$

Table 10.5. *Net earnings differentials between migrants, Jinan and Dongguan*

	Monthly wage (yuan) (1)	Net income[a] (yuan) (2)	(2)/(1) Per cent
Dongguan	792	411	52
Jinan	520	311	60
Differentials (per cent)	52	32	

Note: [a]'Net income' is defined as monthly wage *minus* monthly expenditure.
Source: Author's calculations from Jinan and Dongguan surveys.

where β is a vector of coefficients
X is a vector of individual characteristics
θ is an individual's percentile in the residual distribution
σ is the distribution function of the residuals.

Normally, X and θ are seen as measured and unmeasured individual characteristics, respectively, whereas β and σ are the prices for measured and unmeasured characteristics, respectively.

If an individual migrant were to move from Jinan to Dongguan, the wage level he/she would have received can be specified as:

$$\log w^j_{pred1} = \beta_{DG} X^i_{JN} + \sigma_{DG} \theta^i_{JN} \tag{10.3}$$

That is, Dongguan's prices are used to value the measured and unmeasured characteristics of a migrant from Jinan. If an individual migrant in Jinan were to receive the Dongguan price for unmeasured characteristics, then:

$$\log w^j_{pred2} = \beta_{JN} X^i_{JN} + \sigma_{DG} \theta^i_{JN} \tag{10.4}$$

The difference between (10.1) and (10.3) reveals the wage differential attributable to the difference in measured and unmeasured personal characteristics between the two markets. The difference between (10.3) and (10.4) is due entirely to the difference between the price for measured personal characteristics in Dongguan and Jinan. Finally, the difference between (10.4) and (10.2) represents the impact of the difference in price of unmeasured characteristics between Dongguan and Jinan (wage residuals in Dongguan's wage distribution relative to Jinan's).[3]

---

[3] The three components of regional wage differentials can be expressed as follows:

$(10.1) - (10.3) = (X_{DG} - X_{JN})\beta_{DG} + (\theta_{DG} - \theta_{JN})\sigma_{DG}$
$(10.3) - (10.4) = (\beta_{DG} - \beta_{JN})X_{JN}$
$(10.4) - (10.2) = (\sigma_{DG} - \sigma_{JN})\theta_{JN}$

Table 10.6. *Results of wage equations for Jinan and Dongguan migrant labour markets*

	Jinan				Dongguan			
	Model 1		Model 2		Model 1		Model 2	
	Coeff.	t-ratio	Coeff.	t-ratio	Coeff.	t-ratio	Coeff.	t-ratio
Constant	5.579	98.72***	5.583	99.56***	5.207	17.23***	5.304	19.08***
Years of schooling	0.026	4.44***	0.026	4.45***	0.096	3.52***	0.095	3.54***
City experience	0.015	1.91*	0.010	2.67***	0.081	1.87*	0.040	2.10**
(City experience)^2	0.000	-0.64			-0.003	-1.01		
Rural experience	0.013	3.51***	0.013	3.54***	0.032	1.36	0.026	2.61***
(Rural experience)^2	-0.000	-2.95***	-0.000	-2.98***	-0.000	-0.31		
Total training	0.001	5.32***	0.001	5.29***	0.001	1.48	0.001	1.51
Farmer	-0.055	-3.14***	-0.055	-3.14***	-0.187	-1.96**	-0.177	-1.87*
Married	0.155	6.68***	0.157	6.80***	-0.144	-1.04	-0.136	-1.09
Self-employed	0.633	23.74***	0.634	23.79***	0.387	2.28***	0.378	2.23***
Male	0.186	9.33***	0.185	9.32***	0.100	0.94	0.114	1.09
State sector	0.189	2.10***	0.190	2.10***	-0.599	-1.12	-0.631	-1.18
State × education	-0.026	-2.58***	-0.025	-2.57***	0.028	0.43	0.033	0.50
Adjusted R^2	0.156		0.159		0.493		0.492	
No. of observations	261		261		1,490		1,490	

Notes: *t*-statistic values with *** are significant at the 1 per cent level; ** at the 5 per cent level; * at the 10 per cent level.
Source: Author's estimations.

To undertake the above decomposition, the first task is to estimate wage equations for the two groups of migrants and compare the determinants of wages in the two labour markets. Given that the migrant labour markets in China are highly deregulated, a human capital model should be directly applicable. A single-wage equation that applies to both labour markets is specified and the variables included in the regression are: years of schooling, city work experience, rural experience and total days of training. To control for the possible differences between wage structures in the state and non-state sectors, a dummy variable for employment-ownership and an interaction term for years of schooling and the state sector dummy are included. The latter is included to test if the state sector disregards educational attainment when the wage level is determined.

In addition, demographic variables in the form of dummy variables for marital status (married), gender (males), and type of job (self-employed) are included.[4] Normally, an experience–earnings profile is postulated to be a quadratic shape. In the case of the two migrant labour markets studied here, the relationship between city work experience and wages seems to be approximately linear. For the case of the Dongguan migrant labour market, even rural work experience exhibits a linear relationship with earnings. Hence, a second model of the wage equations with linear specifications for city experience for Jinan and Dongguan, and rural experience for Dongguan, was also estimated. The estimated results for both sets of equations for the two groups of migrants are presented in table 10.6. The discussion that follows will focus on describing the results from model 2 for each market.

Generally speaking, the model fits the Jinan better than the Dongguan data. The adjusted R^2 values are 0.49 and 0.16 for Jinan and Dongguan, respectively. However, the basic human capital variables, such as education and city work experience, are equally significant in determining wages in each labour market.

There are a number of distinctive features of wage determination in the two labour markets:

---

[4] Occupation can certainly contribute significantly to variations in individual wages. However, this is potentially an endogenous determinant of wages. This endogeneity problem is usually handled by the Heckman (1979) two-stage procedure in a wage estimation. When the sample size is small, a group of occupational dummy variables may be included in the wage equation. This assumes that occupational attainment is exogenously determined. In this study, however, not only is the sample size too small for the Heckman approach, but also the occupations in the two regions are so different that apart from the self-employed, hardly any other occupational group matches when the two regions are compared.

- First, the rate of return to education in Dongguan is more than triple that of Jinan. An extra year of education brings about a 3 per cent increase in wages in Jinan, and a 10 per cent increase in Dongguan.

- Second, the rate of return to city work experience in Dongguan is triple that of Jinan. Although the returns to rural work experience (both agricultural and non-agricultural) are higher in Dongguan than in Jinan, the difference (0.026 vs. 0.013) is not as significant as the difference in the returns to city work experience (0.04 vs. 0.01). The fact that both returns to education and to city work experience are much higher in Dongguan than in Jinan may indicate that the demand for skilled labour is higher in Dongguan than in Jinan. This will be discussed in detail later in this section.

- Third, male migrants earn significantly more than female migrants in Jinan after controlling for other variables, whereas there is little gender difference in the Dongguan labour market.

- Fourth, the self-employed earned considerably higher incomes than wage-earners in Jinan, while the same comparison in Dongguan suggests a more moderate difference.

- Fifth, married migrants in Jinan earn more than do those who are single, whereas this relationship is negative and insignificant in Dongguan.

Overall, these differences indicate that migrants in Dongguan are paid mainly according to their labour productivity-related characteristics. Moreover, the market pays more than double, or even triple, prices for education and city work experience in that city in comparison to that which is paid in the Jinan migrant market.

Differences in the price for productivity-related characteristics are determined by market forces through the interaction of the supply of, and demand for, those characteristics. If different levels of skilled workers are imperfect substitutes in production, differences in the demand for, and supply of, skills between the two regions will result in different prices for the skills across regions. In the case under review, as economic development in Dongguan is at a much higher level than in Jinan, the demand for skilled labour will consequently be much higher in Dongguan. The difference between the occupational distributions in the two regions may, therefore, shed some light on the market conditions for skilled labourers. In the Jinan survey, more than 50 per cent of male migrants work in the construction sector and about 40 per cent of female migrants work in the service sector, most of them being employed as domestic servants (a category that accounted for 26 per cent of the total Jinan sample of female migrants). In the Dongguan survey, on the other hand, about 70 per cent of migrants work in the industry sector. Although most industrial enterprises are labour-intensive, the skills required in these factories may well be at a higher level than that for brick layers and domestic servants.

Another difference is that wage differentials between the self-employed and wage-earners seem to be much greater in Jinan than in Dongguan. The reason for this difference might be twofold:

- First, in comparison to Dongguan, Jinan is a large capital city, with a high demand for services. As a newly developed city, more than 50 per cent of the population in Dongguan comprises rural migrants who have lifestyles which differ from those of urban residents. Migrants in Dongguan may have an incentive to minimise their current consumption in order to remit as much as possible to their families back home (Wang and Wang 1995). This, to a large extent would reduce demand for services in Dongguan, which would in turn reduce the return to the services sector.

- Second, most self-employed migrants in Jinan work in restaurants, various repair services and as tailors. The skill levels required for these jobs should be higher and would be likely to require more entrepreneurial skills compared to the construction workers and domestic maids who dominate migrant workers in Jinan. In comparison, in Dongguan the skills required for self-employed service jobs may not be much different from that for the jobs taken up by wage-earners from the factories.

Finally, other non-productivity-related variables, such as gender and marital status, play more important roles in wage determination in Jinan than in Dongguan. The difference in the impact of gender on wage determination between the two labour markets is very interesting indeed. This might be caused by the following two factors:

- First, there is a distinctive difference between men and women in occupational attainments in Jinan. Male migrants dominate construction jobs while female migrants dominate domestic service jobs. The wage levels for the two types of occupations are very different. This is in contrast to the situation in Dongguan where there is no gender wage effect, and the majority of both male and female migrants occupy the same types of industrial jobs.

Table 10.7. *Full-distributional decomposition of wage differential between migrants, Jinan and Dongguan*

(1)	Total wage differential (10.1)–(10.2)		Characteristics effect (10.1)–(10.3)		Price effect (10.3)–(10.4)		Residual effect (10.4)–(10.2)	
	(2) value	(3) per cent	(4) value	(5) per cent	(6) value	(7) per cent	(8) value	(9) per cent
Total sample	0.269	100	0.118	43.9	0.178	66.2	–0.027	–10.0
Primary schooling	–0.149	–100	–0.160	–107.4	0.029	19.5	–0.018	–12.1
Junior high school	0.229	100	0.074	32.3	0.192	83.8	–0.037	–16.2
Senior high school	0.458	100	0.148	32.3	0.288	62.9	0.022	4.8

Source: Author's calculations according to wage equation estimations.

- Second, it may be due to cultural differences. Neo-classical theory suggests that under perfect competition, gender wage discrimination may be caused by the personal tastes of different parties, such as employees, employers and consumers (Becker 1957; Arrow 1972, 1973). The entrenched cultural bias against women in China may explain the gender wage differentials in Dongguan and Jinan. Most migrants in Dongguan are employed in foreign firms which basically produce labour-intensive manufactured products. Foreign investors usually come to China to maximise their profits; they may thus be less prejudiced against hiring women, particularly if women workers are equally, or more, productive in comparison to men. In contrast, the majority of employers in the Jinan migrant labour market are domestic producers; pre-existing attitudes towards women may play a significant role in lowering the wages of women employed relative to those of equally productive men.

In summary, the above analysis of the structural differences in wage determination between the two labour markets suggests that the wage determination pattern is more related to productivity in Dongguan than in Jinan. However, can the structural differences in wage determination fully explain wage differentials between the two markets? The decomposition technique described earlier is adopted to investigate this question (table 10.7).

Column (2) of table 10.7 presents the total log wage differentials between Dongguan and Jinan. Columns (4), (6) and (8) show the effects of differences in measured and unmeasured characteristics, measured prices and unmeasured prices on the total wage gap between the two markets. Columns (5), (7) and (9) list the percentage of their contributions to the total wage differentials. The negative figures in the table suggest that the impact on wages is in favour of Jinan migrants. For example, in columns (8) and (9) the negative values for the residual effect indicate that unmeasured characteristics were paid higher returns in Jinan than they were in Dongguan. In general, the results presented in table 10.7 suggest that the measured price differential is the primary contributor to the wage gap between the two labour markets. In particular, for the higher-educated group (senior high school graduates), the total wage differential is about 0.456, or 45 per cent higher in Dongguan than in Jinan. About 68 per cent of the wage differential between the two markets can be attributed to the measured and unmeasured price effects.[5]

[5] It is interesting to see that at the primary school level, migrants actually earned about 11 per cent more in Jinan than their counterparts in Dongguan. This again confirms that highly educated migrants are, comparatively, in greater demand in Dongguan.

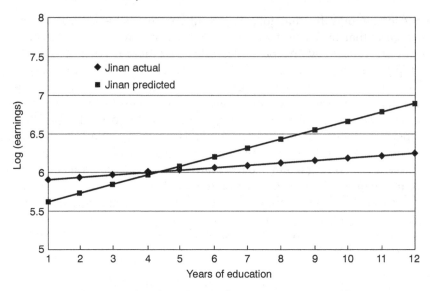

Figure 10.1 Actual and predicted education–earnings profile, an average individual, Jinan

The importance of the price effect in widening the regional wage gap can be further examined by reviewing figure 10.1. The figure exhibits the changes in actual and predicted earnings in accordance with the changes in the years of education for an average migrant in Jinan. The predicted earnings are obtained by using the personal characteristics for an average migrant in Jinan and the coefficients (price levels) for an average migrant in Dongguan. Intuitively, this shows how much an average migrant from Jinan who migrated to Dongguan would have earned in relation to their educational level. The difference between actual and predicted wage levels represents the overall price differentials, and the difference between the slopes of the two curves represents the difference between the rates of return to education in Jinan and Dongguan. It is clear from figure 10.1, therefore, that the wage differentials between migrants in the two regions are mainly caused by the price differentials, especially in relation to the returns to education.

To sum up, it is clear that there is a relatively large wage gap between the migrant labour markets in Jinan and Dongguan. This difference is caused mainly by the difference in the price of acquired human capital. Human capital is paid at a much higher price in Dongguan than in Jinan: a probable reason is that production skills are in much higher demand in Dongguan than in Jinan which is, in turn, caused by the different industrial and ownership structures of the two regions.

Information and migration destination choice

The assumptions of perfect labour mobility and perfect information in a market economy imply that wages should be equal across regions – that is, the market rate of returns to human capital should be the same across regions. This study has demonstrated the opposite: wages differ considerably among regions, and the main cause of this difference appears to be structural variations in regional labour markets. However, the question posed in the beginning of this chapter has yet to be addressed: what are the constraints which prevent migrants from moving to high-wage regions, or what determines an individual migrant's choice of destination?[6] It is identified that the existence of direct constraints on labour mobility (such as government regulations or policies), high direct labour mobility costs and imperfect information are three possible obstacles for migrants moving to high-wage rather than low-wage urban regions.[7] As discussed earlier, however, direct constraints on destination and high direct mobility costs are not a problem for rural–urban migration in China. Information on whether an individual migrant can get a job in the high-wage region may thus be the major factor which limits migrant flows to such regions.

In the migration literature, the probabilistic models, first developed by Todaro (1976), suggest that migrants make migration decisions without specific information on job opportunities. Banerjee's (1984) study, on the other hand, improves our knowledge about information flow and migration in several ways. Banerjee distinguishes specific information from general information and shows that a large proportion of rural–urban migrants had specific information before migration. The wage distribution across regions is considered to be general information, whereas the likelihood of getting a job is specific information; general information is hence less valuable than specific information. Furthermore, Banerjee suggests that the flow of specific information is not through formal channels in some developing countries (in his study, India), but rather through personal contact. In other words, there is no formal market for specific information.

Banerjee's empirical findings were later provided with a theoretical foundation by Vishwanath (1991). The theoretical model, however, ignores the fact presented in Banerjee's study that information flow may not be

---

[6] One could argue that people choose to migrate to Jinan rather than other high-wage regions because of their personal characteristics. Older, married people, especially those with young children, tend to migrate to urban regions which are closer to their home because it is easier for them to look after their families. However, this argument seems not to be valid for our samples as we have shown on p. 163 that an average migrant in Jinan possesses much the same demographic characteristics as an average migrant in Dongguan.

[7] Note again that differences in personal characteristics are not included here as they do not seem to be relevant for the samples used in this study.

through formal channels. Moreover, both Todaro's and Vishwanath's models treat urban areas as uniform entities and so cannot explain why individual migrants choose to migrate to one urban area instead of another. Maier (1987) suggests that search models with imperfect information about the wage offer distribution, such as the one developed by Rosenfield and Shapiro (1981), provide an explanation for this problem. However, these kinds of models do not distinguish between general and specific information. Even though, in general, all migrants 'know' that more developed regions offer higher wages, not all of them have personal contacts in such regions. Rather than choose to go to the region where they would earn the most, they are more likely to go to a region where they have a contact and, hence, are more likely to get a job which has a wage offer higher than their reservation wage[8]. A risk-averse person would rather choose to migrate to an area where he/she has a specific contact than to an area where the wage offer may be higher.

In China, almost everybody knows that Guangdong is richer in comparison to other regions and that the wage rates are much higher there than in any other part of China. However, this kind of general information does not necessarily help individuals to make up their minds on where to go. To further understand key elements for individual migration decision-making, table 10.8 provides information on whether migrants had found a job before they migrated to Jinan.[9] It is clear from the table that more than 70 per cent of sample migrants had pre-arranged jobs before they migrated to Jinan. Among those who did not obtain a job offer prior to migration, 82 per cent found a job within a month after migration.[10] This seems to suggest that when deciding on where to migrate, an individual must be certain that there is a job waiting for him/her or that there is a very high possibility of obtaining a job in a very short period.

In addition, there are other factors that influence an individual's choice of migration destination apart from the possibility of getting a job. In China, one of the common concerns for rural–urban migrants is whether they are going to be paid regularly in the city, as there are many cases where employers delay payment for a substantial period. Hence, specific information may include the assurance of getting paid regularly, being treated fairly, as well as the appeasement of other uncertainties.

[8] Wages they would otherwise earn in their home-town.
[9] The information provided in table 10.8 is not available for the Dongguan sample.
[10] These findings are consistent with what Banerjee found for migrants in India, which is that the majority of migrants had pre-arranged jobs before migration. Rural–urban migration does not therefore necessarily increase the rate of unemployment in urban areas. These findings, however, contradict Todaro's (1969, 1976) model, where he argued that migrants' job searching happens only after they move to the urban area.

Table 10.8.   *Timing of securing a job, Jinan migrants*

	Frequency	Percentage
Found job before migration? **Yes**	1,061	70.6
No	442	9.4
Information source: Relatives and		
friends	1,217	81.0
Others	286	19.0
Among those who did not find a job before migration		
Found job after migration? < 1 month	363	82.1
1–2 months	54	12.2
2–3 months	19	4.3
> 3 months	6	1.4

Source: Author's calculations from the data sets.

Table 10.9.   *First job source of contract*

	Jinan	Dongguan
Relatives and friends	76.0	73.0
Own effort	13.0	16.1
Replacing relatives	0.3	1.1
Government	8.7	4.9
Others	2.5	4.9

Source: Author's calculations from the data sets.

How, then, did the migrants obtain specific information on job opportunities (table 10.8)? Of the total sample, 81 per cent found out about job opportunities from relatives and friends. The figures in table 10.9 also suggest that most migrants surveyed in both Jinan and Dongguan found their first job through such personal channels (76 per cent in Jinan, and 73 per cent in Dongguan).

The high proportion of migrants from both regions being either informed about job opportunities or having found their first job through personal contacts indicates that personal contact rather than a formal information market plays a dominant role in individuals' obtainment of specific information and, hence, migrants' decision-making about destinations.

As such information is often obtained in an ad hoc manner, the efficient allocation of labour may be interrupted by the random nature of the information itself. Suppose that there are two regions, *A* and *B*. The demand for, and supply of, skilled labour are initially in equilibrium in the two regions. Hence, the price for skilled labour is equalised between the two. Now assume that for some reason, economic development proceeds at a faster pace in region *A* than in region *B*; the demand for highly-skilled labour thus increases in region *A*. Suppose also that there is a group of individuals who possess high levels of a skill which is in high demand in region *A*. However, their risk-taking preferences are such that, unless they receive specific job offers and are assured on other uncertainties, they will not migrate. Assume further that this highly skilled group happens to have no personal contacts in region *A*, but does have contacts in region *B*, where they are offered jobs. This group of individuals will thus end up migrating to region *B* to obtain lower but assured wages, rather than to *A* to obtain possibly higher wages. The end result will be that the wage levels for highly skilled labour will increase in region *A* but decrease in region *B*. If only they had had the right personal contacts, the regional price differential would not have developed.[11]

The above analysis strongly suggests that where a rural resident will migrate is basically determined by where his relatives, co-villagers, and/or friends are. This kind of information channel is rather inefficient for the purposes of a fully functioning labour market, in that the matching of demand and supply is an uncertain event. An efficient allocation of resources requires a formal information channel.[12]

Creating an information market

The policy implications of the findings of this chapter are obvious. To eliminate the existing large regional wage differentials in China, it is essential to expand the channels through which specific job information may flow. There are thousands of government and privately-owned job centres throughout China. However, these government agencies are not even as efficient as personal contacts in terms of getting specific information, perhaps because employers are unwilling to go through government channels owing to the high fees they charge or other controls. Another reason that Chinese rural–urban migrants appear to be more risk-averse may be due to the lack of credibility of China's legal system. A common

---

[11] This simple model can be formalised as follows: Suppose individuals' migration decision between regions *A* and *B* is based upon the distribution of expected wages, which is determined by

$$ewage_i = p_i \times wage$$

where p_i is the probability of getting a job in region *i* and $wage_i$ is region *i*'s average wage level. Hence, with a pre-arranged job, $p_i = 1$.

[12] This, of course, is not to say that there is no possibility for informal information flows to be efficient enough to equalise market demand for, and supply of, labour; rather, it says that an informal channel of information flow does not ensure an efficient labour allocation.

feature of China's present labour market is that migrants get paid less than they are supposed to, do not get paid at all, or have payments delayed. Getting information on specific job offers from personal contacts not only ensures a job opportunity, but also provides greater assurance to migrants about the trustworthiness of their prospective employers. To set up an efficient information market, the essential task is therefore to create a law-abiding society. In particular, enforcing labour laws may, to some extent, reduce migrants' fears of being cheated, thus encouraging them to use formal information channels.

Appendix: description of the data

Total, city, and rural work experience

Total experience = age-years of schooling – 7.
City work experience is obtained directly from the survey. Individuals were asked to report the number of months since they had migrated to a city. The variable is then derived by dividing the number of months by 12 to obtain the years of city work experience:

Rural work experience = total experience – city work experience.

Current monthly income is adjusted in the following way

Adjusted total income = current monthly wage + (yearly bonus/12) + other benefits obtained.
The adjustment factors for other benefits are listed in table 10A.1.

Total training days

This variable is obtained by adding the total training days before migration to the total training days after migration.

The self-employed group

The self-employed group includes those who identify themselves as 'self-employed', by occupation, or ownership, or both. In the case of Jinan, it also includes middlemen for construction workers.

Table 10A.1.   *Adjustment factors for other benefits*

Benefit	Adjustment factor (yuan)
Provision or subsidy of housing	50
Provision or subsidy of lunch	100
Subsidy of medical expenditure	10
Travel subsidy for visiting family	5
Other benefit in kind	10

11

The two-tier labour market

The institutional constraints and other restrictions have caused three different wage levels in the economy and also urban hidden unemployment (figure 9.2, p. 151). Eliminating these distortions should bring about further economic gain to the Chinese economy. This chapter investigates the segregation of the urban resident and rural migrant labour markets in terms of wage determination and occupational attainment, and analyses the impact of elimination of segregation on the urban labour market.

Occupational segregation and the wage gap between urban residents and rural migrants

In this section, two survey data sets are employed to analyse the degree of segregation between rural migrant and urban resident labour markets from the point of view of occupational segregation and wage differentials. Both surveys were conducted in Shanghai. The first is the Shanghai Floating Population Survey (FP)[1] and the second is the Shanghai Residents' and Floating Population Survey (RFP). The surveys were conducted by the Institute of Population Studies at Shanghai Academy of Social Sciences in late 1995 and early 1996, respectively. The design of the questionnaires is quite similar and many variables are in common, thus the two surveys provide a good basis for a comparative analysis.

The FP survey comprises 6,609 individuals, of whom 5,614 are migrants from rural areas (accounting for 85 per cent of the sample). Some surveyed individuals were not in the labour force and are not included in the analysis, resulting in a purged data set of 5,167 individuals. The sample size for the RFP survey is 3,000, with 2,453 being Shanghai permanent residents and 547 being in the floating population. Among the former, 2,020 were in the labour force and among the latter, 376 were rural migrants who were in

---

[1] The so-called 'floating population' refers to non-residents of Shanghai who are aged 15 and above, and have come to Shanghai for reasons other than business, tourism, study, or for medical reasons and plan to stay for more than one month.

Table 11.1. *Occupational distribution of rural migrants and urban residents, Shanghai, 1995–1996*

Shanghai	Urban residents		Rural migrants (RFP)		Rural migrants (FP)	
	Frequency	per cent of total	Frequency	per cent of total	Frequency	per cent of total
Professional and managers	491	24.31	6	1.63	125	3.09
Clerks	236	11.68	1	0.27	30	0.58
Trade and service workers	310	15.35	186	50.41	2,185	42.50
Manual workers	983	48.66	176	47.70	2,810	54.49
Total	2,034	100.00	369	100.00	5,141	100.00

Source: Author's calculations from the two survey data sets.

the labour force. The purged RFP data set of labour force participants used in this study is thus 2,020 urban residents and 376 rural migrants. Owing to the small sample size of rural migrants in the RFP survey, the FP survey is also used for more meaningful econometric comparisons.

Occupational segregation

To provide more information on the occupational segregation of urban residents and urban migrants, table 11.1 summarises the occupational distributions for rural migrants and urban residents. The main difference that can be observed from this table is that while the majority of rural migrants worked as trade/service workers or manual workers, more than 35 per cent of urban residents worked as professionals/managers and clerks.

It is unfortunate that the survey questionnaire for the RFP survey defines occupations in very broad categories, but within each of these broad categories occupational segregation can still be very significant. For example, according to the FP survey, within the category of professionals and managers, the majority of rural migrants were small enterprise managers. Among manual workers, construction, garment and transport workers accounted for a large proportion. The majority of tradespersons are agricultural goods merchants and small shop assistants, and among service workers there are domestic servants, barbers, and tailors.[2]

Wage differentials

It is also observed from the surveys that wage differentials between urban residents and rural migrants are very significant. Table 11.2 shows that on average rural migrant monthly earnings are 56–64 per cent of those of urban residents, while their hourly earnings are only 50 per cent of urban residents' hourly earnings. When the occupational segregation is considered, the main wage differentials come from those jobs which have lower status, such as service workers and manual workers.

Although the comparison of gross earnings between the urban residents and rural migrants presented above indicates that a significant wage differential exists, such a comparison is somewhat crude. Economic theory suggests that wage differentials between any two groups of individuals may come from two different sources: labour productivity differences and non-productivity-related wage differences (Becker 1957).

---

[2] See table 11A.1 (p. 196) for the occupational distribution using more detailed occupational categories for rural residents using the FP survey.

Table 11.2.   *Wage differentials between urban residents and rural migrants, by occupation*

Monthly earnings	Urban residents		Rural migrants (RFP)		Rural migrants (FP)	
	Value	SD	Value	SD	Value	SD
Professional and managers	1,044.6	506.0	1,240.0	533.2	1,045.9	755.2
Clerk	918.5	489.0	540.0	0.0	741.1	336.7
Trade workers	922.5	530.5	572.1	421.4	685.7	657.0
Service workers	824.8	511.2	428.1	316.9	537.7	395.9
Manual workers	868.4	524.9	530.5	364.4	560.9	243.5
Total	917.3	520.5	509.8	374.3	590.9	391.5
Hourly earnings	Value	SD	Value	SD	Value	SD
Professional and managers	6.1	3.3	6.9	3.5	5.1	3.3
Clerk	5.4	2.7	2.9	0.0	3.5	2.2
Trade workers	5.0	2.6	3.6	7.3	3.3	4.5
Service workers	4.8	4.1	1.9	2.1	2.3	1.9
Manual workers	5.2	5.7	2.8	2.2	2.6	1.9
Total	5.4	4.6	2.7	3.6	2.7	2.6

Source: Author's calculations from the two survey data sets.

Thus, to understand further why there is a substantial wage differential between urban residents and rural migrants in China, a decomposition technique introduced by Blinder (1973) is adopted. Blinder's decomposition of the wage differential between the two groups may be written as follows:

$$R = \underbrace{(\hat{a}^U - \hat{a}^R)}_{U} + \underbrace{\sum_{j=1}^{n} \bar{X}_j^R(\hat{\beta}_j^U - \hat{\beta}_j^R)}_{C} + \underbrace{\sum_{j=1}^{n} \bar{X}_j^U(\bar{X}_j^U - \bar{X}_j^R)}_{E} \qquad (11.1)$$

where R is the mean wage differential between urban residents and rural migrants, $\hat{\alpha}$ and $\hat{\beta}_j$ are the OLS estimates of the parameters α and β_j from separate wage equations for urban residents and rural migrants. The term E is the portion of the differential attributable to different endowments (or productivity differentials) and the terms U and C are the portions of the unexplained wage differential, the sum of which is usually regarded as the differential attributable to discrimination.

To conduct Blinder's decomposition, a general Mincer (1974)-type human capital earnings equation is specified as follows:

$$\ln(w) = \alpha + \beta_2 OJ + \beta_3 OJ^2 + \beta_4 FT + \beta_5 FT^2 + \beta_6 Train + b7 Workhr + \beta_j Other + u \qquad (11.2)$$

where w is monthly earnings
S is years of schooling
OJ is other job experience
OJ^2 is other job experience squared
FT is current job tenure
FT^2 is current job tenure squared
Train is dummy variable for training
Workhr is hours worked per week
Other is a vector of other individual personal characteristics
u is an error term.

'Current job experience' is separated from 'other job experience' because for rural migrants, 'other job experience' is more likely to be farming experience, which would have less relevance to their current earnings. As the Blinder decomposition requires a consistent specification for both groups, we apply this specification for both rural migrants and urban residents. The summary statistics for the variables used are reported in table 11B.1 (p. 197).

The estimated results of (11.2) are reported in table 11.3. Owing to missing values for various independent variables, the number of observations was reduced considerably for all three samples. Nevertheless, the estimated results are very promising. Most important variables are statistically significant and the adjusted R^2s are reasonable.

The main differences between wage determination for urban residents and rural migrants are as follows:

- First, the rate of increase in wages with current job tenure is initially higher for the rural migrants than for the urban residents.

- Second, the earnings profile for urban residents exhibits a continuously increasing trend, while this is not the case for the rural migrants (figure 11.1). This may suggest that a seniority-related wage determination pattern still exists in the urban sector (see chapter 6).

- Third, for rural migrants the initial returns to current job experience is much higher than for the urban residents in the first 15–18 years. However, when individuals' physical and mental abilities start to decrease, the rate of returns to experience starts to decline.[3]

- Fourth, job training seems to play an important role in urban resident wage determination but it does not appear to affect the wages of rural migrants.

[3] The mean values for years of current job experience for the urban residents, rural migrants (RFP) and rural migrants (FP) are 17, 3 and 2 years, respectively. These are presented as the three grey bars in figure 11.1.

Table 11.3. *OLS estimation of (11.2)*

	Urban residents		Rural migrants RFP		Rural migrants FP	
	Coeff.	t-statistics	Coeff.	t-statistics	Coeff.	t-statistics
Constant	5.7858	30.65	5.3365	34.60	5.3784	104.91
Years of schooling	0.0393	11.36	0.0288	2.16	0.0466	10.91
FT	0.0144	3.77	0.0733	3.91	0.0508	8.98
FT^2	−0.0003	−3.75	−0.0022	−3.03	−0.0021	−5.29
OJ	0.0191	4.77	0.0083	0.94	0.0163	5.03
OJ^2	−0.0006	−3.86	−0.0002	−1.08	−0.0003	−3.35
Dummy for training	0.1517	6.90	0.1244	1.12	0.0176	1.05
Work hours	0.0030	2.07	0.0012	0.78	0.0023	4.92
Dummy for males	0.3091	14.97	0.3149	4.15	0.2165	12.19
Dummy for married	0.0203	0.12	0.2615	2.82	0.0691	3.03
No. of observations	1,974		195		3,545	
Adjusted R^2	0.21		0.29		0.15	

Source: Author's estimations.

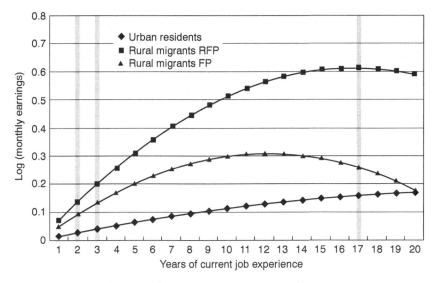

Figure 11.1 Current job experience–earnings profile

- Fifth, marital status seems to contribute significantly to rural migrant earnings but not to urban residents'.

The estimated wage equation results are used to decompose into explained and unexplained portions of the wage differential between urban residents and rural migrants. These results are reported in table 11.4. The mean of the total log wage differential between urban residents and rural migrants using the RFP is 0.51, and using the RFP for urban residents and the FP for rural migrants is 0.44.

The urban and rural weighted decomposition results in table 11.4 refer to the decompositions treating urban or rural wages as the non-discriminatory benchmark, and the bottom panel is the average of the two decompositions. The interpretation below is based upon the average results.

The information presented in table 11.4 indicates that at least 47 per cent of the total wage differential between urban residents and rural migrants cannot be attributable to differences in labour productivity. If the FP survey is used to compare the earnings of the urban residents, the unexplained wage differential accounted for as much as 96 per cent of the total wage differential. This suggests that if rural migrants were treated the same as urban residents, their earnings differential would have been reduced by between 47 and 96 per cent of the current differential, given their personal endowments.

Table 11.4.   *Blinder decomposition results of wage differentials between urban residents and rural migrants*

	Urban vs. rural RFP		Urban vs. rural FP	
	Log wage	Per cent of total	Log wage	Per cent of total
Total wage differential	0.51	100.0	0.44	100.0
Urban weighted				
Explained	0.18	36.0	0.05	12.0
Unexplained	0.32	64.0	0.39	88.0
Rural weighted				
Explained	0.36	71.0	− 0.02	− 4.0
Unexplained	0.15	29.0	0.46	103.0
Average				
Explained	0.27	53.0	0.02	4.0
Unexplained	0.24	47.0	0.42	96.0

Source: Author's calculations based on estimated results from table 11.3.

To further elaborate this point, table 11.5 reports the predicted wages for rural migrants assuming they were facing the same wage structure as their urban counterparts and the predicted wages for urban residents assuming they were facing the same wage structures as rural migrants.

Columns (2) and (3) in table 11.5 show that if urban residents were to face the earnings structure of rural migrants, they would have earned 14–37 per cent less than what they did earn. On the contrary, if rural migrants were treated in the same way as their urban counterparts, they would have earned 38–48 per cent more (see columns (4) and (5) of table 11.5).

Both the decomposition and predicted earnings results suggest that the huge wage gap between urban residents and rural migrants cannot be fully explained by individuals' productivity-related endowments. A significant part of the earnings differential is attributable to discrimination in favour of urban residents which, in turn, is caused by the non-market institutional wage settings in the urban formal sector (see chapter 9).

Economic gains from liberalisation of the two-tier labour market

The elimination of the segregation of the two labour markets will bring about economic gains to the Chinese economy. As mentioned previously, the distortion associated with the two-tier labour market system is two-fold. One distortion is associated with the fact that urban residents' wage levels are set at a rate which is higher than the market equilibrium. The other distortion is that urban residents accept only certain kinds of jobs.

Table 11.5. *Actual and predicted earnings, urban residents and rural migrants*

Earnings (1)	Urban vs. RFP (2)	Urban vs. FP (3)	RFP vs Urban (4)	FP vs Urban (5)
Actual monthly income	811.59	811.59	488.82	521.13
Predicted value	695.76	512.86	675.87	769.70
Difference(act. – pred.)	115.84	298.74	– 187.05	– 248.57
Difference/act. (per cent)	14.3	36.8	– 38.3	– 47.7

Source: Author's calculations based on estimated results from table 11.3.

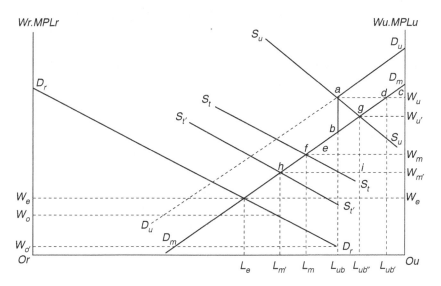

Figure 11.2 Impact of elimination of labour market distortions on urban employment and wages

The removal of the first distortion will reduce labour costs for the urban resident labour market and eliminate urban hidden unemployment; the removal of the second distortion will further reduce urban labour costs and, hence, open unemployment in the cities.

Consider the three-sector model used in chapter 9 (p. 151). The changes associated with the liberalisation of the urban labour markets are presented in figure 11.2. The removal of the institutional wage setting implies that the labour demand curve in the urban sector will merge into one curve, D_mD_m.

Now consider two possible situations. First, assume that government intervenes in a way that jobs are provided to urban residents first, and then to rural migrants.[4] In this situation, the above-mentioned changes will

---

[4] This kind of intervention is a common in urban China.

initially reduce the wage levels of urban residents to $W_u{}'$, and employment to $OuL_{ub}{}''$. Such a change will reduce the hidden unemployment in the formal sector to zero – the surplus workers in the state sector will be laid off. The labour supply curve will thus move from S_tS_t to $S_t{}'S_t{}'$, and the informal sector wages will reduce from W_m to $W_m{}'$. The removal of the institutional wage setting in the urban informal sector will thus reduce urban total labour costs from $OuLu_{tq}aWu + L_{ub}L_mfe$ to $OuL_{ub}{}''gW_u{}'' + L_{ub}{}''L_m{}'hi$.

Second, assume that the government will not intervene in terms of job provision and both urban residents and rural migrants have equal rights in terms of job acceptance. This implies that the division of the urban formal and informal sectors will be eliminated. There will be no special labour supply curve for the urban residents but a total labour supply curve for the urban sector $(S_t{}'S_t{}')$ and the wage levels for the urban formal sector will further reduce to $W_m{}'$. The total labour costs will thus be further reduced from the area of $OuL_{ub}{}''gW_u{}' + L_{ub}{}''L_m{}'hi$ to $OuL_m{}'hW_m{}'$.

Urban unemployment and hidden unemployment

Open unemployment in urban China has never been a serious problem. Official unemployment rates never exceeded 3 per cent up until 1995 (SSB, various years a). However, the official unemployment figure is calculated according to the figures provided by local employment service agencies. The figures provided by these agencies include only those who are registered in such agencies and apply for a job from them. They are likely to be an under-estimation of the actual extent of unemployment, as these agencies are relatively new institutions and hardly used by many unemployed persons. Furthermore, the official unemployment figure does not include hidden unemployment. As mentioned earlier, SOEs can be viewed as over-staffed and about 15 million state sector workers were made redundant between 1990 and 1996 (Zhou 1997), 12 million in 1997 and another 3 million in the first half of 1998 (Meng 1998). Finally, the official unemployment figures do not take account of rural migrants.

Thus, the seriousness of China's urban unemployment in the next few years will, in part, be determined by state sector over-staffing and the continuing impact of rural–urban migration.

Hidden urban unemployment and its solution

To eliminate the negative influence of over-staffing in the SOEs, most firms introduced a system of '*You Hua Lao Dong Zu He Zhi*' (the system of optimal combination of labour) in the late 1980s. This system judges a firm's demand for labour solely according to technical considerations. In other words, the market demand for a firm's products and its financial situation are not considered; instead, only the technical requirements of the enterprise for labour are relevant. After the introduction of this system, some 10–30 per cent of all state sector employees were considered to be redundant (ADB and China's Ministry of Labour 1994; Knight and Song 1995).

To be able to absorb this redundant labour and to stave off possible social and political unrest, most large and medium sized SOEs were asked to set up 'labour service companies'. The nature of tasks that these companies have undertaken varied. Some of them produced a small proportion of the products originally produced by the parent enterprise; some processed byproducts of the parent enterprise which were originally given to TVE firms to process; some worked in service areas, such as restaurants, childcare centres, shops and hotels. Most labour service companies were entitled to pay less tax for a certain period. The wage levels for the redundant staff who were transferred to the labour service companies were usually set according to the average wage levels of the parent enterprise. In some cases, as they paid less tax, the wages and welfare paid were even higher than levels in the parent enterprise. In other words, redundancies were, in some ways, still a burden to the enterprises. This is a so-called 'internal labour market solution'.

However, this kind of solution to over-staffing problems can be applied only by successful enterprises. For those enterprises with production restricted by market demand or those making losses, there is no possibility of looking after their redundant workers. The situation became extremely serious in the 1990s, when at least 40 per cent of SOEs were making losses (see World Bank 1996b). The situation has been worsening because of China's macroeconomic situation. The government deficit had reached 40 billion yuan per annum for more than 4 years (this figure was close to 57.5 billion yuan in 1994 and 58.2 billion yuan in 1995). In 1993, inflation started to reach double-digit figures and in 1996, SOEs made losses exceeding their total profits. Both central and provincial governments no longer had any means of financially supporting loss-making state enterprises; consequently, the government had no choice but to let enterprises retrench workers. In some cases, everyone in a given enterprise lost their jobs.[5] Workers who lost their jobs were entitled to receive a low living allowance from the enterprise,[6] and at the same time, they had

---

[5] Being forced to accept such an outcome can be considered as a passive mode of reform rather than an active, purposeful process arising from government directives and economic policy.

[6] The rate, however, varies from region to region and from firm to firm. The range is somewhere between 80 yuan and 200 yuan (US$ 9 and US$ 22) per month.

to find a job in the external labour market by themselves.

The widespread retrenchments initially resulted in a social and political backlash, especially in Northeast China, where most SOEs were heavy industries that had out-of-date technology and equipment. Thousands of unemployed workers demonstrated against these reforms in some cities and some managers who were considered to be directly responsible were killed. The initial anger, however, gradually dissipated in the harsh realisation that the government was not able to provide an immediate solution. This forced displaced workers to focus on finding a solution by themselves. According to the author's interview information, those who had family responsibilities started to try very hard to find whatever work was available with some assistance from the government, while those who were relatively financially better off decided to quit the labour force (also see Chen 1997).

Most job opportunities existed in the informal sector, mainly in the service sector. In most cases workers were able to find a new livelihood in the informal sector a few months after they had been made redundant (Mai and Perkins 1997).[7] The redundant urban workers often accepted jobs they had previously regarded as low-status migrant jobs, including hotel housekeeping, office cleaning, waitressing and construction work.

Small restaurants, small shops and street markets have proliferated in the cities. Some of them are owned by the rural migrants, and others by redundant SOE workers. (In Beijing, a large number of taxi drivers are redundant state sector workers.[8]) If we consider that roughly 60–80 million rural migrants were able to find jobs in urban China without any help from the government, there seems to be no particular reason to worry about redundant state sector workers, especially when most of them still have access to government housing, food and other welfare subsidies.

In this regard, Hong Kong's experience is extremely relevant. One of the most important reasons for Hong Kong's sustainable rapid economic growth is its extremely flexible labour market and the development of its informal sector. For example, it is reported that although the garment

---

[7] Needless to say, being in the centrally planned economy for more than 40 years means that most employees in the state sector have difficulty in adjusting themselves to accept the fact that there is no one but themselves to take care of their own living; this psychological adjustment may take some time. However, as economic reform has been taking place for more than 15 years, numerous employees have entered the labour market, and for these workers, the psychological adjustment may be relatively easy. Furthermore, when the issue of survival is concerned, the psychological adjustment may quickly become a relatively trivial matter.

[8] In the large cities of China, there are also some 'underground' occupations, such as prostitution, which are taken up by migrants, as well as by some redundant state sector workers.

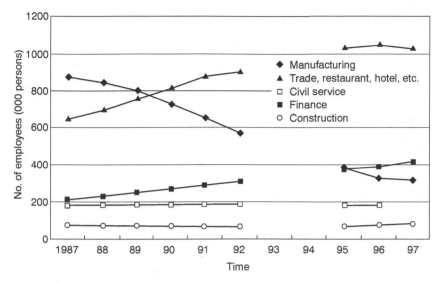

Figure 11.3 Structural change of employment, Hong Kong, 1987–1997
Sources: 1978–92: Choi Po King and Lok-Sang (1995); 1995–7: Census and Statistics Department, Hong Kong, website information (March 1998).

industry had contributed significantly to Hong Kong's growth, in the 1980s, following the development of SEZs in South China, the Hong Kong garment industry has almost completely shifted to China. Has unskilled labour in Hong Kong suffered? 'Individuals lost their jobs in garments production, but other jobs were being created rapidly, ... the unemployment rate has remained below 3 per cent' (World Bank 1995).

Figure 11.3 presents the structural change to employment in the main sectors for Hong Kong over the last 10 years. It is clear that reduced employment in the manufacturing sector was offset by an increase in employment in services (including wholesale, retail trade, restaurant, hotel and other service sector), and the finance and insurance sector. During this 10-year period, the reduction of manufacturing jobs was about 561,000, with the annual reduction rate being 9.7 per cent. At the same time, the increase in the number of jobs in the service sector about 380,000 and in the financial sector was about 205,000. The annual increase in employment in the service sector was 4.7 per cent and in the financial sector about 7.0 per cent.

This rapid increase in employment in the service sector is related to Hong Kong's flexible wage-setting system. According to the limited available information, real wages for unskilled and semi-skilled workers in Hong Kong increased very little over 1991–6 owing to supply-side pressures.

Table 11.6.   *Employment/investment ratio, by sector, 1995*

	New employment (1,000 persons)	New investment (million yuan)	Employment/ investment (person/million yuan)
State sector	470	108,982.4	4
Collective	1,380	9,217.4	150
Shareholding	10	1,184.8	8
Joint venture	250	8,639.9	29
Foreign-owned	460	15,552.5	30
Overseas Chinese	610	6,736.3	91
Other ownership	20	599.9	33
Self-employed	3,350	5,523.9	606

Source: Authors calculations from SSB (various years a), tables 4.4 and 5.2.

With 1992 set to 100, the real wage index is 99.8, 101.6 and 102.8 for 1991, 1995 and 1996, respectively. For these three years, the percentage changes over the preceding years are – 0.3, – 1.5 and + 1.2, respectively (Census and Statistics Department 1997). The reduction in real wages for unskilled workers may well indicate that the flexibility of the Hong Kong labour market is a very important contributor to its low unemployment rate.

Apart from the flexibility of the labour market, the reason that the development of an informal sector is important in absorbing state sector laid-off workers is its high employment/investment ratio. Table 11.6 presents information on the ratio of new employment over new investment in China. As aggregated data for the urban informal sector is not available, the self-employed sector is used as a proxy here. It is clear that with the same amount of investment, the self-employed sector employs the most workers, whereas the state sector is the poorest performer in this regard.

One important question here is how the East Asian economic slowdown will affect employment growth in urban China – and, hence, affect the absorption of redundant SOE workers. To test the extent to which GDP and export changes will affect the change in employment, a simple cross-section time-series analysis using data for 30 regions over the period 1993–5 is conducted (table 11.7). The estimated results suggests that a 1 per cent increase in real GDP will increase employment by about 0.62 per cent, whereas a 1 per cent increase in exports will increase employment by 0.15 per cent. This implies that a given percentage change in exports has a much smaller impact on employment than a change in real GDP.

If one believes that GDP growth is not heavily dependent on export growth owing to the large size of the domestic market, it is possible that the GDP growth rate will not fall too much for the next few years. The

Table 11.7. *OLS results from employment regression*

Dependent variable = Log(employment at year end)

	Coefficient	*t*-ratio
Log (real GDP)	0.627	12.66
Log (average annual wage)	− 1.210	− 7.73
Log (export)	0.147	4.01
Dummy for 1993	0.019	0.31
Dummy for 1994	0.079	1.27
Constant	9.280	8.87
No. of observations	90	
Adjusted *R*²	0.92	

Source: Author's estimations.

Asian crises should thus not have too much of a negative impact on employment growth.

What is more interesting from the results obtained in table 11.7 is the strong negative effect of the average wage on employment. This result indicates that every 1 per cent reduction in average wages will bring a 1.2 per cent increase in employment. It further confirms that introducing a flexible labour market is the most effective way of resolving the unemployment problem. This result reconciles very well with the analysis provided earlier, which shows that jobs are available as long as urban employees can adjust themselves to accept lower-paid work. In summary, this result implies that under the situation of an economic slowdown, reforms of the labour market which encourage wage flexibility should be speeded up to encourage employment growth.

Impact of liberalisation of the two-tier labour market on urban unemployment

Given that the informal sector provides a great opportunity for laid-off state sector workers, the next relevant question is whether this implies that these workers have to compete with rural migrants for the limited jobs available in the informal sector. Figure 11.4 presents an amended version of the three-sector model used in this book. When state sector hidden-unemployed workers are laid off, the total urban supply curve moves from $S_t S_t$ to $S_{t'} S_{t'}$, with the distance $L_m L_{m'}$ being equal to the distance $L_{ub'} L_{ub}$. Employment in the formal sector is reduced from $O u L_{ub}$ to $O u L_{ub''}$.

Now consider two situations. In the first situation the institutional distortion to wage-setting in the state sector does not change. This will result in an unchanged labour demand curve for the urban formal sector.

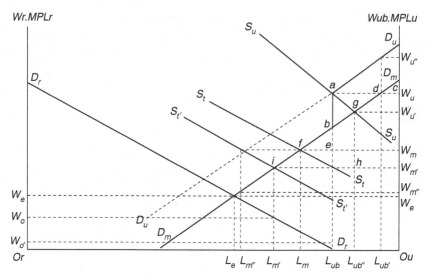

Figure 11.4 Impact of state sector redundancies on urban employment and unemployment

The new wage levels for the state sector will be at $W_{u''}$, *ceteris paribus.* Initially, workers who are redundant may refuse to accept jobs from the informal sector due to the lower wages and status of the jobs in the informal sector. Thus, open unemployment in the urban sector may appear as the amount of $L_{ub}L_{ub''}$. However, most redundant workers will gradually realise that the opportunity cost of being unemployed (wage levels in the informal sector) is higher than marginal benefit of being unemployed (redundancy-payments, normally 80–200 yuan per month) and, hence, accept jobs from the informal sector. Assuming that wage levels in the informal sector are fixed at W_m, the number of jobs available in the sector are, therefore, fixed. Redundant state sector workers entering the informal sector will thus generate one of two possible results. First, if the government does not intervene, competition between rural migrants and urban redundant workers over available informal sector jobs will occur which, in turn, will generate open unemployment of $L_mL_{m''}$. Second, if the government does intervene, say, to give urban redundant workers priority for employment or to restrict the number of rural migrants, the number of jobs for rural migrants will be reduced. Given the fact that rural migrants still hold on to their land in the countryside, this may cause rural migrants to move back to rural areas rather than adding to urban open unemployment. The numbers of migrants moving back to rural region will be $L_mL_{m''}$.

However, the assumption that the wage level in the informal sector is fixed is not a necessary condition. Given Hong Kong's experience and the empirical study on China's urban labour market (table 10.7, p. 193), it is clear that an urban service sector with flexible labour market settings has great potential for generating jobs. If wage levels in the urban informal sector are reduced, say from W_m to $W_{m'}$, employment in the urban sector will increase from OuL_m to $OuL_{m'}$. Thus, both rural migrants and urban redundant workers can be employed in the urban informal sector without causing a serious unemployment problem. Given the fact that most redundant urban workers are unskilled or semi-skilled, the simple model presented here does not violate reality.

In the second situation, the institutional distortion of urban sector wage-setting is eliminated. Thus, the labour demand curve in urban sector merges from $D_u abD_m$ to $D_m D_m$. This will result in a reduction of wage levels in the urban formal sector from W_u to $W_{u'}$, rather than increasing it from W_u to $W_{u''}$. This will not change informal sector wage-setting and employment levels, though.

An important implication may be drawn from this simple model, which is that government intervention creates distortions to the market and, hence, reduces economic efficiency. For example, if the government intervenes in informal sector wage-setting, say at level W_m, urban unemployment will become a serious problem. On the other hand, if the government restricts rural–urban migration, rural MPL will reduce, and hence reduce the income of the rural population.

To sum up, Hong Kong's experience as well as the empirical results provided in table 11.7 indicate that so long as labour market institutional settings are flexible enough, the informal sector has great potential to generate jobs. The liberalisation of the two-tier labour market may create an opportunity for China to resolve its urban unemployment, especially hidden unemployment. Although state sector redundant workers may temporarily suffer from unemployment, they should be able to find jobs in the informal sector at a lower wage. Some of the redundant workers may quit the labour market if their opportunity cost of staying at home is lower than their marginal benefit of staying at home. But this should not be a concern to policy-makers as this is an individual's rational choice. More importantly, if wage levels in the informal sector are flexible enough, one should not fear that rural migrants would take up jobs from state sector redundant workers.

Appendix A

Table 11A.1.   *Detailed occupational distribution for rural migrants*

Occupation	Freq.	Per cent
Professionals and managers		
Professionals	34	0.66
Managers and party leaders	1	0.02
Contractors	61	1.19
Shift leaders	16	0.31
Other managers	13	0.25
Clerks		
Security guards	16	0.31
Secretary and public relation workers	1	0.02
Other clerks	13	0.25
Merchants		
Merchants	1	0.02
Agricultural goods merchants	629	12.23
Food product merchants	197	3.83
Recycling workers	21	0.41
Shop assistants	391	7.61
Sales persons	85	1.65
Other merchants	39	0.76
Cigarette merchants	2	0.04
Daily general goods merchants	7	0.14
Service workers		
Service workers	3	0.06
Restaurant/hotel/motel service workers	114	2.22
Domestic servants	65	1.26
Barbers	100	1.95
Tailors	187	3.64
Repairing trade persons	57	1.11
Cleaners	58	1.13
Scavengers	11	0.21
Cooks and kitchen hands	156	3.04
Other service workers	70	1.36
Manual labourers		
Agricultural workers	148	2.89
Industrial, transportation and other labourers	321	6.24
Spinners	57	1.11
Weavers	69	1.34
Sewing workers	399	7.76
Carpenters and painters	149	2.9
Construction workers	731	14.22
Metal workers	221	4.3
Electricians	82	1.6
Transport workers	335	6.52
Odd-job persons	103	2
Other labourers	81	1.58
Mobile carpenters	34	0.66
Self-employed	59	1.15
Gold processors	2	0.04
Operators	1	0.02
Lock-smith	1	0.02
Total	5,141	100

Appendix B

Table 11B.1. *Summary statistics of variables*

	Urban		Rural 1		Rural 2	
	Mean	SD	Mean	SD	Mean	SD
Log(earnings)	6.699	0.497	6.192	0.580	6.256	0.514
Years of schooling	10.484	2.898	7.303	3.057	7.907	2.151
FT	16.738	10.193	3.095	4.186	2.003	2.753
$(FT)^2$	384.004	389.632	27.010	101.020	11.589	36.864
OJ	4.297	7.960	5.882	9.707	10.217	8.546
$(OJ)^2$	81.794	203.445	128.339	372.860	177.412	306.353
Dummy for males	0.541	0.498	0.533	0.500	0.659	0.474
Dummy for married	0.996	0.059	0.795	0.405	0.548	0.498
Dummy for training	0.299	0.458	0.118	0.323	0.349	0.477
Weekly work hours	41.177	7.089	56.851	22.915	54.228	17.027
No. of observations	1,974		195		3,545	

12

Reforming China's labour market

This book has examined various aspects of labour market reform in China over the period of the economic evolution towards a market economy. This chapter summarises the main findings of the book and its contributions to enriching our understanding of Chinese labour market reform.

Problems with pre-reform labour arrangements

For nearly half a century China did not have labour markets in the conventional sense. These started to emerge only following the economic reform that began in 1978. The main characteristics of the country's labour arrangements before that were the segregation of the rural and urban economies, the extreme immobility of labour and the disincentives implanted in the income distribution system. The separation of the rural and urban economies eliminated possible economic gains from efficient labour allocation. Within each sector, the immobility of labour resulted in serious problems of hidden unemployment and low productivity. The situation was made worse by the way income was determined in both the rural and urban economies.

In the countryside, income distribution followed a work point system, where an individual's work points were evaluated against each day of work among the members of the team. At the end of each year, the net distributable income of the production team was divided by the total work points earned by all members. This system separated individual effort and the distribution of benefits – an individual's earnings were not only determined by his/her own efforts but also by the efforts of other members of his/her team. Because the nature of farming is such that monitoring work effort is very difficult, this system encouraged individuals to shirk in the hope that they could share in other people's effort and in the belief that no matter how hard they worked, the results of their extra effort would be shared by all the members of the team in any case.

In the urban economy, wages were determined by the central government on the basis of an individual's education, experience, occupation and location of the work unit. Although human capital was the basis for wage differentials, the rate of returns to schooling and work experience were extremely low.

Furthermore, an individual's human capital stock is only an indicator of potential productivity. Without the right mechanism to encourage individuals to work efficiently, human capital stock in itself will not lead to high productivity. In a market economy, an incentive to high productivity is provided by labour mobility: firms are able to hire and fire workers according to their own will, and workers are free to choose jobs. However, in pre-reform urban China, such a mechanism did not exist. Thus shirking was widespread.

Impact of rural economic reform on the rural labour market

The years 1977 and 1978 marked a turning point in contemporary China. After 40 years under a centrally controlled economy, Chinese farmers reacted to their extremely poor living conditions by deciding to work on a family basis, ignoring the possible punitive repercussions from authorities. Their success in dramatically increasing agricultural production enlightened the Chinese government. In 1978, a new system – the household responsibility system (HRS) – was gradually introduced throughout the country.

Once agricultural production and income distribution began to be based on the family unit, labour allocation and income determination became family decisions. This provided for a better incentive system, in that the returns to farm household production were directly linked to the effort of the family. In comparison, in the pre-reform collective system, income distribution was essentially egalitarian and bore little relation to individual effort. Mere attendance (regardless of effort) was rewarded by work points, therefore individuals tended to supply more labour in terms of attendance than was needed. Moreover, the value of the work point had no impact on an individual's labour supply because it was unknown until the end of each year (Burkett and Putterman 1993).

It was found in chapter 3 that after the change of the production and income distribution system, household income variation was determined primarily by productivity-related variables, such as household average education level, average work experience and labour and capital inputs. Moreover, labour supply appeared to respond to wages in a normal way. An increase in the wage rate had a positive and significant impact on household labour supply to a certain extent then, when a household was rich enough, further increases in wages gradually reduced labour supply.

A similar and more gradual change also occurred in the rural non-agricultural sector. The rapid growth of a rural non-agricultural sector was a result of the introduction of the household responsibility system (HRS). After the introduction of the HRS and the increase in grain prices in 1979, the rural economy experienced a sharp rise in labour productivity, which generated two important changes: a resultant increase in the agricultural surplus and an increase in surplus agricultural labour. As a consequence of these changes and of the fact that rural surplus labourers were barred from moving to the cities to find jobs, Chinese peasants found their own way to increase their income. Surplus agricultural output and labour were invested into already existing rural non-agricultural enterprises and hundreds of thousands of new rural non-agricultural enterprises were soon set up. These enterprises were originally entirely owned by the collective authorities (that is, the townships and villages), but later on private ownership was also encouraged.

After the introduction of the HRS, the communes, brigades and production teams lost most of their administrative and economic functions. When production and income distribution decisions in the agricultural sector were made within the household, it was impossible and meaningless for those who worked in the non-agricultural sector to have their income transferred back to their production teams. Logically, the income distribution system needed to be changed to a within-enterprise distribution system. Nevertheless, for quite a long time, employment in the rural non-agricultural enterprises was still controlled by the authorities. Township and village-owned enterprises (TVEs) were given the right to determine wages but not the right to hire and fire; this situation did not change until the middle-to-late 1980s.

However, the inflexible employment system in the township, village and privately-owned enterprise (TVP) sector did not seem to stop enterprises from paying workers according to their labour productivity. The analysis conducted in chapter 4 indicated that the wage determination structures for those who were paid by piece-rates and those paid by time-rates were similar. If one believes that piece-rate payments reflect labour productivity, the consistent wage determination structures for the two groups suggested that workers in the TVPs were paid according to their labour productivity.

Why is it, then, that the inflexibility in hiring and firing workers did not stop the wage determination system in the TVP sector becoming similar to that found in market economies? The answer may be twofold. On the one hand, TVPs operated in a very competitive market and under fairly tight budget constraints. To be successful, firms had to, and were motivated to, operate efficiently, which necessitated setting up good incentive systems for workers. On the other hand, the only alternative employment opportunity for TVP workers was agricultural employment, which paid much less; hence, employees would not quit jobs. Although managers were not allowed to fire workers, the right to determine wage levels and bonuses enabled them to reward hard work and punish shirking.

The empirical work conducted in chapter 4 used data for 1985. Since then, the flexibility of employment in the TVP sector has increased rapidly. One survey of 300 TVEs indicated that by 1991, 96 per cent of firms were allowed to make recruitment decisions and 95 per cent could dismiss workers. More importantly, privately-owned enterprises in the rural non-agricultural sector have grown rapidly; by 1995, about 53 per cent of total TVP employment was in the private sector.

Although rural employment and the wage determination structure in both the agricultural and non-agricultural sectors have moved towards a market-oriented system, one phenomenon remains puzzling: the persistent and widening wage gap between the rural agricultural and non-agricultural sectors. Chapter 5 was devoted to an investigation of this interesting feature of the rural labour market.

Neo-classical economic theory suggests that in a flexible labour market, when the wage level reflects the marginal productivity of labour (MPL), wages between two sectors should be equalised. This theory, however, assumes that both sectors under consideration adopt technology characterised by a high degree of substitution. This does not suit the case of the rural agricultural and non-agricultural sectors in China.

A theoretical explanation was provided in chapter 5 to show how limited substitutability of capital and labour in the non-agricultural sector and perfect substitutability in the agricultural sector might cause wages to differ. In the short run, technology with limited substitutability implies a non-continuous and nearly horizontal labour demand curve and a high degree of substitutability induces a downward-sloping labour demand curve. Thus, when capital resources are limited in the short run, the marginal product of labour in the non-agricultural sector will be higher than that in the agricultural sector.

In the long run, however, if the relative price of capital to labour is held constant, an increase in capital supply will eventually allow the non-agricultural sector to absorb labour from the agricultural sector so as to equalise the marginal product of labour between the two. Nevertheless, if the relative price of capital to labour is declining in the long run, enterprises in the non-agricultural sector will tend to choose more capital-intensive technology, which will in turn reduce labour demand in the non-agricultural sector. If this happens, the marginal productivity in the non-agricultural sector will be persistently higher than that in the agricultural sector, and a persistent wage gap between the two sectors will be observed.

The empirical tests conducted in chapter 5 confirmed that

- the rural non-agricultural sector adopted technology characterised by limited factor substitution

- the relative factor price of capital to labour has been declining over time.

Urban labour market reform

Urban economic reform started in the early 1980s following the success of the agricultural reforms. These reforms, however, met with much more resistance as socialist ideology clashed with the attempts to introduce market-based institutions. From a labour market perspective, such conflict is twofold.

On the one hand, socialist ideology implies public ownership and as a corollary, that workers should have the right to full and lifetime employment. Thus, labour market reform was (and still is) politically sensitive. This was one of the most important reasons why urban economic reform bypassed factor markets and concentrated on the goods markets for a long time. Labour market reforms did not begin until as late as the middle of the 1980s, and even then, reforms were implemented with great caution. On the other hand, public ownership and its consequent soft-budget constraints prevented enterprises from operating efficiently. There were insufficient incentives for efficient labour allocation and labour cost minimisation, which further undermined the already tentative reforms.

A labour contract system was formally introduced in 1984–6, and by 1995 involved about 39 per cent of state sector workforce. However, as managers in the SOEs were not responsible for the state's assets but rather were responsible for their employees' well-being, this system did not produce the desired flexible hiring and firing outcome either. Workers hired under such contracts had guarantees that their contracts would be extended. For the same reason, although managers were given the right to dismiss workers, they tended not to do so even when their firms were seriously over-staffed. Managers of state enterprises were trying to maximise employees' benefits rather than minimising labour costs because, if a manager was not popular with his/her employees his/her own career could be damaged. As a result, a rapid and unchecked rise in labour compensation unrelated to gains in productivity was widely observed (Walder 1989).

Because of these difficulties, urban labour market reform in China has had limited success. Chapter 6 investigated the changes in individual wage determination in this sector. Although economic reforms had brought about a structural change in the system of individual wage determination, the rate of returns to human capital-related variables changed only slightly and wages still appeared to be seniority- rather than productivity-related. Much of the change in wage structure was induced by the changes in industrial wage differentials which, in turn, may have been caused by the introduction of enterprise profit retention.

Chapter 7 examined the impact of the current ownership structures of the state sector on firms' labour compensation and employment systems. The chapter used a data set comprising the state, collective and private sectors to test how enterprises in the state (and collective) sectors behaved differently from the private sector. The empirical results obtained indicated that state ownership prevented enterprises from behaving in a profit-maximising manner and, in the public sector (both state and collective enterprises), labour compensation was related to a firm's retained profits rather than to productivity. Labour compensation in private enterprises, however, was determined solely by labour productivity.

Furthermore, although both state and collective firms had public ownership, the degree of separation between risk-bearing and decision-making was much higher in the state than in the collective sector. This implied that the former had softer-budget constraints. As a result, the productivity incentives induced by profit-sharing were much stronger in the collective than in the state sector. It was also found that over-staffing was more a problem for the state and collective than for the private sector. All these results indicated that labour market reform in urban China is more difficult and requires deep-rooted changes in urban ownership structures. Of course, ownership reform is not a simple task. One major obstacle is how to transform the current social security system without causing significant social and political instability. In the pre-reform era, the state provided a lifelong social security system in the cities. The system included free childcare, free education, lifetime employment, free medical care, subsidised housing and a full pension. To complicate matters, the provision of these benefits was enterprise-based. This internal social security system had two major flaws. First, it was costly for state enterprises at a time when they were trying to become efficient and financially independent: some enterprises had to pay pensions equivalent to their wage bills. Second, it prevented efficient labour allocation by reducing the possibility of labour mobility. Enterprises did not dare to lay off workers for fear of reprisals, and individual employees were unwilling to move for fear of losing their benefits.

Two social security models are discussed in chapter 8: a Western social welfare model and the East Asian private welfare model. A review of the functioning of the two models revealed that most OECD countries which followed the welfare state model encountered high unemployment, rapid growth of government expenditure and low economic growth, while the countries that followed the private welfare system tended to have low unemployment rates, low government expenditure and high economic growth rates. More importantly, simple predictions of the necessary expenditures on unemployment benefits and pensions if the government were to provide them indicated that it was beyond the Chinese government's financial ability to follow the welfare state model. The answer is thus clear. China needs and can only afford a welfare system which can encourage individuals to take care of themselves. Such a system would induce more private saving, reduce labour costs, reduce unemployment and encourage economic growth.

Rural–urban migration

After over 40 years of separation, the rural and urban economies were finally linked by rural–urban migration in the late 1980s and early 1990s. Like the rural economic reform, rural–urban migration was not initiated by the government. Rather, it was a result of rural surplus labour and excess labour demand in the urban sector. The government reacted passively to this movement, but the controls on migration have been gradually loosened: in 1996, about 80 million rural migrants were working in the urban areas. China's rural–urban migration has two unusual features. The first is the labour market segregation between rural migrants and urban residents. As a result of the lengthy separation of the rural and urban economies, urban residentship entitled city dwellers to generous subsidies and benefits that were not available to rural residents. Although rural residents are now allowed to work in the cities, they are excluded from the welfare benefits of urban jobs. The jobs that rural migrants take pay less and have no job tenure and other benefits; more importantly, rural migrants are not entitled to get jobs in the formal sector. The second feature arises from the existing institutional constraints on rural–urban migration, including the household registration system, and the compulsory agricultural production quota.

These features of Chinese rural–urban migration made the impact of rural migration on economic growth in China somewhat different from that in some other developing countries. The most important difference is that rural–urban migration was not to be blamed for urban unemployment. Chapter 9 set up a theoretical model to analyse the impact of migration on economic growth in China. The model indicated that the main impacts were the reduction of labour costs in the urban sector and the increase of income in the rural sector. While these gains have been significant, there are other features of rural–urban migration which prevent optimal labour allocation. An important one was found to be inadequate job market information. A symptom of this problem is the existence of considerable wage differentials among different regional migrant labour markets. Analysis carried out in chapter 10, using two cross-sectional data sets for rural migrants in Jinan City (Shandong Province) and Dongguan City (Guangdong Province), indicated that the significant wage differential between the two migrant labour markets was mainly caused by the difference in the price of individual acquired human capital. In Dongguan, the demand for human capital was much higher than in Jinan; thus, it was paid a higher price than in Jinan.

Further analysis suggested that the reason why the higher demand for more skilled migrants in Dongguan could not be met by more migrants moving to the region was a lack of specific job information. As migrants in China were risk-averse, they moved to a region only when they had a guaranteed job offer. However, such job offers could not be obtained unless one had friends, relatives, or co-villagers who already worked in the region. Thus, the information flows about jobs and job markets are rather random, insufficient and depend on personal contacts. It is the accidental nature of the information flows which inhibits an efficient allocation of labour across regions.

Nevertheless, creating efficient information channels is no easy task. An important problem has been the lack of credibility of China's legal system. Private job agencies have a reputation for cheating job-seekers; government agencies charge high fees and tend to be inefficient. Furthermore, job-seeking migrants do not trust employers unless they have evidence to the contrary. Migrants are often cheated by employers because labour and other relevant laws are not enforced.

Another important factor which prevents efficient allocation of labour is the existence of a two-tier labour market in urban China – the segregation of the urban labour market between urban residents and rural migrants. In chapter 11 the degree of this segregation was examined and the impact of eliminating this segregation on the urban labour market was analysed.

The analysis indicated that rural migrants were almost exclusively employed as trade, service and manual workers, while more than 30 per cent of urban employees were professional, managerial and office workers. Moreover, the wage gaps between rural migrants and urban employees were huge. The former, on average, earned 50 per cent of urban employees' hourly wage. Further analysis indicated that about 40 per cent of this wage differential could not be explained by labour productivity and other personal endowment differentials between the two groups. This suggested that it might be attributable to discrimination in favour of urban residents owing to the non-market institutional wage settings in the urban formal sector.

The removal of such distortions will bring about economic gains to the Chinese economy. However, the fear that these reforms might generate a serious unemployment problem in China. Nevertheless, the analysis in chapter 11 found that although the removal of the non-market wage setting in the urban formal sector would release its hidden unemployment, this would not create serious unemployment if the labour market institutional setting was flexible enough. Furthermore, if this condition held, the release of hidden unemployment would not clash with rural–urban migration either. In this regard, Hong Kong's experience is extremely relevant. Over the last 10 years or so, as a result of the development of labour-intensive manufacturing in mainland China, about 560,000 manufacturing jobs were lost in Hong Kong; the garment industry there having almost completely shifted to China. Unskilled labour has not suffered from this structural change because jobs were being created rapidly. During the same period, 380,000 new jobs were created in the finance sector and 205,000 in the service sector; Hong Kong's unemployment rate never exceeded 3 per cent because of the flexibility of the Hong Kong labour market.

Of course, as part of a centrally planned economy for more than four decades, urban employees are used to the idea of being looked after in every aspect of their lives. The removal of labour market inefficiencies implies for some workers a reduction in wages and the possibility of ending up with lower-status jobs. However, psychological adjustment can be quick when it is a matter of survival: most of the 30 million state sector workers who were made redundant have accepted jobs which they previously regarded as low-status migrant jobs.

Establishing a flexible labour market in China

The detailed analysis of China's pre- and post-reform labour market in this book shows that many of the deficiencies of the earlier period will increasingly impede China's economic growth unless there is a thorough overhaul of the country's labour markets. There are three keys to freeing up China's labour markets:

- Eliminating existing restrictions on rural–urban migration at both ends.

- Changing the labour market system within the urban sector. The majority of SOEs should be gradually privatised so that managers of enterprises will be responsible for long-run growth and profits rather than for employees' short-run benefits. Labour market segregation between urban residents and rural migrants should be eliminated so that everybody has an equal right to compete in the labour market. All these changes will facilitate a flexible labour market which, in turn, will assist economic growth, generate jobs and induce higher income.

- Designing a new welfare system, whereby individual employees play an important role in the provision of their own safety nets.

References

Adam, K. J., Chenery, B. S., Minhas, B. S. and Solow, R. M., 1961. 'Capital–labour substitution and economic efficiency', *Review of Economics and Statistics*, 43(3): 225–50

ADB and China's Ministry of Labour, 1994. *Social Welfare and Labour Adjustment in Enterprise Reform*

Ahn, N. and Ugidos-Olazabal, A., 1995. 'Duration of unemployment in Spain: relative effects of unemployment benefit and family characteristics', *Oxford Bulletin of Economics and Statistics*, 57(2): 249–64

Arrow, K., 1972. 'Models of job discrimination and some mathematical models of race discrimination in the labour market', in Pascal, A. H. (ed.), *Racial Discrimination in Economic Life*, Lexington, Mass.: Heath: 83–102, 187–204

1973. 'The theory of discrimination', in Ashenfelter, O. and Rees, A. (eds.), *Discrimination in Labour Markets*, Princeton: Princeton University Press: 3–33

Banerjee, B., 1983. 'The role of the informal sector in the migration process: a test of probabilistic migration models and labour market segmentation for India', *Oxford Economic Papers*, 35 (November): 399–422

1984. 'Information flow, expectations and job search', *Journal of Development Economics*, 15: 239–57

Barr, N., 1992. 'Economic theory and the welfare state: a survey and interpretation', *Journal of Economic Literature*, 30: 741–803

Bartel, A., 1979. 'The migration decision: what role does job mobility play?', *American Economic Review*, 69(5): 775–86

Becker, G. S., 1957. *The Economics of Discrimination*, Chicago: University of Chicago Press

1962. 'Investment in human capital: a theoretical analysis', *Journal of Political Economy*, 70(5) pt. 2: 9–49

Beijing Bureau of Labour, 1996. *Beijing Manual for Urban Labour Force Pensions in Beijing Enterprises*, Beijing: Beijing Bureau of Labour (in Chinese)

Bhargava, S., 1994. 'Profit sharing and the financial performance of companies', *Economic Journal*, 104: 1044–55

Birdsall, N. and Sabot, R. H., 1994. 'Virtuous circles: human capital growth and equity in East Asia', World Bank, Policy Research Department, Washington, DC, mimeo

Birdsall, N., Ross, D. and Sabot, R. H., 1995. 'Inequality and growth reconsidered: lessons from East Asia', *World Bank Economic Review*, 9(3): 477–508

Blinder, A. S., 1973. 'Wage discrimination: reduced form and structural estimations', *Journal of Human Resources*, 8: 436–55

1990. *Paying for Productivity: A Look at the Evidence*, Washington, DC: Brookings Institution

Bonin, J. P., 1977. 'Work incentives and uncertainty on a collective farm', *Journal of Comparative Economics*, 1: 77–97

Borland, J., 1996. 'Earnings inequality in Australia: changes and causes', paper presented in *Labour Research from Three Countries Workshop*, Centre for Economic Policy Research, Research School of Social Sciences, Australian National University, Canberra (March 1997)

Borland, J., Vella, F. and Woodbridge, G., 1995. 'Inter- and intra-industry earnings variation in Australia and the United States: what explains the difference?', Australian National University, unpublished

Burkett, J. P. and Putterman, L., 1993. 'The supply of labour by individuals to a Chinese collective farm: the case of Dahe Commune', *Economica*, 60: 381–96

Byrd, W. A., 1987. 'The market mechanism and economic reforms in Chinese industry', dissertation, Department of Economics, Harvard University

1992. *Chinese Industrial Firms under Reform*, New York: Oxford University Press

Byrd, W. and Lin, Q., 1990a. *China's Rural Industry*, Oxford: Oxford University Press

1990b. 'China's rural industry: an introduction', in Byrd, W. and Lin, Q. (eds.), *China's Rural Industry*, Oxford: Oxford University Press: 3–18

Byron, R. P. and Manaloto, E. Q., 1990. 'Return to education in China', *Economic Development and Cultural Change*, 38: 783–96

Caballe, J., 1993. 'On endogenous growth with physical and human capital', *Journal of Political Economics*, 101(6)

Cable, J. and Wilson, N., 1989. 'Profit-sharing and productivity: an analysis of UK engineering firms,' *Economic Journal*, 99: 366–75

1990. 'Profit-sharing and productivity: some further evidence', *Economic Journal*, 100: 550–5

Castles, F. and Mitchell, D., 1994. 'An institutional view of the Australian welfare state', in *Perspectives on Shaping Our Future*, Conference Proceedings, EPAC, Canberra: Australian Government Publishing Service

Census and Statistics Department, Hong Kong, 1998. Web site information

Centre for Rural Economic Research in the Ministry of Agriculture (CRER), 1996. 'Research on rural labour mobility in China: migrants and their home towns', paper presented at the International Conference on the Flow of Rural Labour in China, Beijing

Chen, J. Y and Yu, D. C., 1993. *Rural Labour Migration in China (Zhonggou Nongye Laudongli Zhuanyi)*, Beijing: People's Publishing House

Chen, Y., 1995. *Chen Yun Wen Xuen (Selected Works by Chen Yun)*, Beijing: People's Publishing House

Chen, Z. X., 1997. 'Social transformation and layoff workers' behaviour', Masters thesis, Department of Sociology, Peking University

Choi Po King and Lok-Sang, K., 1995. *The Other Hong Kong Report*, Hong Kong: Chinese University Press

Chow, N. W. S., 1981. 'Social security in Hong Kong', in Jones, J. (ed.), *The Common Welfare: Hong Kong's Social Services*, Hong Kong: Chinese University Press

Clarke, G. R. G., 1995. 'More evidence on income distribution and growth', *Journal of Development Economics*, 47: 403–27

Cotton, J., 1988. 'On the decomposition of wage differentials', *Review of Economics and Statistics*: 236–43

Council for Economic planning and Development Executive Yuan (CEPDEY), various issues. *Industry of Free China*, Taipei

Dickens, W. T. and Katz, L. F., 1987. 'Inter-industry wage differences and industry characteristics', in Lang, K. and Leonard, J. S. (eds.), *Unemployment and the Structure of Labor Markets*, Oxford: Basil Blackwell: 48–89

Domar, E. D., 1966. 'The Soviet collective farm as a producer cooperative', *American Economic Review*, 56(4): 734–57

East Asia Analytical Unit (EAAU), 1997. *China Embraces the Market*, Canberra: East Asia Analytical Unit, Department of Foreign Affairs and Trade

Eckaus, R. S., 1955. 'The factor proportions problem in underdeveloped areas', *American Economic Review*, 45(4): 539–65

Economic Commission of Shanghai, Labour Bureau of Shanghai and Industrial Economic Union of Shanghai (ECS, LBS and IEUS), 1994. *Labour, Wage, and Insurance Reform*, Shanghai: People's Publishing House of Shanghai

Economist, 1995. 'The changing face of the welfare state', *Economist* (26 August): 41–2

Estrin, S. and Svejnar, J., 1993. 'Wage determination in labor-managed firms under market-oriented reforms: estimates of static and dynamic models', *Journal of Comparative Economics*, 17(3): 687–700

Estrin, S., Moore, R. E. and Svejnar, J., 1988. 'Market imperfections, labour management, and earnings differentials in a developing country: theory and evidence from Yugoslavia', *Quarterly Journal of Economics*, 103(3): 465–78

Feng, L. R., 1982. 'Six questions concerning the problem of employment', *Selected Writings on Studies of Marxism*, 1, Beijing: Institute of Marxism–Leninism–Mao Zedong Thought, Chinese Academy of Social Sciences

Fields, G. S., 1975. 'Rural–urban migration, urban unemployment and underemployment, and job-search activity in LDCs', *Journal of Development Economics*, 2(2): 165–87

Florkowski, G. W., 1988. 'The organisational impact of profit sharing', PhD Dissertation, Syracuse University

Garrett, G. and Mitchell, D., 1995. 'Globalisation and the welfare state: income transfers in the industrial democracies, 1965–1990', Centre for Economic Policy Research, *Discussion Paper*, 330

Greenwood, M., 1975. 'Research on internal migration in the United States: a survey', *Journal of Economic Literature*, 13: 397–433

    1985. 'Human migration: theory, models and empirical studies', *Journal of Regional Science*, 25: 521–44

Gregory, R. R. and Meng, X., 1995. 'Wage determination and occupational attainment in the rural industrial sector of China', *Journal of Comparative Economics*, 21(3): 353–74

Griffin, K. and Griffin, K., 1984. 'Institutional change and income distribution', in Griffin, K. (ed.), *Institutional Reform and Economic Development in the Chinese Countryside*, London: Macmillan

Griliches, Z. and Ringstad, V., 1971. *Economies of Scale and the Form of the Production Function*, Amsterdam: North-Holland

Groves, T., Hong, Y., McMillan, J. and Naughton, B., 1994. 'Autonomy and incentives in Chinese state enterprises', *Quarterly Journal of Economics*, 109(1): 183–209

Ham, J. C. and Rea, S. A., 1987. 'Unemployment insurance and male unemployment duration in Canada', *Journal of Labor Economics*, 5(3): 325–53

Han, Xiaoyun, 1995. 'The characteristics of migrant labourers' income, consumption and occupation – A study on rural labour mobility', *Zhongguo Nongcun Jingji (Chinese Rural Economy)*, 1995(5): 40–4

Harding, A., 1997. 'The suffering middle: trends in income inequality in Australia 1982 to 1993–4', National Centre for Social and Economic Modelling, *Working Paper*, DP21, Canberra

Harris, R. and Todaro, M. P., 1970. 'Migration, unemployment and development: a two-sector analysis', *American Economic Review*, 60: 126–42

Hashimoto, M. and Raisian, J., 1985. 'Employment tenure and earnings profiles in Japan and the United States', *The American Economic Review*, 75(4): 721–35

Hay, Donald A., Morris, D., Liu, G. and Yao, S., 1994. *Economic Reform and State-Owned Enterprises in China 1979–1987*, Oxford and New York: Oxford University Press and Clarendon Press

Heckman, J., 1979. 'Sample selection bias as a specification error', *Econometrica*, 47: 153–61

Higgins, B., 1968. *Economic Development*, New York: W. W. Norton: 17–20, 296–300

Hong, N. S., 1990. 'Labour and employment', in Wang, R. and Cheng, J. (eds.), *The Other Hong Kong Report*, Hong Kong: Chinese University Press

International Labour Organisation (ILO), 1972. *Employment, Incomes and Equality: A Strategy for Increasing Productive Employment in Kenya*, Geneva: ILO

International Monetary Fund (IMF), 1993. *China, at the Threshold of a Market Economy*, prepared by Bell, M., Khor, H. E. and Kochhar, K., with Ma, J., N'guiamba, S. and Lall, R., *Occasional Paper*, 107(9), Washington, DC: IMF

Johnson, D., 1988. 'Economic reform in the People's Republic of China', *Economic Development and Cultural Change*, 36(3): S225–45

Jones, D. C., 1987. 'The productivity effects of worker directors and financial participation in the firm: the case of British retail cooperatives', *Industrial and Labour Relations Review*, 41(3): 79–92

Juhn, C., Murphy K. and Pierce, B., 1993. 'Wage inequality and the rise in returns to skill', *Journal of Political Economy*, 101(3): 410–42

Kao, C., Polachek, S. W. and Wunnava, P. V., 1994. 'Male–female wage differentials in Taiwan: a human capital approach', *Economic Development and Cultural Change*, 42: 351–74

Karunaratne, N. D., 1995. 'Paradox of hysteresis and real wage flexibility in Australia', *Journal of Post Keynesian Economics*, 17(4): 503–14

Khan, A. R., Griffin, K., Carl, R. and Zhao, R., 1993. 'Household income and its distribution in China', in Griffin, K. and Zhao, R. (eds.), *The Distribution of Income in China*, New York: St Martin's Press, London: Macmillan: 25–73

Kidd, M. and Meng, X., 1997. 'Trends in the Australian gender wage differential over the 1980s: some evidence on the effectiveness of legislative reform', *Australian Economic Review*, 36(68): 85–9

Kidd, M. P. and Shannon, M., 1996. 'The gender wage gap: a comparison of Australia and Canada', *Industrial and Labor Relations Review*, 49(4): 729–46

Kmenta, J., 1967. 'On the estimation of the ECS production function', *International Economic Review*, 8(2): 180–9

Knight, J. and Song, L., 1995. 'China's labour market', *Bulletin of Rural Labor Mobility Studies*, Centre for Rural Economic Research, China's Ministry of Agriculture

Kornai, J., 1980. *Economics of Shortage*, Amsterdam: North-Holland

Korzec, M., 1992. *Labour and the Failure of Reform in China*, London: Macmillan

Krueger, A. B. and Summers, L. H., 1987. 'Reflections on the inter-industry wage structure', in Lang, K. and Leonard, J. S. (eds.), *Unemployment and the Structure of Labor Markets*, Oxford: Basil Blackwell: 17–47
    1988. 'Efficiency wages and the inter-industry wage structure', *Econometrica*, 56(2): 259–93

Kruse, D. L., 1992. 'Profit sharing and productivity: microeconomic evidence from the United States', *Economic Journal*, 102: 24–36

Lal, D., 1973. 'Disutility of effort, migration and the shadow wage rate', *Oxford Economic Papers*, 25 (March): 112–26

Lee, E., 1984. 'Employment and incomes in rural China: the impact of recent organisational changes', in Griffin K. (ed.), *Institutional Reform and Economic Development in the Chinese Countryside*, London: Macmillan

Lewis, W. A., 1954. 'Economic development with unnlimited supplies of labour', *Manchester School*, 22(2): 1139–91

Lin, J. Y., 1988. 'The household responsibility system reform in China: a peasant's institutional choice', *American Journal of Agricultural Economics*, 69: 410–15
    1992. 'Rural reforms and agricultural growth in China', *American Economic Review*, 82(1): 34–51

Lucas, R. E., 1988. 'On the mechanics of economic developments', *Journal of Monetary Economics*, 22: 3–42

Luo, X., 1990. 'Ownership and status stratification', in Byrd, W. and Lin, Q. (eds.), *China's Rural Industry*, Oxford: Oxford University Press: 134–71

Mai, Y. and Perkins, F., 1997. 'China's state owned enterprises: nine case studies', *Briefing Paper Series*, 7, Canberra: Department of Foreign Affairs and Trade

Maier, G., 1987. 'Job search and migration', in Fischer, M. M. and Nijkamp P. (eds.), *Regional Labour Markets*, Amsterdam and Oxford: North-Holland: 189–204

Mazumdar, D., 1976. 'The rural–urban wage gap, migration and the shadow-wage', *Oxford Economic Papers*, 28(3): 406–25
    1977. 'Analysis of the dual labour market in LDCs', in Kannappan, S. (ed.), *Studies in Urban Labour Market Behaviour in Developing Areas*, Geneva: International Institute of Labour Studies

McMillan, J., Whalley, J. and Zhu, L., 1989. 'The impact of China's economic reforms on agricultural productivity growth', *Journal of Political Economy*, 97(4): 781–807

Meng, X., 1992. 'Individual wage determination in township, village and private enterprises in China', PhD dissertation, Australian National University

1996a. 'An examination of wage determination in China's rural industrial sector', *Applied Economics*, 28(1): 715–24

1996b. 'Regional wage gap, information flow, and rural–urban migration', paper presented at the International Conference on the Flow of Rural Labour in China, Beijing

1998. 'Recent developments in China's labour market', paper presented in China Update Conference, Canberra, Australian National University

Meng, X. and Kidd, M., 1997, 'Wage determination in China's state sector in the 1980s', *Journal of Comparative Economics*, 25(3): 403–21

Meng, X. and Wu, H. X., 1998. 'Household income determination and regional income differential in China', *Asian Economic Journal*

Miller, P. W., 1987. 'The wage effect of the occupational segregation of women in Britain', *The Economic Journal*, 97: 885–96

Mincer, J., 1958. 'Investment in human capital and personal income distribution', *Journal of Political Economy*, 66(4): 281–302

1974, *Schooling, Experience and Earnings*, New York: National Bureau of Economic Research

Mincer, J. and Higuchi, Y., 1988. 'Wage structures and labor turnover in the United States and Japan', *Journal of the Japanese and International Economies*, 2: 97–133

Murphy, K. and Topel, R., 1987. 'Unemployment, risk and earnings', in Lang, K. and Leonard, J. S. (eds.), *Unemployment and the Structure of Labor Markets*, Oxford: Basil Blackwell: 101–40

Myint, H., 1971. *Economic Theory and the Underdeveloped Countries*, Oxford: Oxford University Press

OECD, 1994. *The OECD Job Study*, Paris: OECD Publication Service

1996. *OECD Economic Outlook*, 59: 25, Paris: OECD Publication Service

Pagan, A., 1984. 'Econometric issues in the analysis of regressions with generated regressors', *International Economic Review*, 25(1): 221–47

Perkins, D. and Yusuf, S., 1984. *Rural Development in China*, Baltimore: Johns Hopkins University Press

Polachek, S. W. and Siebert, W. S., 1993. *The Economics of Earnings*, Cambridge: Cambridge University Press

Prasnikar, J. and Svejnar, J., 1994. 'Behaviour of participatory firms in Yugoslavia: lessons for transforming economies', *Review of Economics and Statistics*, 76(4): 728–41

Preston, A., 1995. 'Where are we now with human capital theory in Australia?', paper presented at PhD student conference in business and economics, The University of Western Australia (November)

Psacharopoulos, G., 1985. 'Returns to education: a further international update and implications', *Journal of Human Resources*. 20: 583–604

1994. 'Returns to investment in education: a global update', *World Development*, 22(9): 1325–43

Putterman, L., 1987. 'The incentive problem and the demise of team farming in China', *Journal of Development Economics*, 26: 103–27

1990. 'Effort, productivity and incentives in a 1970s' Chinese people's commune', *Journal of Comparative Economics*, 14: 88–104

1993. 'Ownership and the nature of the firm', *Journal of Comparative Economics*, 17(2): 243–63

Qu, Y. L., 1997. 'Analytical report on the survey of employment of migrants', in Employment Bureau, Ministry of Labour (ed.), *Chinese Rural Labour Employment and Migration*, unpublished manuscript

Ranis, G., 1995. 'Another look at the East Asian miracle', *The World Bank Economic Review*, 9(3): 509–34

Ranis, G. and Fei, J. C. H., 1961. 'The theory of economic development.' *American Economic Review*, 56: 533–65

Rawsni, T. G., 1979. *Economic Growth and Employment in China*, Oxford: Oxford University Press

Research Group on Reform in Employment System, 1991. 'On further reform in employment system', in Ling, H. (ed.), *Reform of Labour, Wage, and Social Security System*, Beijing: China's Labour Press (in Chinese)

Reynolds, L. G., 1986. *Labor Economics and Labor Relations*, Englewood Cliffs: Prentice-Hall

Romer, P. M., 1986. 'Increasing returns and long-run growth', *Journal of Political Economics*, 94(5): 1002–37

Rosenfield, D. B. and Shapiro, R. D., 1981. 'Optimal adaptive price search', *Journal of Economic Theory*, 25: 1–20

Salop, J. and Salop, S., 1976. 'Self-selection and turnover in the labour market', *Quarterly Journal of Economics*, 90: 619–28

Schmitt, J., 1993. 'The changing structure of male earnings in Britain, 1974–1988', *Discussion Paper*, 122, Centre for Economic Performance, London School of Economics

Sen, A. K., 1966a. 'Labor allocation in a cooperative enterprise', *Review of Economic Studies*, 33: 361–71

1966b. 'Peasants and dualism with or without surplus labor', *Journal of Political Economy*, 74: 424–50

Shan, C., 1991. 'Within firm income distribution', in Ling, H. (ed.), *Reform of Labour, Wage, and Social Security System*, Beijing: China's Labour Press (in Chinese)

Shao, L., 1992. 'Income differentials within the state enterprises', in Du, H. (ed.), *The Foundation for Efficient Management: Employees' Feelings and Behaviour*, Shanghai: People's Publishing House of Shanghai: 156–72

Sicular, T., 1994. 'Going on the dole: why China's state enterprises choose to lose', unpublished paper

Slichter, S., 1950. 'Notes on the structure of wages', *Review of Economics and Statistics*, 32: 80–91

Sloane, P. J., 1985. 'Discrimination in the labour market', chapter 3 in Millward, R., Sumner, M. T. and Zis, G. (eds.), *Labour Economics*, New York: Longman

Smith, S. C., 1995. 'Employee participation, I: China's TVEs', *China Economic Review*, 6(1): 157–67

Solow, R. M., 1979. 'Another possible source of wage stickiness', *Journal of Macroeconomics*, 1: 79–82

—— 1985. 'Insiders and outsiders in wage determination', *Scandinavian Journal of Economics*, 87(2): 411–28

Stark, O., 1993. *The Migration of Labour*, Cambridge, MA and Oxford: Blackwell

State Council of China (SCC), 1993. 'Regulation on the state sector employees' unemployment insurance', in Economic Commission of Shanghai, Labour Bureau of Shanghai and Industrial Economic Union of Shanghai (ed.), *Reform on Labour, Wage and Social Security System*, Shanghai: People's Publishing House of Shanghai

State Statistical Bureau of China (SSB) various years a. *China Labour Statistical Yearbook*, Beijing: Chinese Statistical Publishing House

—— various years b. *China Statistical Yearbook*, Beijing: China Statistical Publishing House

—— 1995. *China Population Statistical Yearbook*, Beijing: China Statistical Publishing House

Stephen, F. H., 1984. *The Economic Analysis of Producers' Cooperatives*, London: Macmillan

Stigler, G., 1961. 'The economics of information', *Journal of Political Economy*, 69: 213–25

—— 1962, 'Information in the labour market', *Journal of Political Economy*, 70: 94–105

Stiglitz, J. E., 1974. 'Alternative theories of wage determination and unemployment in LDC's: the labour turnover model', *Quarterly Journal of Economics*, 88: 194–227

—— 1975. 'The theory of "screening", education, and the distribution of income', *American Economic Review*, 65: 283–300

—— 1982. 'Alternative theories of wage determination and unemployment: the efficiency wage model', in Gersovits, M. (ed.), *The Theory and Experience of Economic Development: Essays in Honour of Sir Arthur Lewis*, London and Boston: Allen & Unwin

Suits, D. B., 1984. 'Dummy variables: mechanics V: interpretation', *Review of Economics and Statistics*, 66(1): 177–80

Sun, L., 1995. 'Background information about Changan township, Dongguan City, Guangdong Province', interview paper

Takahara, A., 1992. 'The politics of wage policy in post-revolutionary China', London: Macmillan

Tan, H. W., 1980. Specific training in technological change: a case study of Japan', PhD dissertation, Yale University

Tao, J., 1981. 'Growing old in Hong Kong: problems and programmes', in Jones, J. (ed.), *The Common Welfare: Hong Kong's Social Services*, Hong Kong: Chinese University Press

Thornber, E. H., 1966. 'The elasticity of substitution: properties of alternative estimators', unpublished paper presented at the meeting of the Econometric Society (San Francisco); abstract in *Econometrica*, 35(5): 129

Todaro, M. P., 1969. 'A model of labour migration and urban unemployment in less developed countries', *American Economic Review*, 69 (March): 486–99

1971. 'Income expectations, rural–urban migration and employment in Africa', *International Labour Review*, 104 (5): 391–95, 411–13

1976. *Internal Migration in Developing Countries: A Review of Theory, Evidence, Methodology and Research Priorities*, Geneva: ILO

United Nations (UN), 1995. *Statistical Yearbook for Asia and the Pacific, 1995*, Bangkok: Economic and Social Commission for Asia and the Pacific

Vanek, J., 1970. *The General Theory of Labor-Managed Market Economies*, Ithaca: Cornell University Press

Vanek, J. and Jovicic, M., 1975. 'The capital market and income distribution in Yugoslavia', *Quarterly Journal of Economics*, 89: 432–43

Varian, H. R., 1984. *Microeconomic Analysis*, New York: W. W. Norton

Vishwanath, T., 1991. 'Information flow, job search, and migration', *Journal of Development Economics*, 36: 313–35

Walder, A., 1987. 'Wage reform and the web of factory interests', *The China Quarterly*, 109: 22–41

1989. 'Factory and manager in an era of reform' *China Quarterly*, 118: 242–64

Wang, H. L. and Li, S., 1995. *Industrialisation and Economic Reform in China*, Beijing: New World Press

Wang, H. S., 1996. 'Industrial-community mobility: a special type of rural–urban migration in China – A case study of Zhejiang Village', paper presented at the International Conference on the Flow of Rural Labour in China (Beijing) (in Chinese)

Wang, H. S. and Wang, X. Q., 1995. 'Strategy of migration and newly emerged large city', *Strategy and Management*

Wang, X. L., 1997. 'What contributed to China's rapid rural industrial growth during the reform period?', PhD dissertation, Canberra: The Australian National University

Ward, B., 1958. 'The firm in Illyria: market syndicalism', *American Economic Review*, 48: 566–89

Weitzman, M. L. and Kruse, D. L., 1990. 'Profit sharing and productivity', in Blinder, A. S. (ed.), *Paying for Productivity: A Look at the Evidence*, Washington, DC: Brookings Institution: 95–142

West, L. A., 1996. 'Pension reform in China: some implications for labor markets', paper presented at the Association for Asian Studies Annual Meeting, Honolulu (11–14 April)

White, G., 1988. 'State and market in China's labor reforms', *Journal of Development Studies*, 24: 180–202

White, H., 1980. 'A heteroskedasticity consistent covariance matrix and a direct test for heteroskedasticity', *Econometrica*, 46: 817–38

Williamson, J. G., 1988. 'Migrant selectivity, urbanization, and industrial revolutions', *Population and Development Review*, 14(2): 287–314

World Bank, 1993a. 'China's state industry: a paradox of rising productivity and declining profitability', *Transition* (February–March): 7–8

1993b. *The East Asian Miracle*, Oxford: Oxford University Press

1995. 'Involving workers in East Asian growth', *Regional Perspectives on World Development Report*, Washington, DC: World Bank

1996a. *China: Pension System Reform, Report* 15121-CHA

1996b. *China: Reform of State-Owned Enterprises, Report* 14924-CHA

Wu, H. X. and Li, Z., 1997. 'Rural to urban migration in China', *Asia-Pacific Economic Literature*, 7(2)

Xiang, B., 1996. 'Mobility, traditional networking marketisation and the development of a "non-government" controlled space', paper presented at the International Conference on the Flow of Rural Labour in China (Beijing) (in Chinese)

Xu, W., Jefferson, G. and Rathja, D., 1993. *China Data Documentation*, Manuscript, Transition and Macro-Adjustment Division, Washington, DC: World Bank

Yao, S., 1995. 'Does profit-sharing work in a centrally planned economy? Evidence from the Chinese state industries', *Applied Economics Letters*, 2: 26–129

Zhang, J. 1988. 'Overview of development of China's Township and Village Enterprises', in chen, J. Y and Xia, D. F. (eds.), *Studies on Township and Village Enterprises*, Beijing: China Social Sciences Press (in Chinese)

Zhou, Q. R., 1997. 'System transformation, structural change, and urban employment', *Comparative Economic and Social Systems*, 97(3): 8–15 (in Chinese)

Index